THE TRAVELER'S GUIDE TO
DAMANHUR
The Amazing Northern Italian Eco-Society

Esperide Ananas and Stambecco Pesco

Illustrated by Cinzia di Felice, Ape Soia, and Pangolino Tulipano

North Atlantic Books

Berkeley, California

Published by
North Atlantic Books
P. O. Box 12327
Berkeley, California 94712

Cover photograph by Albatros: Children playing in the Labyrinth
Title page photograph by Esperide Ananas: The Open Temple in Damjl
Back cover photographs by Esperide Ananas and Roberto Benzi: The Open
    Temple and the Sun Door
Cover and book design by Brad Greene
Printed in Malaysia

Photos by Albatros (pages vi, 102, 212), Esperide Ananas (pages iii, 2, 6, 18, 27, 31, 40, 54, 70, 186, 198, 200, 201, 202, 203, 204, 205, 206, 207, 208, 209, 211), and Shed Bedsole (page 194).

Photos on back cover, page 11, 16, 84–85 by Roberto Benzi and diagram on page 11 by Eli Morgan are from *Damanhur: Temples of Humankind* (New York: CoSM Press) and are reprinted by permission of the publisher.

The Traveler's Guide to Damanhur: The Amazing Northern Italian Eco-Society is sponsored by the Society for the Study of Native Arts and Sciences, a nonprofit educational corporation whose goals are to develop an educational and cross-cultural perspective linking various scientific, social, and artistic fields; to nurture a holistic view of arts, sciences, humanities, and healing; and to publish and distribute literature on the relationship of mind, body, and nature.

North Atlantic Books' publications are available through most bookstores. For further information, call 800-733-3000 or visit our Web site at www.northatlanticbooks.com.

Library of Congress Cataloging-in-Publication Data

Ananas, Esperide.
    The traveler's guide to Damanhur : the amazing northern Italian eco-society / Esperide Ananas and Stambecco Pesco ; illustrated by Cinzia di Felice, Ape Soia, and Pangolino Tulipano.
        p. cm.
    ISBN 978-1-55643-761-8 (alk. paper)
    1. Damanhur (Italy)—Description and travel. I. Pesco, Stambecco, 1960- II. Title.
    BL980.I8A53 2009
    299'.93—dc22
                                                    2008028808
                                                    CIP

1 2 3 4 5 6 7 8 9 TWP 14 13 12 11 10 09 08

To all the creative builders of peace,
who know how to believe in their dreams,
and
through them transform the world.

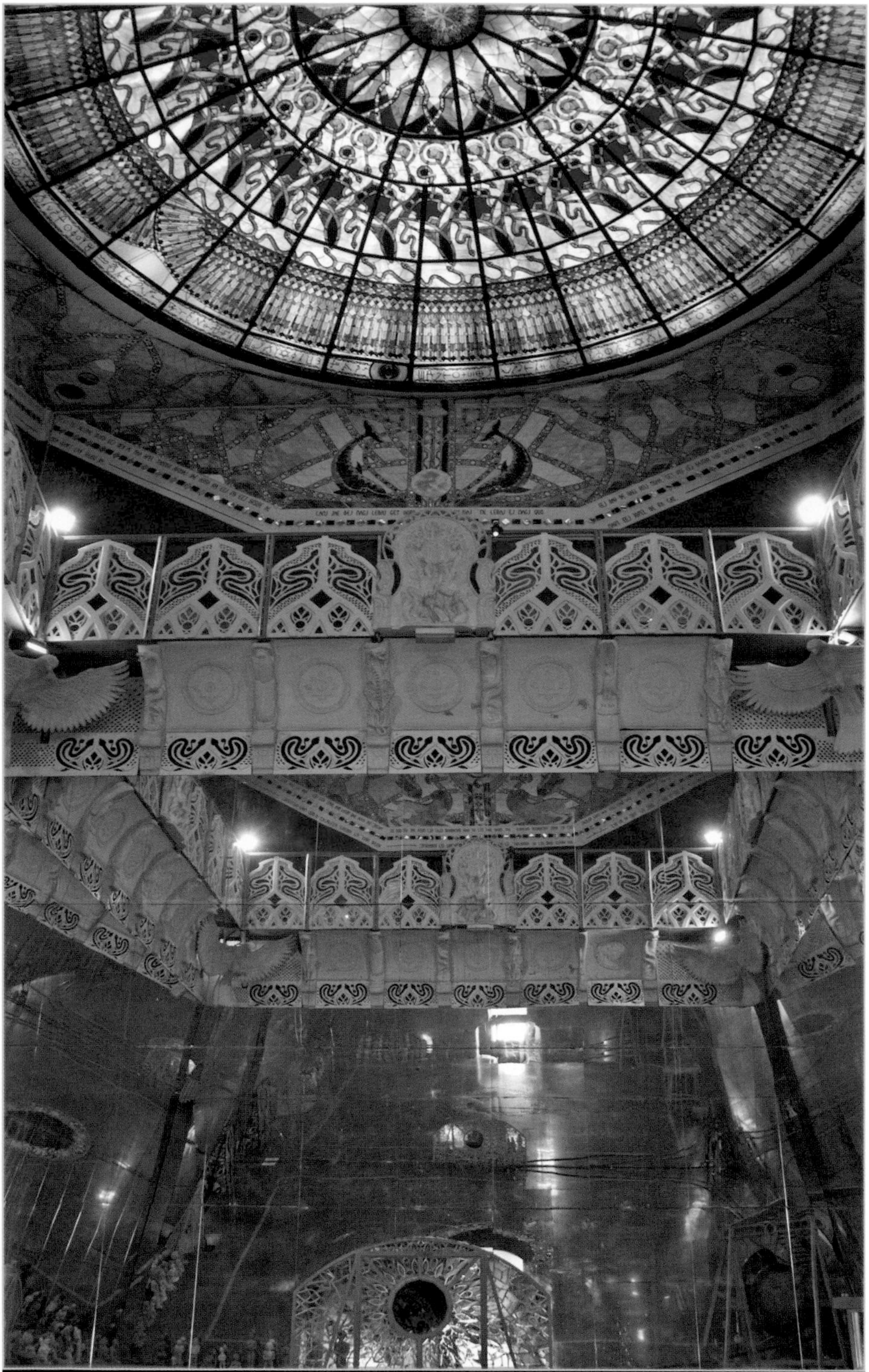

The Hall of Mirrors

CONTENTS

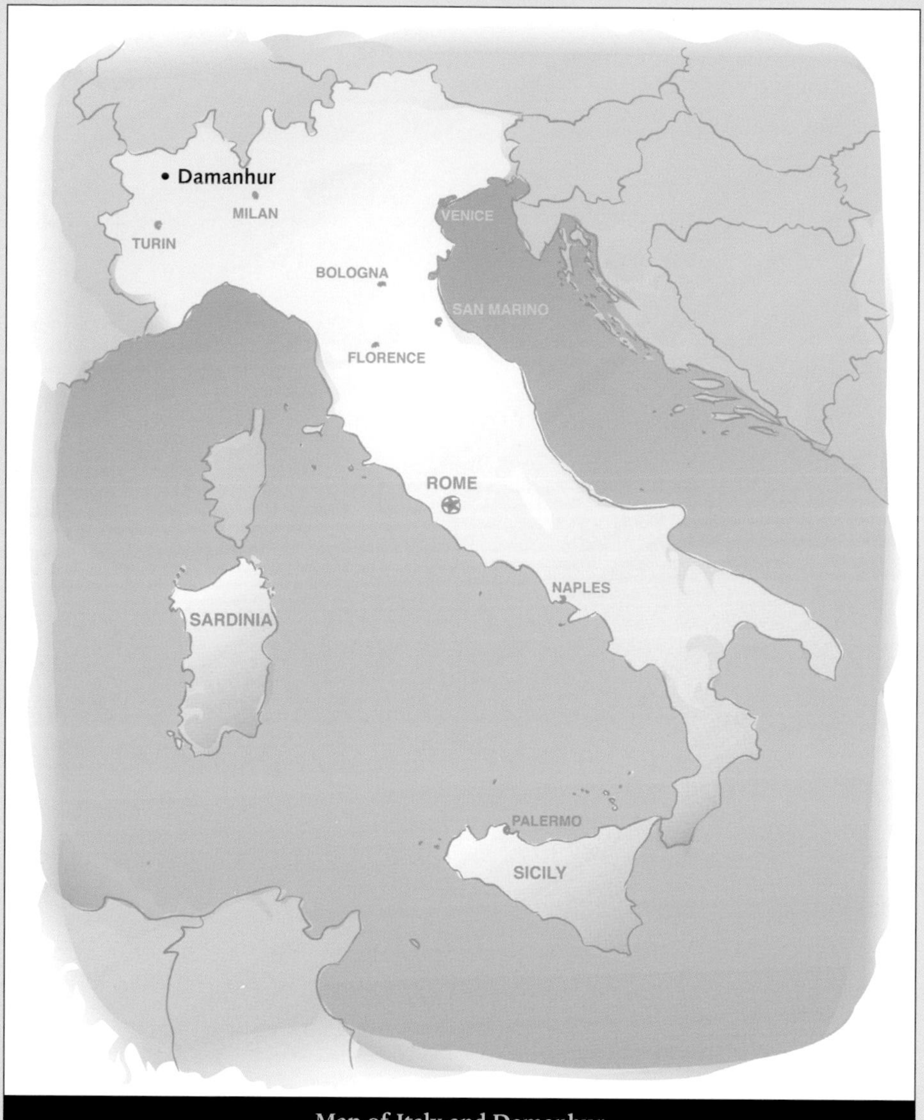
Damanhur
MILAN
TURIN
VENICE
BOLOGNA
SAN MARINO
FLORENCE
ROME
SARDINIA
NAPLES
PALERMO
SICILY

Map of Italy and Damanhur

PART ONE

Traveling to Damanhur

D amanhur is truly an amazing place. Dubbed "a laboratory for the future" by philosopher-scientist Ervin László, this intentional community with its own currency, healthcare system, schools, and spiritual practices has been in existence since the 1970s—and yet, until a few years ago, it was kept hidden from most of the world. Damanhur is centered on the astonishing underground Temples of Humankind, nine ornate temples on five levels carved into a mountainside, which have drawn comparisons with the fabled city of Atlantis and have been called "the Eighth Wonder of the World" by the British newspaper *The Daily Mail*.

Damanhur is situated in a special region with its own profound and magical history. Within ten minutes' drive of Damjl, the center of Damanhur, you will be able to enjoy the natural beauty of the green Valchiusella valley— a picturesque valley dotted with medieval villages and close to the Alps—or visit the wealthy city of Turin with its fascinating esoteric history, less than an hour away.

The purpose of this eclectic guide is to give readers a taste of just some of the many treasures within Damanhur and the surrounding region, as well as presenting an entertaining overview of Damanhur's dramatic history through the comic book *Checkmate to Time*.

Sleeping Beauty mountain in Valchiusella

What Is Damanhur?

Founded in 1975, the Federation of Damanhur in Italy is an internationally renowned center for spiritual, artistic, and social research.

Its philosophy is based on action, optimism, and the idea that every human being lives to leave something of themselves to others and to contribute to the growth and evolution of humanity at large. Its founding values are positive thinking, kindness, solidarity, and creativity.

Damanhur was born in the early seventies when a group of seekers gathered around the philosopher and healer Oberto Airaudi, who, in keeping with the Damanhurian custom of taking a new name, goes by the name "Falco." Together, Falco and his friends planned the creation of a new society, in which everyday life could be the practical application of spiritual values.

The aims of Damanhur are: the freedom and reawakening of the human being as a divine, spiritual, and material principle; the creation of a model of life based on the principles of good communal living and love; and harmonious integration and cooperation with all the forces linked to the evolution of humankind.

In Damanhur, the uniqueness of every individual is considered as an important value. Everybody's talents contribute in creating an innovative and complex society that is constantly evolving and growing.

The Federation is most famous for its underground Temples of Humankind, an extraordinary work of art created *by hand* by its citizens over two decades and dedicated to the reawakening of the divine in every human being. Constructed like a three-dimensional book narrating the history of humanity, the temples are linked by hundreds of yards of richly decorated tunnels. The nine chambers are embellished with stunning murals, mosaics, statues, secret doors, and stained glass windows. In the words of Falco, the purpose of the temples is to "to remind people that we are all capable of much more than we realize, and that hidden treasures can be found within every one of us, once we know how to access them."

Damanhurians are also a highly pragmatic people who see themselves as focusing on the ability of humans to transform dreams and visions into concrete realities. Their Web site states:

> Damanhur is a collective dream transformed into reality through the creative power of positive thought. It is a seed that has been growing for over thirty years, constantly transforming and renewing itself. The reality it has created is the fruit of its citizens' shared ideals.

From the initial dozen founders, 800 people now live in the community and nearby villages, with more than 1,112 acres of territory comprising woodland, farmland, and over 100 houses, workshops, and studios. Damanhur Crea, housed in the former Olivetti factory in nearby Vidracco, acts as a hub for eco-businesses and creative ventures started by Damanhurians. Damanhur Crea is the site of the Damanhur Family School; the offices of the ValdiChy Project, an initiative to attract cultural creatives to the Valchiusella valley; Tentaty, a market selling organic food and natural products; an eco-architecture studio; a consultancy business for renewable energy systems; a Center for Integrated Medicines; a physio-kinesiotherapy and rehabilitation center; a beauty institute; fine arts and restoration workshops, craft workshops, and a goldsmith; a musical instruments workshop; an art gallery; the selfic research laboratory; a café, and a refined organic restaurant.

The building also hosts a modern conference center named after the industrial and social reformer, Adriano Olivetti, who in the 1950s created

The Founder of Damanhur

Damanhur was born of a dream. A dream of a society based on optimism and the idea that human beings can be the masters of their own destiny.

It all began in the early sixties when visionary founder Oberto Airaudi was ten years old. Born in Balangero, near Turin, in 1950, Oberto is a philosopher, healer, writer, and painter. He claims to have had a vision of a new civilization, with amazing temples at its heart. Around these temples, he dreamed there lived a highly evolved community who enjoyed a meaningful existence in which all the people worked for the common good.

"My goal was to recreate the temples from my visions," he says.

Oberto—who now prefers to use the name "Falco" ("falcon" in Italian)—began by digging a trial hole under his parents' home to more fully understand the principles of excavation. But it was only many years later, after he had founded a center for esoteric research in Turin, that he began searching for the perfect site.

In 1977, he selected a remote hillside in the Valchiusella valley, where the hard rock would sustain the structures he had in mind. Strangely enough, it was not far from his parents' home.

An old house on the hillside was restored, and became a base for Falco and his friends who shared his vision. Using hammers and picks, they began their dig to create the temples of Damanhur—named after the ancient subterranean Egyptian temple meaning "City of Light"—in August 1978. As no planning permission had been granted, they decided to share their scheme only with like-minded people and keep the temples secret.

Volunteers worked to create the temples for the next sixteen years with no formal plans other than Falco's sketches and visions, funding their project by setting up small businesses to serve the local community.

Today, Oberto Airaudi is Damanhur's Spiritual Guide, but unlike other leaders of spiritual groups, he is not put up on a special guru pedestal. His teachings encourage the awakening of the inner master through study, experimentation, overcoming dogmatic attitudes, and the complete expression of individual potential. ■

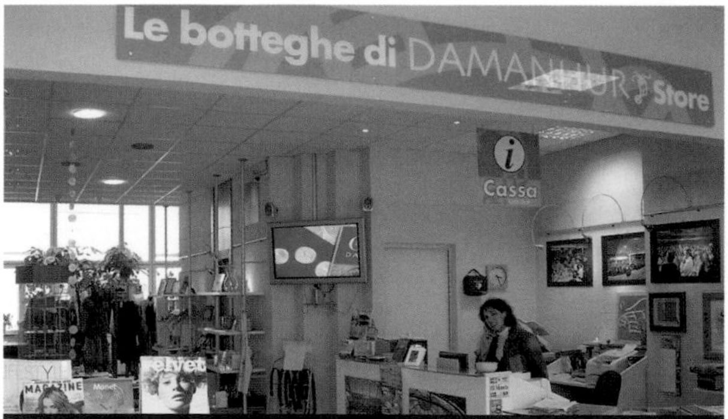
Le botteghe di
Store
Cassa

Damanhur Crea reception area

this complex to counter the growing exodus of the population from the valley, allowing the inhabitants of the place to stay and work in the area. The new use of this complex is an excellent example of renewing an abandoned industrial area. The structural work required great care to adapt the building to the needs of the Damanhur Crea Consortium, while at the same time respecting the characteristics planned by Adriano Olivetti, which stand as testimony to an advanced concept of the relationship between the individual, business, and the local region.

The people of Damanhur have a profound connection to the land and at the same time are concerned with global issues, and embody a deep and idealistic vision with their feet firmly planted on the ground. Thinking positively and translating ideas into actions and concrete achievements are indispensable steps towards the peace consciousness that is called for in our time. This is Damanhur's commitment to the future.

The Social and Spiritual Organization of the Damahurian Community

The Federation began with what are called the three "bodies" of Damanhur, which each focus on particular aspects of human experience: The School of Meditation (ritual tradition), Social (social theory, social realization), and the Game of Life (experimentation and dynamics, life as a game, change). A fourth body was recently added called Tecnarcato, which emphasizes individual inner refinement.

Citizens participate at one of four levels of involvement, depending on each individual's inclination: A, B, C, or D. Group A citizens share all resources and live on site full time. Group B citizens contribute to financial goals and live on site a minimum of 3 days a week. Group C and D citizens live anywhere. Group A and B citizens participate fully in the School of Meditation, Social, and the Game of Life. Group C citizens participate fully in The School of Meditation (Merrifield 2006, 106).

Citizens follow one of several Ways, depending on their personal nature. Ways include the Way of the Oracle, the Way of the Monks, the Way of the Knights, the Way of Health, the Way of the Word, the Way of Integrated Arts and Work, and others.

An Ecologically Sustainable Society

Damanhurians see our planet as a living being to be respected and protected. This principle is maintained in the ecological development of all the Federation's settlements.

The pursuit of energy self-sufficiency is one the Federation's most important objectives. Currently Damanhur is 60% self-sufficient in domestic hot water through solar panels; 30% self-sufficient in electricity through photovoltaic plants; and 90% self-sufficient in heating through firewood obtained through Damanhur's vast reforestation and forest management program.

Several green building companies created by Damanhurian citizens build state of the art eco-homes in the valley and surrounding areas, paying great attention to the best use of water, energy, and thermal resources. In 2007, two of the most recent buildings—a home hosting twenty-five people and a large farmhouse—were internationally recognized for their sustainability. Older Damanhurian houses, on the other hand, are converted to eco-homes through the installation of solar and photovoltaic panels and systems for rainwater collection.

Organic agriculture and food self-sufficiency are high priorities. The Federation produces vegetables, fruit, milk, cheese, olive oil, cereals, bakery products, wine, and honey; it also raises poultry, pigs, cows, and fish. These and many other organic foods can be purchased from the Tentaty Cooperative market at the Damanhur Crea complex in Vidracco. Tentaty is the first organic food store in the Valchiusella valley. Damanhur's researchers have patented a technique to "create" meat in a laboratory from cells. Damanhur's laboratory of bio-molecular research constantly conducts random tests on its products, to ensure that they are free of genetically modified ingredients.

Social and Political Commitment

The Federation has created many bodies recognized by the Italian government as "Associations of Social Promotion." Approximately 250 Damanhurians are engaged in local volunteer work in Civil Protection teams, the Red Cross, blood donation banks, and care of the elderly.

Damanhurian volunteers created the first Red Cross station in Vidracco to guarantee emergency coverage of the Valchiusella area and specialized transport for local hospitals and private citizens.

The Damanhur Civil Protection Association shares the experience of its individual members gained from working for many years in the volunteer sector. Damanhurian teams have participated in the "Rainbow" mission in Albania and in many local, national, and international emergencies caused by earthquakes.

Damanhur has founded a new independent political movement called *"Con Te, per il Paese"* ("With You, for the Country") which supports Italy's Green Party. *Con te, per il Paese* is very active in the political life of Valchiusella: twenty-two Damanhurians have been elected on valley councils and the Mayor of Vidracco is a citizen of the Federation. The achievements of *Con Te per il Paese* are examples of how spiritual ideals can create growth and development that benefit all.

In Valchiusella, Damanhur is also in the process of promoting the "ValdiChy Project," an initiative to facilitate individuals and groups from all philosophies and walks of life who want to settle in the valley and together create the "first autonomous spiritual region of the new world."

Sharing the Experience

In recent years, Damanhur has been welcoming more and more politicians, architects, city planners, business consultants, and economists from many nations, all interested in exploring the insights and models an established and structured intentional community can offer toward the creation of an environmentally responsible, pluralistic, and more awakened world. Many scientists and concerned politicians warn us that our human civilization is at risk, and that we need to immediately transform our relationship to the planet. They call for urgent new policies, for a world governance capable of meeting the challenges not as "zero sum" problems, but as opportunities for the creation of a new planetary balance in social, economic, human, and cultural terms. In this context, a new society like Damanhur is a laboratory where new paradigms, systems, and norms can be tested. From this experience, it is possible to distil elements and ideas that can be applied to society at large. For more information, e-mail futurelab@damanhur.org

The Temples of Humankind

The Halls of Water, Earth, Spheres, Mirrors, Metals, the Blue Temple, and the Labyrinth: The Temples of Humankind are an underground work of art, a three-dimensional book that narrates human history through all forms of the arts.

The following temples are open to the public for guided tours and visits. See "Programs for Visiting Damanhur and the Temples" on page 17 for more information.

The Blue Temple	The Labyrinth
The Hall of Water	The Hall of Mirrors
The Hall of the Earth	The Hall of Spheres
The Hall of Mirrors	

Detailed descriptions and 3D models of the chambers of the temples can be viewed on the Damanhur Web site, http://www.thetemples.org.

The Future of the Temples

The Temples of Humankind are constantly being developed and enriched; they are not a monument of the past, but an answer and a hope for the world of today and of the future.

The present complex is only ten percent of the development envisaged inside the mountain. A new project sees the reclamation of a vast natural area, ruined in the past by stone quarries, in the woodland adjacent to the already built Temples of Humankind. Inside the rock the "Temple of Peoples" will be built, to represent and celebrate the preciousness of human diversity. It will be a modern cathedral to honor the importance of safeguarding all peoples, their culture, their language, their traditions, and their expressions of contacting the Divine.

The Temple of Peoples will be a magic place which will have a positive influence on those who visit because, like the Temples of Humankind, it will be sited at a special point on the planet: the meeting place of the Synchronic Lines, the roads that carry spiritual energy throughout the universe.

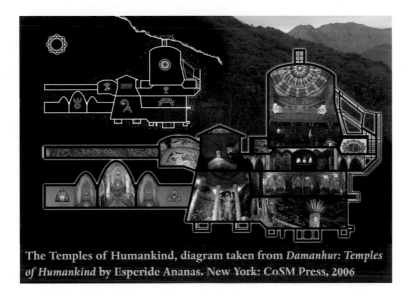

The Temples of Humankind, diagram taken from *Damanhur: Temples of Humankind* by Esperide Ananas. New York: CoSM Press, 2006

The Temple of Peoples will become a meeting point for different traditions and arts, for science and politics. It will also be a place in which the powerful of the planet can meet as human beings in the spirit of understanding rather than opposition; it will be a place to create new hope for humanity and construct the path towards a planet of peace and harmony.

The Temple of Peoples will host modern theater seating over a thousand. A part of the original rock walls will be left untouched to create a special acoustic and energetic effect. It will be the ideal space for meetings and artistic expressions from all over the world.

There will be a library of sacred and spiritual texts, innovative spaces for art and research, underwater hot pools, and spaces for health and well-being. A small underground electric train will link the present Temples to the new area, and a cable car will carry visitors to the complex from the village below.

The new spaces will be enclosed within a huge dome, constructed with innovative technological solutions. All the environments will be rich in works of art, so that artists from all over the world can participate in the realization of this dream.

The Music of the Plants

Experience an extraordinary event during your stay at Damanhur—hear plants sing! The desire for a strong connection to nature has inspired many original experiments at Damanhur: one of them is a village in the trees for dreaming and being in contact with the forces of the forest and for experimenting with communication with plants and trees.

Damanhurian researchers have invented a special device that, using sensors, picks up the variations of a plant's electrical conductivity. The signals are then translated into music. The results are very evocative—the trees seem to be aware of the meditation music they are creating by harmonizing and improvising along with accompanying human musicians. Each plant has its own specific sound, which varies with the different times of day and when they interact with human beings.

Many experiments have been conducted in cooperation with Florence's Botanical Gardens, and Concerts of the Trees are performed regularly in Italy and all over the world. These sound experiences have also been presented at the Sound Symposium Festival 1998 in Newfoundland, Canada; with Steven Halpern in 1999 in Miami, USA; and in large auditoriums in Delhi and Chennai in India in 2002 and 2008. Recordings of concerts in the Sacred Woods and in Florence's Gardens are available at Damanhur and online.

Soon a small device called "PlantTunes" will be available for sale so that everybody can enjoy the company of their beloved green friends! Damanhur's intention is to educate people to consider plants not as inanimate objects but as living beings. ■

The Synchronic Lines

Damanhur is located on a very active energetic point of the planet. In Valchiusella four Synchronic Lines meet. The Synchronic Lines are rivers of energy that wind their way horizontally and vertically, deep inside the Earth and around the poles to link the planet with the galaxy. The ancient Chinese called these lines the "Back of the Dragon." These eighteen subtle roads carry ideas, thought, intuition, dreams, and ways of thinking, enveloping all the planets that host life. The founders of Damanhur traveled the world to complete the map of these Lines of Energy. Besides the temples, the territories of the Federation host a variety of structures that allow everyone to take advantage of the extraordinary energy of the Lines for their own well-being and spiritual growth.

Damjl Energy Circuits and the Open Temple

In order to tap into the energies of Synchronic Lines—besides the temples of course—Damanhurians have built stone labyrinths, dedicated specific places to the Elements, and erected standing stones. Damanhur's territory, from this point of view, can be considered as a large piece of circuitry, where everything is integrated so that synchronic energies can be naturally tapped for one's well-being and spiritual growth.

Damjl is the name of the first territory to be inhabited in 1979. In Damjl five circuits of painted stones pathways can be walked along a stretch of land between the Open Temple and the Ritual Circle, used for Solstice and Equinoxes celebrations. Based on the principle of correspondence between physical movement and the activation of specific synapses in the brain, these geometric figures are an experiment in seeing how effective they are in helping people with goals such as increasing optimism, experiencing good dreams and reducing insomnia, facilitating digestion, relieving headaches and fatigue, and stimulating memory. A spiral made of stones can also be walked by guests in order to improve clarity of mind and general well-being.

In the same territory are four special points dedicated to the connection with the different elements: fire, water, earth, and air. The meditation points are clearly indicated by colored posts that give simple instructions on how to connect to that element. Water is near the ceramic fountain, earth at the standing stone circle, and air and fire are in the Open Temple. Situated in Damjl, the Open Temple, considered an extension of the Temples of Humankind, offers a sacred space open to people of all philosophies and religions to perform their own rituals.

Built with a stage and an amphitheater, it is used in Damanhur for theater performances, weddings, special events (like the Global Peace Meditation held in May), and the monthly Rite of the Oracle.

At the top of one of the columns at the side of the fire altar is the Damjl bell, which is rung at different moments of the day to remind citizens of the aims and ideals of Damanhur.

In the morning at 7:30 a.m. it invites everyone to unite in a spirit of prayer as they begin their individual days.

At sunset it rings three times, as a reminder of the present, and everyone stops for a moment to send out a loving thought to all their fellow Damanhurians, to all their friends and people committed to spiritual transformation, and to every human being in the world.

It rings again at 11:30 p.m. to wish everyone a good night.

Damanhurian Spirituality

Damanhurian spiritual research is based on the premise that all that is, is part of an all-comprising Being that can be defined as the Unmovable Motor, the ultimate God. Thus, every human being also has a divine origin: It is our task to become aware of our primeval condition, in harmony with the complex ecosystem of which we are a part. This ecosystem includes plants, animals, the forces of nature, and the different divine forces. In this vision, the search for oneself and that of the divine coincide, as the human being is a "bridge form" between the spiritual and the material plane.

Damanhurian Philosophy

Damanhur's philosophy is based on positive thinking, an element that has the power of directing our best energy to create a path between our inner world and aspirations and our spiritual and human growth.

The Eight "Quesiti"

Damanhurian philosophy is synthesized in eight formulas called *Quesiti,* the steps of the human and spiritual growth of individuals, groups, and organizations.

The Quesiti are dynamic formulas, meditation themes, and directions for practical actions. Their content is the result of Damanhur's collective achievements. Every individual can interpret them according to their own inclination and characteristics.

Here are the formulas of the Eight Quesiti in an extremely simplified format:

1. Act in order to *be,* with pure-minded intent.
2. Continue to act, to continue being.
3. Change your logic to transform yourself, from the I to the We.
4. Be aware, be available.
5. Harmoniously revolutionize your inner self.
6. Become the Artist of your Life.
7. Search for what is True, beyond all certainties.
8. Choose your Ideal, and be open to others with Love. ■

A small group of spiritual people sharing dreams and ideals can achieve extraordinary objectives, if everybody gives a common direction to their thoughts with purity and optimism. Every Damanhurian citizen commits to always think positively of the future, of others, and of oneself.

Another founding principle of Damanhur's philosophy is the importance of being open to change. New, unimaginable horizons can be discovered with each new step on the path. As a consequence, Damanhur is a constantly evolving society, based upon the celebration of individual differences.

A characteristic element of change is the new name that Damanhurian citizens choose to take: the animal and the plant name. The new name— which co-exists with the legal one—symbolizes a will to renew oneself through a playful attitude and the desire for a deep contact with nature.

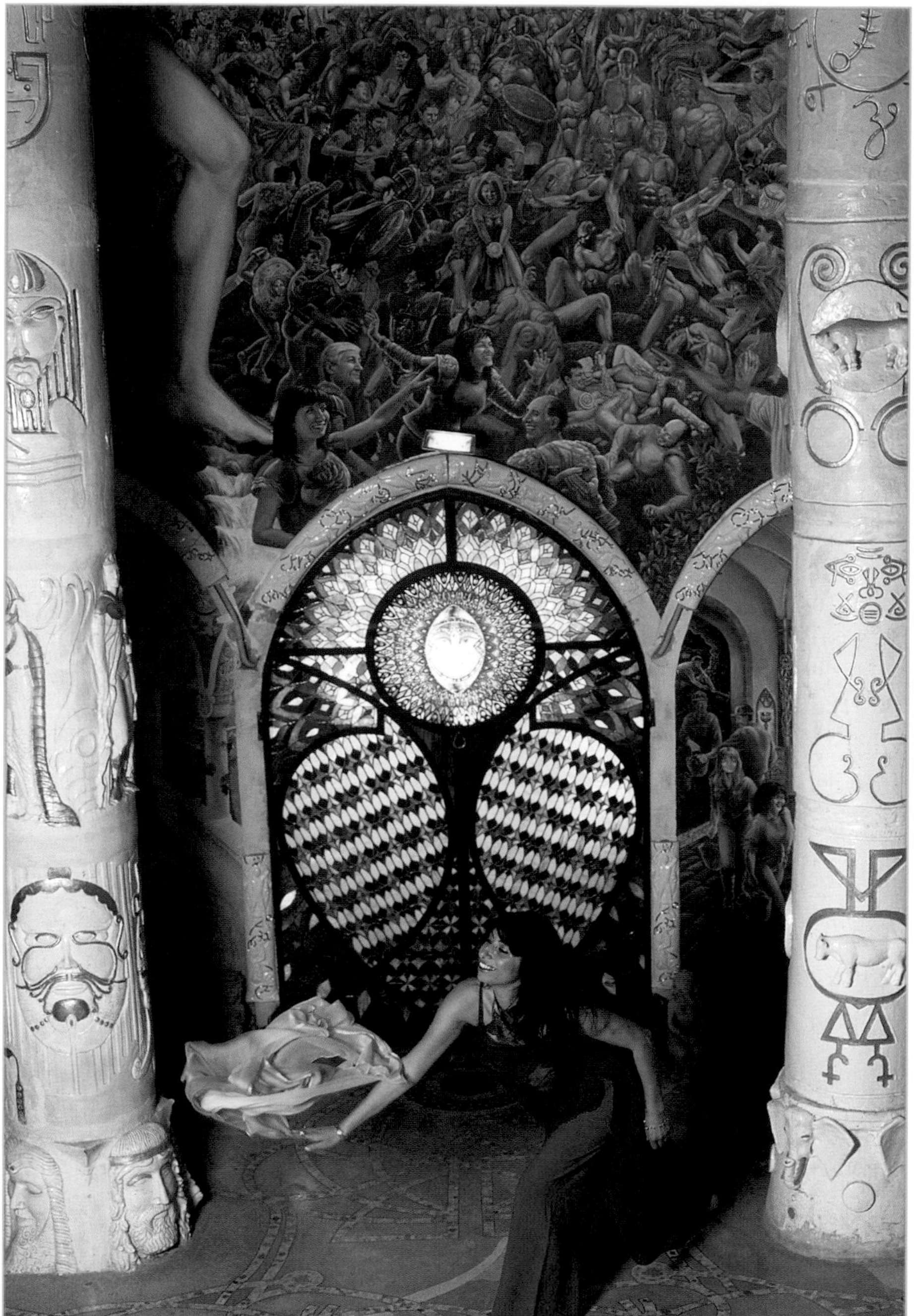

Dance in the Upper Chamber of the Hall of the Earth

Programs for Visiting Damanhur and the Temples

Every year thousands of people come to Damanhur from all over the world to explore a unique and extraordinary reality. Damanhur's Welcome Center offers events and seminars all year round to suit the needs of individual travelers and groups alike.

The Federation and the Temples of Humankind can be visited for short periods or long stays for study, vacation, healing, or regeneration. The Federation is happy to welcome all visitors: those who are attracted by a cultural and artistic interest, as well as spiritual seekers who wish to stay for a longer period of time. Their programs are therefore very diversified. Some meet the needs of those pilgrims who have only limited time available; others provide the time and conditions for those who wish to use the temples as a sacred space to awaken the divine within themselves. The Welcome Center is happy to assist with logistics, transport, and any practical detail concerning your stay—contact information is given at the bottom of this section.

First-time visitors who wish to have a comprehensive introduction to the life of the Federation can take a half-day tour, the ICAL program, or a one-day tour, the LAOR program. They may also choose between stays of three or seven days. The three-day ALMOA and seven-day ELA programs run throughout the year and are offered in English.

The programs include visits to the various territories and activities of the Federation, a visit to the Temples of Humankind, and a presentation introducing Damanhurian philosophy and its practical applications. For information about each Damanhur nucleo and its specialty, see "Living

Global Meditation Day 2005 in the Open Temple of Damjl

in a Nucleo Community" on page 42. It is also possible to visit Damanhur throughout the year and stay for as long as one wishes, providing that visits are booked at least three days in advance. At the Solstices and Equinoxes, Damanhurians celebrate special moments of communion with Nature, just as many peoples and civilizations on our planet have done for thousands of years. The Commemoration of the Dead takes place at the beginning of November, and every month at the full moon the Rite of the Oracle is celebrated. For more details on visiting Damanhur during seasonal celebrations, see "Festivals of Damanhur" below on page 25. These seasonal and monthly appointments are open to all by prior arrangement with the Olami Welcome Center: Ⓣ (+39) 0124 512236/(+39) 0124 512205; welcome@damanhur.it

Damanhur also hosts international conferences and special events that bring together inspiring speakers and participants from around the world. For up-to-date information on special events, visit Damanhur's Web site, http://www.damanhur.org.

Guided Tours of Damanhur

1. ICAL Program

DURATION: Four hours

TOURS: Morning or afternoon, by prior booking—groups of three people minimum. If you are coming alone or with just one other person, the welcome office staff will organize a group for you with other guests.

ICAL includes a tour of Damjl, the central area of the Federation, and Damanhur Crea, the Center of Art, Research, and Well-being, as well as a tour of the Temples of Humankind. The tours are facilitated by specialized guides who are all citizens of the Federation. They will share with guests the history, the ideals, and the motivations of Damanhur's social and spiritual endeavors. At the end of the visit, the visitors will be accompanied back to Damjl.

2. LAOR Program

DURATION: One day, 9 a.m. to 6 p.m.

TOURS: LAOR includes a tour of Damjl, the central area of the Federation, and Damanhur Crea, the Center of Art, Research and Well-being, as well as a longer tour of the Temples of Humankind.

MORNING: Tour Damjl and Damanhur Crea.

VISIT THE TEMPLES (first part): Hall of Earth and Hall of Metals.

AFTERNOON: Walking meditation in the Stone Labyrinths (circuits of Ogni Dove) to prepare for the second part of the visit to the Temples of Humankind.

VISIT THE TEMPLES: The Labyrinth, Blue Temple, Hall of Water, Hall of Spheres, and Hall of Mirrors.

3. VELJ Program

DURATION: Two days

DAY ONE: 11 a.m. to 1 p.m. and 3 p.m. to 6 p.m.

MORNING: Tour of Damjl, the central area of the Federation, and Damanhur Crea, the Center of Art, Research and Well-being.

AFTERNOON: Preparation for visiting the Temples of Humankind, with a special meditation in the Gallery of Selfic Paintings. Visit to the Temples (first part): Hall of Earth and Hall of Metals.

DAY TWO: 10 a.m. to 1 p.m.

MORNING: Walking meditation in the Stone Labyrinths (circuits of Ogni Dove) to prepare for the visit to the Temples of Humankind. Visit to the Temples (second part): the Labyrinth, Blue Temple, Hall of Water, Hall of Spheres, and the Hall of Mirrors.

The program VELJ offers a profound visit to the temples and contact with their energies. The sessions of preparation, thanks to specific disciplines of the School of Damanhur, help pilgrims to fine-tune their sensitivity so that they can perceive the energetic characteristics of the Temples. In this way the contact with the energies of each Hall will be optimal. ∎

The ALMOA and ELA Programs:
Stay in Damanhur for Three or Seven Days

These multiple-day programs are available with prior booking only, for a minimum of four people. If you are traveling alone or with fewer people, the Welcome Center will add you to a group with other guests.

The ALMOA Program

This three-day program takes place over a long weekend from Thursday to Sunday. It offers a detailed introduction to Damanhur and a deep immersion in the spiritual energies of the Temples of Humankind.

SCHEDULE

ARRIVAL (Thursday) Visit Damanhur and the Temples of Humankind.

Welcome to Damanhur! Settle into your accommodations.

DAY 1 (Friday)

9–11 a.m.: Guided tour of Damjl, the central area and "capital" of the Federation and Damanhur Crea, the Center of Art, Research, and Well-being.

11 a.m.–1 p.m.: Visit to the Temples of Humankind (part one): Hall of Earth and Hall of Metals.

LUNCH BREAK

2:30 p.m.–3:30 p.m.: Walking Meditation in the Stone Labyrinths (circuits of Ogni Dove), in preparation for the second part of the visit to the Temples of Humankind.

3:30 p.m.–5:30 p.m.: Visit to the temples (part two): Labyrinth, Blue Temple, Hall of Water, Hall of Spheres, and Hall of Mirrors.

This program provides profound contact with the Temples of Humankind and with its energies. The sequence of the visits is in the order that optimizes the emotional and spiritual experience of being in each hall.

DAY 2 (Saturday)

9:30–10:30 a.m.: Visit the Standing Stones and walk the Spiral in Damjl to contact the element of Earth, in preparation for meditation in the Temples.

11 a.m.–12:30 p.m.: Meditation in the temples in the Hall of Earth, facilitated by Damanhurian guides.

LUNCH BREAK

3–6 p.m.: Introduction to Esoteric Physics: learning more about Damanhurian philosophy, our spiritual model and research.

DAY 3 (Sunday)

10 a.m.–1 p.m.: Guided tour of the Sacred Wood, the open-air extension of the temples; visit the Tree Village and enjoy the Music of the Trees; walking meditation in the Stone Circuits in the Sacred Wood.

AFTERNOON: Time for you to fully absorb your experience of visiting the temples.

DEPARTURE

The ELA Program

SCHEDULE

DAY 1 (Sunday) ARRIVAL

Welcome to Damanhur! Settle into your accommodations.

DAY 2 (Monday) VISIT TO DAMANHUR

AND THE TEMPLES—FIRST PART

MORNING: Guided visit to Damjl, the central area of the Federation, with questions and answers on Damanhur's philosophy, art, and social structure. Visit the research and art center Damanhur Crea, with time to view the studios and activities.

AFTERNOON: Participate in a guided meditation with the Selfic Paintings to prepare for the visit to the Temples, followed by a guided visit to the Temples of Humankind (first part): the Hall of Earth and Hall of Metals.

DAY 3 (Tuesday) VISIT TO THE TEMPLES —SECOND PART

MORNING: Walk the Stone Circuits in the Sacred Forest.

Enjoy a guided visit to the Temples of Humankind (second part): the Labyrinth, the Blue Temple, the Hall of Water, the Hall of Spheres, and the Hall of Mirrors.

AFTERNOON: Free time.

DAY 4 (Wednesday) MEDITATION IN THE TEMPLES—THE SACRED WOOD

During the morning, walk the Spiral in Damjl and contact the Element Earth at the Standing Stones to prepare for mediation in the Temples.

MORNING: Meditate in the Hall of Earth.

AFTERNOON: Guided visit to the Sacred Forest and to the Tree Village, enjoying the experience of the Music of the Plants.

EVENING (optional) 7:30 to 8:30 p.m. Community meeting with Damanhur's Guides and founder Falco at Damanhur Crea.

DAY 5 (Thursday) GUIDED TOUR OF TURIN AND ITS MAGICAL HISTORY

All day in town. Guided visit to the city to discover the secrets of its esoteric history.

EVENING (optional) 7:30 to 8:30 p.m. Community meeting with Damanhur's Guides and founder Falco at Damanhur Crea.

DAY 6 (Friday) MEDITATION IN THE TEMPLES—FROM COMMUNITY TO FEDERATION OF COMMUNITIES

In your free time during the morning, walk the Spiral in Damjl and contact the element Air at the Open Temple to prepare for the meditation in the temples.

MORNING: Meditation in the Blue Temple and Hall of Mirrors.

AFTERNOON: Guided visits to some of the communities that form the Federation, focusing on agriculture, ecological building, and research laboratories.

DAY 7 (Saturday) CREATIVITY AS AN INSTRUMENT OF PERSONAL TRANSFORMATION

MORNING: Clay workshop experience with Damanhurian master sculptors. The importance of art and creativity in Damanhur's history. Everybody is an artist.

AFTERNOON: continue your piece of art.

DAY 8 (Sunday) LEARN MORE ABOUT DAMANHUR'S PHILOSOPHY

MORNING: Learn about Damanhur's philosophy and research, an opportunity for questions.

FREE TIME. Departure during the day. ∎

Meditations in the Temples

Thousands of people from all over the world use the Temples of Humankind every year as an instrument for inner research and contact with the divine, and to open inner channels to inspiration, dreams, and creativity. These new paths of meditation allow a deep level of access to the spiritual energies of the halls, and offer an extraordinary opportunity of communion and dialogue with one's soul.

1. TECO Program

All meditations in the TECO Program are guided by expert facilitators. The meditations are different for each hall, with specific activation patterns, sounds, mantras, and movements to reach a complete harmonizing with oneself and the temples. Pilgrims will also have personal meditation time. To participate in a TECO Program, it is necessary to have already visited the Temples of Humankind.

Before meditating, pilgrims prepare according to specific instructions. The preparation is an indispensable part of each meditation session. These meditation sessions can be done singly or in a sequence, and can be repeated more than once.

Meditation sessions normally take place in groups, according to requests. For special individual needs, please contact the Welcome Center staff. It is possible to request individual meditations following the TECO program.

The duration of each meditation is approximately 90 minutes.

TECO 1: THE HALL OF EARTH

Preparation: Walk the Spiral and contact the Earth element in Damjl.

TECO 2: THE HALL OF SPHERES AND THE HALL OF METALS

Preparation: Walk the Spiral and contact the Fire element in Damjl.

TECO 3: THE LABYRINTH

Preparation: Walk the Spiral and contact the Earth element in Damjl.

TECO 4: THE HALL OF WATER

Preparation: Walk the Spiral and contact the Water element in Damjl.

TECO 5: BLUE TEMPLE AND THE HALL OF MIRRORS

Preparation: Walk the Spiral and contact the Air element in Damjl.

2. Meditations for Creativity and Inspiration

The temples are the ideal space to open inner channels of creativity and inspiration.

The Halls are available to those who wish to gather inside themselves, to compose, research, write, sing, or dance. . . . A Damanhurian facilitator is present during these sessions.

3. Damanhurian Sacred Dance

Damahurian Sacred Dance is the transposition in movements of an archetypal ideogrammatic language. This language—the basis of Damanhurian artistic expression—comprises signs and gestures that belong to the ancestral memories of our human species and offers keys to the reawakening of inner knowledge. Sacred Dance, moreover, is a powerful means to activate the energy lines of the human body, and can be used for well-being and health.

A Damanhurian Sacred Dancer will guide this meditation in movement, preparing the participants with simple exercises of breathing and relaxation.

Each session lasts approximately 90 minutes. These sessions can be repeated.

4. Dreaming in the Temples:
The Talej Program

The program TALEJ is open to those who have already done at least one of the following things:

- spent a night in the Temples of Humankind
- attended the VELJ program (or a full-day visit to the temples, according to the programs offered by the Olami Welcome Center in the past years)
- attended one meditation session of the TECO program
- attended the course "Reawakening the Inner Senses"

After a period of preparation, you will spend the night in the hall of your choice to tune into its energies while you sleep and receive intuitions through inspired dreams.

DURATION: Evening to the following morning.

6 p.m.: Walking meditation in the Circuit for Dreaming in Damjl, and a special meditation in the Gallery of Selfic Paintings.

DINNER

9 p.m.: Drive to the Temples of Humankind.

Halls available for the TALEJ program:

1. Hall of Mirrors
2. Hall of Metals
3. Hall of Earth (upper and lower parts of the hall) ∎

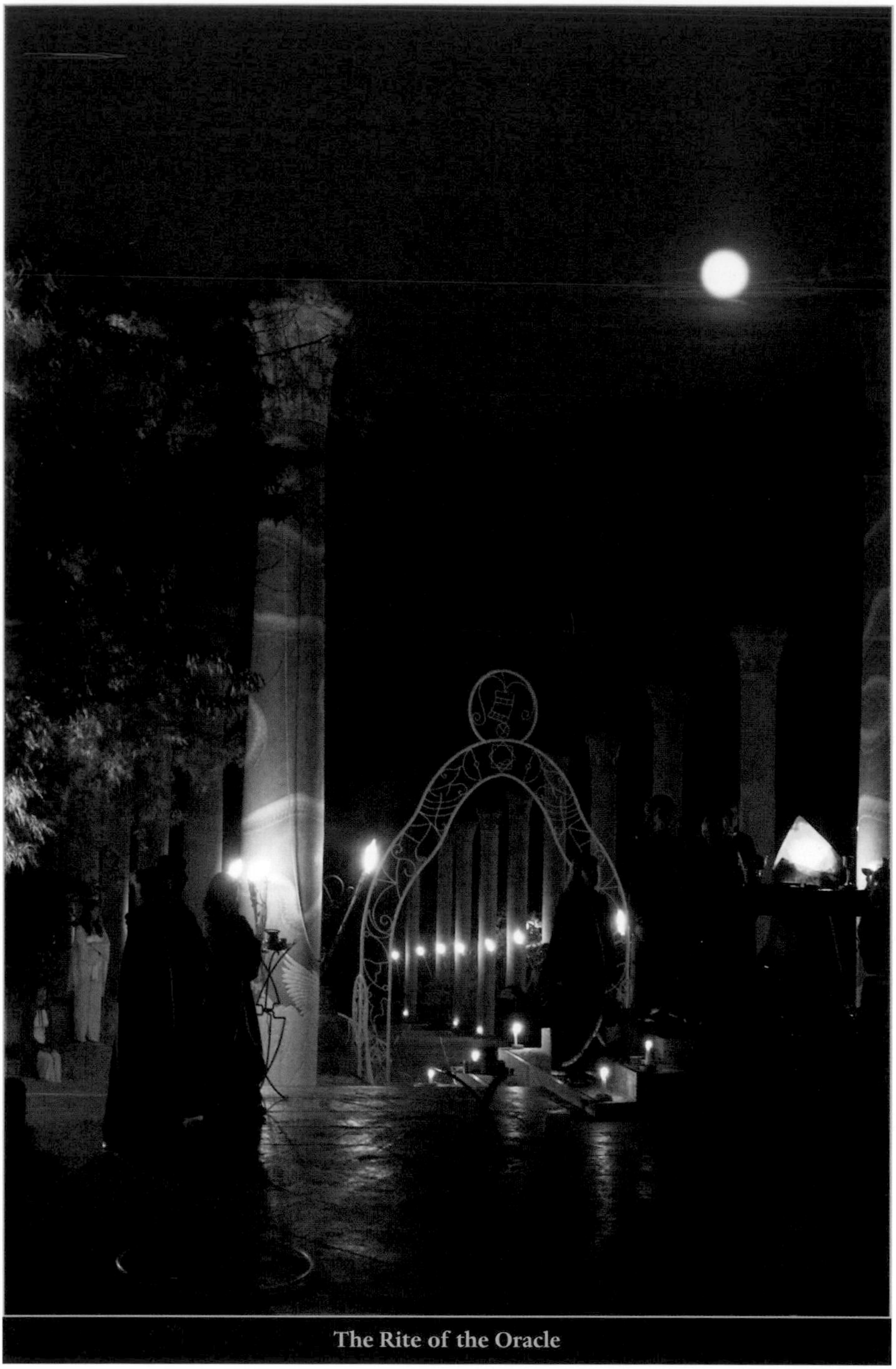

The Rite of the Oracle

Festivals of Damanhur
The Rite of the Oracle of Damanhur

The Rite of the Oracle is one of the most important celebrations of Damanhur. Since September 1985, it has taken place every month at the full moon. The public phase of this rite in the Open Temple is the culmination of profound and attentive ritual work, carried out by the members of the Way of the Oracle throughout the lunar month.

In Damanhur the Oracle is not a person. The "Oracle" is a group of divine forces, which comprises all the Oracles of ancient times. Integrated with the new forces of the third millennium, they can once again perform their role of guide for humanity. The forces of the Oracle not only give answers and directions, but they also interact with all the possible branches of time, scheduling events so that they can be the most propitious for the spiritual evolution at many levels for many people: the people receiving an Answer, those who participate in the ritual, and the community of Damanhur as a whole. During the ritual a window of spiritual light opens and everybody present can feel the contact with the divine dimension.

The Rite is accompanied by drumming, while the dancers of the Way of the Oracle trace prayers and propitiations with their movements. For all participants, this is a time of silence, insight, and inner contact with the realm of the sacred.

Those people who had previously requested an Answer are accompanied onto the stage to receive it. Responses are given to questions presented in writing one or more months ahead—the ritual work for the compilation of a response requires time and care. The Answer is written on a chestnut leaf and, before being given to the recipient, it is read by a Priestess. The sound of her voice is covered by music, so that only the recipient of the Answer can hear it.

How to Request an Answer

The Oracle of Damanhur can be consulted by all those who wish to take advantage of this opportunity for human and spiritual growth. Individuals and groups from all over the world have requested an Answer as a precious source of inspiration and insight. If you wish to consult the Oracle, contact Gazza Solidago at the Welcome Center, Ⓣ (+39) 0124 512205; welcome@damanhur.it

Spring, Summer, and Winter Festivals

The Spring, Summer, and Winter Festivals combine tours of the Federation and the Temples of Humankind with short seminar courses that give an in-depth overview of the philosophy and organizing principles of the People of Damanhur. Here is a typical sample schedule of presentations and workshops at one of the festivals:

First Day

9:30 a.m. • The opening of the festival

10 a.m.–11:30 a.m. • Session on Alien Civilizations and Atlantis

12 p.m.–1 p.m. • Damanhurian therapies and the School for Spiritual Healers

1 p.m.–3 p.m. • Break for lunch and group sessions

3 p.m.–5 p.m. • Contact with the plant world and Music of the Plants

5:30 p.m.–6:30 p.m. • Session on Inner Personalities

6:30 p.m.–9 p.m. • Free time for dinner, therapies, and relaxation

Second Day

9:30 a.m.–10:15 a.m. • Inner Harmonizing and Damjl Circuits

10:30 a.m.–1 p.m. • Spiritual Physics (Cosmogenesis and Time)

1 p.m.–3 p.m. • Break for lunch

A class during the Summer Festival

3 p.m.–4 p.m. • Contact with the Cosmos and the Synchronic Lines

4:30 p.m.–5:30 p.m. • Astral Travel

6:30 p.m.–9 p.m. • Free time for dinner, group sessions, and relaxation

Third Day

9:30 a.m.–10:30 a.m. • Damanhurian massage and self-massage exercises

11 a.m.–12 p.m. • The Path to the Inner God

12:15 p.m. 1:15 p.m. • Past Life research

1:15 p.m.–3 p.m. • Break for lunch and therapies

3:30 p.m.–5 p.m. • Inner Senses and contact with the Spheroself

5:30 p.m. 6:30 p.m. • Questions & Answers

6:30 p.m. • Final Celebration Party

7 p.m.–9 p.m. • Free time for dinner, group sessions, and relaxation

Classes and Workshops

In order to share and draw upon the experience of the life and research of the Federation, Olami Damanhur University offers short-term courses and seminars in many subjects linked to the development of human potential, in addition to one- to three-year courses offered by Damanhur's Mystery School, School for Spiritual Healers, School of Colour Therapy, and School of Massage (see "Staying On" on page 41).

The courses and schools are based upon the teachings of Oberto Airaudi and the research of the citizens, and are grounded in the experience of life in the Federation.

The short courses offered by Olami University run the gamut from those that sound down-to-earth ("How to Create a Successful Community") to the intriguingly "out-there" ("Astral Travel"):

How to Create a Successful Community

Personalities Within

The Dream Path

Reawakening the Inner Senses

The Inner Artist

Lateral Thinking

The Transformation of Memories

Past Life Research

Astral Travel

Alien Civilizations and Atlantis

Many seminars include exercises and meditations in the Temples of Humankind. Sessions are scheduled so that people who live abroad can attend intensive periods of study. Many of the university's courses are also held at venues outside of Damanhur.

Olami University ⊤ (+39) 0124 512236; dhcorsi@damanhur.it

Contact the Intelligence of the Galaxy in the Temples of Humankind

After guided preparatory exercises to open and reawaken your sensitivity, you will enter the Temples of Humankind and live a unique experience. There you will find the optimum conditions to receive messages that can arrive from inside you or from very far away. This workshop is a whole night devoted to this form of contact, with the support and guidance of specialist instructors.

How to Create a Successful Community

Harvesting more than thirty years of experience, Damanhur presents a workshop that provides all the basic elements needed to build a successful intentional community capable of renewing itself and lasting over time. Over the course of many years, a group of ordinary citizens can transform themselves and manifest solid values while creating a truly successful human group. Building spiritual community parallels the inner journey and requires concentration, cooperation, and determination on the part of each individual. Living in a spiritual community means each person is faced with a mirror image of "the ideal" within a harmonious but also imperfectly human framework.

Every person in the world is already part of many communities, although in most cases they participate unconsciously. The communities of one's nation, state, city, political party, charitable organizations, and family help us define who we are.

In this seminar Falco, the founder of Damanhur, and his associates will help you recognize the most important aspects required to transform an intentional community into a spiritual community. They will also provide clear guidelines for the necessary and gradual steps needed to walk upon this path. The topics covered include:

Philosophy:

Ethical principles, solidarity and sharing, critical numbers theory

Creating rules, the importance of playing, defining responsibilities

Leadership, ethical banking, relationships with other communities

Philosophy of money, voluntary work, dreaming the future

Economy:

Economic self-sufficiency, shared finances, working businesses

Research and development, personal contributions

Communal expenses and investments, banking

Complementary currency, exchanging goods and services with other communities

Social:

Living communally, community services, continuous research

Social organizations, decision-making processes, food self-sufficiency

Health care, schools, elders, changing generations

Relations with the state, political relationships

Relations with other communal groups

Territory:

Researching a territory, optimal characteristics of property

Choosing the land, relationships with the surrounding area

Energy self-sufficiency, renewable energies and technologies

Sustainable living

Summer School for Children

Damanhur Family School is open to all children from all countries who would like to participate in Damanhur during the Summer season in August, when the School organizes Summer Games for children from six to thir-

Damanhur Family School children with their teacher

teen years old, as well as a weeklong residential Summer Arts Camp for children between ages ten and thirteen.

Healing and Other Alternative Therapies
Healing in Damanhur

Health has represented one of the fields of constant research ever since the beginning of Damanhur. Many visitors to Damanhur come with a specific health issue that they wish to work on during their stay.

Damanhurian medicine is characterized by a humanistic vision of healing in which the individual is the protagonist. Healing is never seen as a passive event to be demanded from the miraculous intervention of other specialized individuals or from a means outside of oneself. Healing, for

The Atlantean Discipline of Selfica

One of the most interesting fields of research that Damanhur has developed is linked to "Selfica," a discipline that involves the concentration and direction of vital and intelligent energies. Selfica was widely used in Atlantis and traces of its use can also be found in Egyptian, Etruscan, and Celtic cultures. The ancient Arabs used Selfica until the eighth century BC.

Selfica, introduced to Damanhur through the research of Oberto Airaudi, creates structures based on the spiral and the use of metals, colors, inks, and minerals that are able to host intelligent energies. With a simple structure known as a Self based on metals, particular substances, and geometric combinations, Selfica facilitates the superimposition of the complex functions. The particular energies that selfic structures known as Selfs call upon are "border intelligences" that pass from one reality to another, acting as intermediaries between planes of existence. The intelligence of the Self is in fact the energy that manages the physical part of the structure and which continues to use the laws of its own plane of existence in order to act in ours.

The interaction of a Self with an individual is always based upon mutual advantage. The Self attracts useful conditions for the physical life of an individual person or for the development of his or her personal potential, connecting to the aura through "microlines": the energy lines of the human body. In exchange, the selfic intelligence has the opportunity to gain experience of a different world from that in which it originates. Selfs and human beings do not live all aspects of their existence in reciprocal interaction, only those that bring specific mutual advantages.

The largest selfic structure on the planet is hosted by the Temples of Humankind. The temples, seen in the context of a laboratory, create the ideal conditions for interacting with higher forces for the evolution of humanity. The use of the selfic structures of the temples has allowed for the development of new areas of research, both in the field of health and the exploration of time and space. ■

Damanhurians, is not just a profession but an art that springs from a holistic view of the individual and which, in addition to scientific knowledge, also makes use of sensitivity and attentiveness towards others.

The body, in Damanhurian philosophy, is considered to be a temple, a precious tool for the soul and for the divine principle contained within every human being; for this reason, physical and spiritual well-being are equally

Sel Et: The Selfica Laboratory at Damanhur Crea

The Selfica laboratory Sel Et conducts research in the field of energies linked to the use of metals. Experts in Selfica direct their research to the creation of "live" objects with functions that are aimed specifically at the user to encourage personal and environmental harmony and to amplify sensorial capacities.

The simplest Selfs are made of metal and resemble handmade copper bracelets or other personal ornaments, but the Sel Et workshop also creates more complex structures that combine metals with spheres containing specially prepared liquids for the transformation of energy. Other structures unite precious metals with microcircuits constructed in specially prepared inks, to carry out complex energetic functions. These Selfs can be programmed for multiple functions and can be used by more than one person at the same time for different purposes.

The selfic laboratory is located next door to the healing center. Sel Et hosts an experimental selfic cabin for the treatment of minor ailments.

⊤ (+39) 0125.7891144; selet@damanhur.com
Web site http://www.sel-et.com ■

important for health. A harmonious lifestyle and way of thinking, prevention, and identifying suitable cures in each case are all part of the Damanhurian concept of health, making use of the principles of maximum benefit and minimum risk. From home births to organic foods; from pranatherapy to regular health screening; from phytotherapy to emergency medicine; from Selfica to genetic screening tests; from hypnosis to art in all its forms as therapy; from the fight against GMOs to research into the divine essence within oneself: this is the territory covered by the original Damanhurian model of health.

It is important to Damanhurians to choose natural methods that respect humans and the environment, without neglecting our present scientific and technological innovations and discoveries. In a step-by-step model, one moves from prevention (pranatherapy, diet, deep breathing exercises, prenatal and birth care) to maintenance medicine (disciplines of well-being), to curative medicine (phytotherapy, homeopathy, flower remedies, conventional medicine, surgery).

The Damanhur Health Association is composed of Damanhurian specialists and professionals who have different skills and therapeutic training. It is a social organization whose members are dedicated to research, to the experimental application of collective discoveries, and to training in the field of health and therapy. The training of the doctors and therapists who are part of the association also comprises a series of treatment methods from traditional and Damanhurian medicine, such as pranatherapy, chromatherapy, and Selfica. Surgery and conventional drugs are used if necessary, but these other methods work as non-invasive alternatives in many cases.

In the Damanhurian model, doctors ideally have a broad training that covers various fields and may include homeopathy, homotoxicology, Traditional Chinese Medicine, hypnosis, and relaxation techniques. Reaching a diagnosis also makes use of mixed systems, ranging from the typical tools of scientific/technological medicine, applied strictly according to the instructions, to techniques closer to a "shamanic" vision of health: chiromancy, pulsology, birth chart and astrological reading, dowsing, and channeling. Nothing is excluded; every element is added to the others to obtain as broad a view as possible.

House of Health: A Center for Integrated Medicines

Under the supervision of three highly experienced doctors, the House of Health, located on the lower floor of Damanhur Crea, hosts a medical clinic that provides first aid services and medical consultations during the day. The center provides specialized consultations and personalized programs in stress-relief medicine, diet and fitness, allergy treatment, gynecology, and midwifery. The doctors offer sessions of acupuncture, hypnosis therapy, and homeopathy. The center also hosts a dentistry clinic operated by fully qualified professionals from the prestigious Traversa Clinic in Turin, one of the best in Italy.

Damanhurian doctors are also available to evaluate if Damanhur's unique selfic healing treatments can be beneficial for the healing of specific conditions, even serious ones. The healing instruments available at Damanhur include complex healing devices based on selfic technology that can be used for cellular and organ rejuvenation, for prevention, and as an aid in the cure of serious diseases. Their functioning principle is based on the possibility of conveying correct information to the body and its cells and organs, so that it can correct a malfunction, and the body can achieve a state of harmony and health.

All therapeutic interventions with selfic technology are done under the supervision of Dr. Maria Luisa Ravaioli. A medical doctor, surgeon, anesthetist specializing in Life Support, and psychotherapist, Dr. Ravaioli is also a specialist in acupuncture and Traditional Chinese Medicine. Dr. Ravaioli is the head of Damanhur's internal health service and has been working side by side with Oberto Airaudi in the field of alternative medicines for several years.

FisioCrea Rehabilitation Center

Practitioners at FisioCrea are highly specialized in post-traumatic physical rehabilitation, using innovative technologies such as the **Tecar® Technique** (Capacitive and Resistive Energetic Transfer, http://www.fitenergy.it/tecar.html). Appointments for treatments should be booked well in advance.

Ⓣ (+39) 0125 789922

The "Medicines" of the Damanhurian Tradition

Two beautiful rooms at the medical center in Damanhur Crea are completely dedicated to alternative Damanhurian healing treatments.

Contact: Damanhur Health

healing@damanhur.it

T (+39) 0125 7899

Damanhurian energy healing

Damanhurian energy rejuvenation

Damanhurian selfic treatments

Damanhurian massage and sound and color therapy

Pranatherapy

Beauty pranatherapy

Damanhurian massage and self massage

Hypnosis

Selfica

Stiloselfs

Some of the most popular treatments:

Pranatherapy is the most ancient form of healing. It rebalances the body through the flow of *prana,* which means "universal energy" in Sanskrit. Damanhurian healers do not transmit a personal flow of energy to their patients; they are channels for a pure, vital energy that helps the physical and subtle bodies to reestablish their equilibrium and return to an optimum state of health. Pranatherapy—or spiritual recovery as it is more accurately termed—is beneficial in a great variety of diseases, and a very effective complement to all other forms of treatment.

Prana affects the subtle bodies positively, and strengthens and repairs them where necessary. The result is to fortify the immune system and the organism's self-defense capacities, to open the psychic and spiritual pathways for individual evolution, and to support and accelerate the healing process.

Damanhurian spiritual healers are aided by the use of highly evolved multi-functional Selfica, such as the new generation Spheroself and the gold Stiloself. The outcome of the most advanced research of the Damanhurian laboratories at the boundaries of science, the Selfs are structures made from metals and specially prepared liquids and ink—see "The Atlantean Discipline of Selfica" on page 32 above. They can become intelligent healing tools, working in symbiosis with the organism by re-imprinting information onto the functional aspects of the body that are weak at the time.

Gold Stiloselfs

Stiloself—a selfic instrument that is applied without puncturing to energy points and meridians of the body—obtains results that are similar to those of Chinese acupuncture. The application of Stiloself affects the various levels of the physical body, from cells to organs, and reestablishes the correct energetic balance. This ensures a perfectly safe, clear, and effective transmission of energy.

Beauty Pranatherapy acts with the same principles as pranatherapy, and is applied as a specific treatment for tissue regeneration and for aesthetic purposes.

Damanhurian Massage is a refined and original system of bodywork with the active participation of the person treated. It has a profound effect on rebalancing the different body parts and enhancing the connection between the organism and the universal sources of vital energy.

Hypnosis allows a person to make the best use of their physical and psychical resources, with the aim of overcoming damaging behavioral patterns. ■

Other Practitioners

A variety of techniques are also offered by quality practitioners in the valley. Many healing professionals are drawn to live in Valchiusella to incorporate the energy of the Synchronic Lines into their work and to share their knowledge with others. Some of these holistic healers are listed here. All are English speakers.

Essential Coaching

CONTACT: Lida de Koning, Inigolida.henning@gmail.com

Enneagram/astrology method. Aura reading and healing.

Magical Massage and EFT

CONTACT: Adam Déjamour, EFT Practitioner, adam@yes-to-life.com

Utilizing techniques from an extensive background of almost forty years of experience in diverse healing modalities, Adam will take you on a magical journey that is much more than a massage, beneath his sensitive and skilled hands. Or, you can try a session of EFT, a gentle work of "emotional acupuncture without needles," a quick yet very profound and permanent reprogramming system to reach a blissful state of emotional freedom.

Intuitive Healing and Psychic Readings

CONTACT: Gabrielle Déjamour, readings@yes-to-life.com, http://www.yes-to-life.com

Magical journeys into your psyche and your energy, these metaphorical readings give you profound insights and unlock blockages. Sessions in English, French, or Italian.

International phone readings are toll-free for Western Europe, the USA, and Canada.

Polarity and Craniosacral Energywork

CONTACT: Liz Welch, lizwelc@yahoo.co.uk

Liz offers gentle assistance with your transmutation of physical, emotional, or spiritual issues.

Yoga, Meditation and Ayurveda

CONTACT: Franziska Richter, Frani.Ri@web.de

Individual sessions and/or weekends with B&B accommodation. ■

Pré-Saint-Didier Spa

The closest spa to Damanhur is at Pré-Saint-Didier, a beautiful European-style hot-spring resort offering a variety of treatments: thermal mud baths, Turkish baths and saunas, hydrotherapy, and massage. It is a one-and-a-half hour drive on the A5 from Damanhur in the direction of Aosta; exit at Courmayeur.

The source of the Pré-Saint-Didier natural thermal springs flows out from a cave in the Pré-Saint-Didier ravine. The warm waters of Pré-Saint-Didier flow out from the heart of the mountain at a temperature of around 98.6°F (37°C). The water of Pré-Saint-Didier is a saline-acidulous-arsenious-ferruginous water with moderate radio-activity. It also contains silica, arsenicated acids, iron oxide, and calcium carbonate.

The warm thermal waters were used for many years to treat rheumatic and muscular disorders, as well as skin ailments and blood circulation problems. They were also famous for possessing tonic and fortifying properties and for soothing both the body and the mind.

English language Web site: http://www.termedipre.it/spa_italy.asp. ■

Kythera Day Spa

Kythera offers Damanhurian and other rejuvenative techniques such as massage and energy treatments. It also offers slimming and anti-aging treatments with innovative machines for professional esthetic treatments. The spa features a steam bath, a tanning cabin, a floating bed, Proellixe vibrational equipment, and different kinds of massage modalities.

T (+39) 0125 789936; kythera@kythera.it

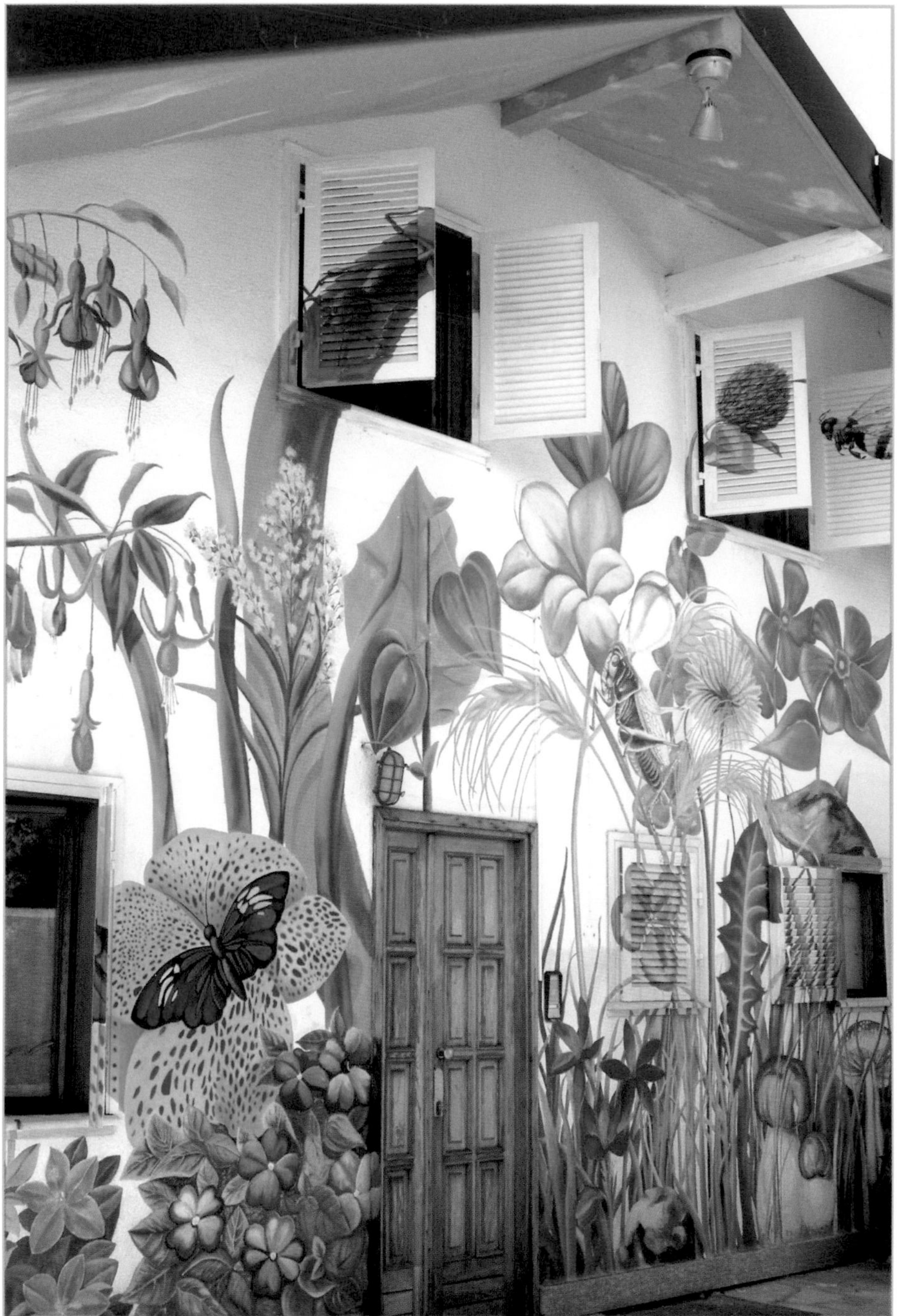

A painted house in Damjl

Staying On: Nucleos, Eco-homes, Eco-Villages, and Schools for Personal Growth

Visitors who wish to deepen their participation in Damanhurian life are invited to consider returning for an extended stay, to study at Olami University in one of their professional certification programs, or simply to live and join in the life of the community. Daily life is based upon sharing, exchange with others, and the commitment of everyone to bring alive their individual and their shared dreams.

The social structure and the political system have been changed many times over the course of the years from the first communities up to the present Federation, giving rise to a democratic system with representatives and elected bodies based upon the active participation of all the citizens in public debate. All the changes to the rules and regulations are ratified in accordance with the Constitution, which has been updated several times, so that it always reflects the aims of the citizens of Damanhur. Damanhur offers various possibilities for citizenship according to the level of commitment that each person chooses: from those who live full time within the community to those who are linked to the project of the Federation while still living outside.

The citizens who choose the community formula live in large houses or in houses close to one another called "nucleos," where nucleo-families are formed of around twenty people. There are couples, couples with children, single people, young and old people living in the communities, and this variety in generational groups permits an exchange of experiences among all the different ages.

Each member has their own personal space to live in and they share with the others the communal areas such as the kitchen and the meeting rooms, the gardens, and the territory. The houses and land belong to building and agricultural cooperatives, of which all the resident Damanhurians are associate members and shareholders.

According to their own preferences, the Damanhurians live in apartments in the villages of the valley or on farms, or in the woods and rural areas in contact with nature. Work is aimed at self-sufficiency in food and energy. Every Damanhurian chooses where and with whom to live, according to their own personal inclinations and their own goals. The children live with their parents while they are small and every citizen feels responsible for their well-being and is involved in looking after them and supporting them.

For the elderly people, there are structures set up to take care of each person's needs. Giving attention to the elderly is a point of excellence in the Damanhurian social system, which aims to guarantee the very best conditions for a senior individual, both with their daily well-being and with the assistance that might eventually be needed. Above all, Damanhur elder care values the experience that each elderly person can bring to others.

Living in a Nucleo Community

But what is daily life like in a Damanhurian nucleo-community? How do twenty or so people of different ages, cultures, and habits manage to live together in harmony for a long time?

Of course there are no standard answers, and every person and every family has a path of research facing them to find the optimal balance between individual and group needs, which permits not only living together in a harmonious and pleasant manner, meeting the needs of everyone, but also allows growth through confrontation with others. In thirty years of existence, the Damanhurians have had the opportunity to explore these themes in great depth and, beyond the differences of each individual case, they have managed to identify the following common ingredients to successful communal living:

KINDNESS, listening and showing respect for the needs and the space of others

PERSONAL SPACE suited to everyone's needs

LARGE COMMUNAL SPACES for meetings and activities

SHARING ONE'S OWN TALENTS and experiences through actively taking part in family life

OPENNESS TO CHANGING ONESELF, allowing others to be a mirror for one's own strengths and weaknesses

SHARING TASKS to look after small children, cook, clean the house, and take care of the surrounding land

ACTIVELY TAKING PART in bringing up the children, taking care of them and their well-being

GROUP SPIRIT AND A SENSE OF HUMOR to get through difficult personal or family moments with a smile

ADAPTABILITY TO CHANGE, for example when the family welcomes a newborn, or when new members arrive, or when others leave for other family nucleos

CHOICE OF NUCLEO-COMMUNITY according to one's own affinity with the household and its projects

SHARING MOMENTS OF MEETING in which one gives and receives support and personal acknowledgment, makes decisions, and develops projects

ELECTIONS every year of one or more heads of groups, who meet regularly with other heads of families and with the representatives of the other Damanhurian bodies to decide communal politics and treasure one another's experiences, ensuring the cohesion of the whole community

CHOICE OF A COMMON GOAL linked to improving the territory, the house, and the quality of life within a nucleo

SHARING THE EXPENSES of rent, maintenance, management, and improvement of the house and the territory

There are many nucleos in Damanhur, and new ones may be created at any time. However, to give readers concrete examples of how nucleos work, just three will be described here.

Nucleo example 1: Porta del Sole (Sun Gate)

Porta del Sole is one of the oldest nucleos in Damanhur. The original small house the nucleo is housed in was already on the hillside when the building of the Temples of Humankind started in August 1978. It has now been completely renovated and a new extension is currently being built, which will be dedicated to guest accommodation.

The house has many solar and photovoltaic panels, and residents collect firewood from the woods and undergrowth, making both the house and the temples self-sufficient in their heating needs.

The members of this nucleo dedicate a large part of their time to the upkeep of the temples and serving the people who use and visit them. Guests will be able to enjoy this special area close to the temples for their spiritual retreats.

Nucleo Example 2: Aval

The nucleo-community of Aval takes care of the production of the vine-yards and wines of the "Aval" appellation, a D.O.C. white *erbaluce* and a red *passito* wine whose production from vine to distribution is coordinated by the community whose name it bears.

Aval is situated in Cuceglio and comprises two connected houses, the original Aval and the new building completed in summer 2007. The construction of the new house saw great activity on the part of the Damanhurians, who completed the building in record time (less than six months!).

This house was built according to the most modern eco-building criteria and has avant-garde technological systems installed for air conditioning and energy production. The house has been given an award for environmental sustainability by the FEE Green Home program. The inhabitants of the house are extremely careful to sort and recycle waste. They choose to follow an organic diet free from genetically modified organisms. They use ecological cleaning materials and take care not to waste resources.

Aval is characterized by work in scientific and social experimentation. Advanced laboratories are working on *in vitro* reproduction of meat cells, hydroponics, the extraction of hydrogen from algae, and personalized anti-aging cosmetics, in addition to carrying out biological, chemical, and clinical analyses.

A bed and breakfast is currently being organized, thus giving Aval a place in the cultural circuit linked to the oenogastronomic tradition that is so strong in the Piedmont region (Piedmont is the headquarters of the international Slow Food movement). The property has a large hall to host courses and meetings; on one of the walls a planetarium is vertically depicted, where those who are fond of the Damanhurian version of the game of Risk discover, in playing, new methods of logical deduction and games of strategy.

Aval is a jewel of eco-building: 800 square meters that bring together the use of traditional organic materials with the most modern technologies in the field of construction and building engineering. Advanced technologies in the field of air conditioning and the use of solar energy reduce to a minimum the emissions of CO_2 and greenhouse gases. The entire building is insulated by cladding made from wood fiber that reduces the heat loss.

A thermal control center, one of the largest in Europe for private use, regulates the winter and summer air conditioning. The heating and the cooling of the house is effected by radiator panels and walls which maximize living comfort with the minimum expenditure of energy. Heat production is integrated by solar heating panels. Temperature regulation is also assured by a ventilation system that passes the air through pipes in the ground that are able to mitigate the heat in summer and preheat the air in winter, so as to reduce to a minimum the energy needed by the air conditioning system.

It is not necessary to open the windows to get fresh air, because ventilation ducts were inserted throughout the whole house. Integrated ventilation is a fundamental prerequisite for green building energy certification and gives tax benefits for the owners of the house.

Control of the summer air conditioning is facilitated by the presence of a heated swimming pool, which helps to keep down the temperature of hot fluids during the period when heat production would be too much.

Great attention has been given to water management. Rainwater is saved in two underground tanks and is used for all purposes except where drinking water is needed.

For electricity production, the house has a 20 kW-powered installation able to produce 20,000 kW annually; plans are in progress to increase the power of the installation to 60 kW.

Nucleo Example 3: Ogni Dove

The nucleo-community of Ogni Dove (which means "everywhere" in Italian) is situated in a very special territory from the point of view of its energy; from here the Sacred Wood opens up to the stone Labyrinths that represent the outdoor continuation of the Temples of Humankind. On the territory there are also stone altars dedicated to the elements of nature, which complete the energy circuit of the place.

From a geographical point of view, the nucleo of Ogni Dove is situated at the highest point of the council district of Vidracco and owes its name to the spectacular 360-degree view to be enjoyed from the house. In Ogni Dove there live around twenty people, both adults and children, plus two dogs, several cats, and many guests who regularly come to visit from Italy, from various parts of Europe, and from the United States.

Ogni Dove's projects are linked in particular to the Sacred Wood, to its spiritual pathways, to the stone circuits, and to the development of the Temples of Humankind.

They include the new project of the Temple of the Peoples in the area of the Buche, which is situated right in front of Ogni Dove.

Family dinner at Ogni Dove

The Damanhur Family School (DFS): Awakening the Human Potential of Children

Damanhur Family School (DFS) was initiated in 1985 within the Federation of Damanhur and today more than seventy students of several nationalities between the ages of six months and fourteen years attend the school's small classes, which range from a nursery for infants to eighth grade.

At Damanhur learning is linked with life experiences and life is viewed as an ongoing source of learning; so, in a sense, all are students and all are teachers. Teachers are expected to continue to learn and to grow more deeply rooted in their jobs and interactions with young people. Personal, verifiable experience is the guiding principle, and education, like so many other "mundane" aspects of life in Damanhur, is seen as a multifaceted art form.

At Damanhur parents invite other adults into their family circle: people they think will be beneficial for their child's development. Godparents, surrogate grandparents, and other extended family members weave a tapestry of desirable qualities around the child, beginning before conception and extending throughout their lives. This extended family network is an integral component of the child's education.

At DFS, a child's main teacher is no longer merely a skilled transmitter of knowledge but a "preceptor" who carefully observes each child to discover their innate talents and inclinations. The preceptor guiding each student also ensures respectful space for emotional and spiritual development, coordinating class teachers and volunteers and presenting learning experiences in an innovative and creative format that far surpasses the standard curriculum required by the state government.

Travel is another form of experiential learning with the entire world viewed as an ideal classroom. Travel was a core learning experience for Falco and his friends in the early days of forming the Damanhur community. Through travel, students learn to gather knowledge and experiences, using traveling itself as a field of experience. Students explore the local environment and region in frequent field trips, and the school organizes longer trips to different parts of Italy and foreign countries. For example, in 2007 the nursery school children went to the Ligurian coast, where they observed sea mammals; one group traveled to Sicily to study the geography and culture of the region; and a third group went to France to participate in a program with a group of French children. In 2008 the fourth grade went to both Rome and Florence to give presentations on their project pertaining to the rainforest in Central America, and the eighth graders traveled to New York.

The family component of the DFS curriculum was created in order to bridge the gaps in cultural growth that tend to form between school, home, and society. The primary extended family works in conjunction with the nucleo family and takes upon itself the commitment of helping the child express their talents, strengthen their weak points, and prepare for the future. Each child's growth is followed with great interest by both school and family, and includes other educational activities such as sports, Scouts, and extracurricular activities.

The DFS incorporates an integrated curriculum and uses projects, or learning modules, to achieve many aspects of the curriculum. In keeping with Damanhur's goal of practical idealism, teaching objectives are realized through practical projects using real life situations as a starting point, moving on to discovering more "traditional" subject matter within the base project, such as mathematics, literature, etc. Some projects involve mixed age groups of children to promote cooperation and improve social skills through arts, sports, theater, and music.

Peace, individual responsibility, active sharing, and inclusion are pursued as fundamental values. These values prompt young people to take responsibility for the planet and to feel themselves to be citizens of the world.

Children are expected to develop deep awareness towards the environment and its ecology and to become fully responsible members of society.

Seeds of an International Boarding School

Many Italian and international children upon visiting DFS express their wish to attend the school, which of course is not possible living outside the Valchiusella area. It has therefore become one of Damanhur's dreams to create an international boarding school. Starting in August 2008, DFS is opening Damanhur's first experimental boarding school with interested children whose parents wish them to spend one or more years as students in Damanhur, not only benefiting from Damanhur's Family School, but also from their being immersed in the overall culturally and spiritually stimulating environment of the Federation. Children will be assigned an extended family upon registration for DFS.

In addition to an excellent academic education, Damanhur's boarding Family School wishes to stimulate important human and social values, such as good communication skills, sensitivity toward others, responsibility, and reliability, thanks to the child's close daily social interaction with teachers, schoolmates, and the whole of Damanhur's variegated broader social context. As a consequence of this, pupils learn to set a high standard for themselves, and to be open to those values that they gain by experience in dealing with real life situations. Damanhurians propose that this boarding school will offer opportunities for learning that cannot be acquired in an ordinary school setting or simply by contact with family and friends.

Olami, the Damanhur University

In addition to the workshops and classes offered to short-term visitors, Olami Damanhur University also offers certification programs in healing and spirituality that integrate theoretical and practical aspects of those fields. In May 2007 Damanhur started a collaboration with Wisdom University that now offers part of their internationally recognized Master and PhD programs in the Federation, with the presence of international artists, healers, and sociologists. Describing all the programs is beyond the scope of this guide but descriptions of two popular courses are given here as examples of the curricula available.

To register or request information, contact: seminars@damanhur.org; T (+39) 0124 512236

The Mystery School

The Damanhur Mystery School, a part of Olami Damanhur University, is a three-year journey of self-discovery that will also reveal the hidden reality around us. The seminars are guided by expert instructors to help students embody a new approach to self and life.

How vast is the reality around us? How rich is the world within us? Where do human beings come from? The Mystery School gives participants practical and useful tools to find the answers to these questions resounding loudly within themselves.

The first year is dedicated to self-discovery, to connecting with our deepest nature, the different facets of our soul, and our ancient human origins. Within us are unimaginable treasures waiting to be discovered and shared, and the first year opens a window onto that inner world, allowing us to enjoy a very unexpected landscape.

Participants in the second year, now conscious of their wholeness, are ready to discover the surrounding reality. The vast world composed of natural and spiritual ecosystems is a dimension that needs to be sensitively and energetically approached. The Mystery School offers a series of experiences that teach how to participate with the life surrounding us, to understand its nuances and expressions, and not merely be observers.

The third year once again brings our attention back to ourselves. Conscious of who we are, and in harmony with our surroundings, we now feel ready to know the unique role that we serve in the Universe. The course will lead us step by step to perceive the spiritual mission that guides our growth and evolution. Each life has a precise purpose in the Universe; when we discover our purpose and become an active participant in fulfilling it, we begin to weave a tapestry using all the threads of our existence.

The Mystery School's courses are selected from Damanhur's thirty years of experience. All seminar instructors have themselves been through this school. Damanhur offers the Mystery School journey to all people sensitive to these subjects as a way of expressing gratitude to life.

School for Spiritual Healers

The School for Spiritual Healers is a three-year course of training in healing with Pranatherapy. Founded in 1975, the School is based upon the principles and teachings of Oberto Airaudi and guides students on a pathway of self-knowledge, accompanied by a theoretical-practical training by a variety of specialist tutors. The objective is to provide students with a holistic preparation that will awaken their inherent therapeutic powers and encourage them to become truly holistic healers.

The Damanhur School for Spiritual Healers is designed for practitioners already operating in the sector who are seeking further qualifications as well as for beginners with no previous experience in the field. The School provides the instruments for a profound and positive transformation in the student through individual and group experiences. The course offers a technical training and also encourages the opening of students' energetic channels so that they can effectively direct the cosmic healing energy of *prana*.

Even though the main focus of the school concerns the use of pranic energy, learning to work with selfic healing instruments is also included in the program to extend the range of the healer's capabilities; studies include experimentation with selfic instruments from the basic Stiloself to the most complex Spheroself.

One of the unique characteristics of the Damanhurian School for Spiritual Healers is the use of the Temples of Humankind as an integrated part of the training. The temples are used for sessions of inner research and to explore the correspondence of the different halls with the physical organs of the body and psychophysical equilibrium.

The three-year course is split into yearly units of 200 hours, offering a total of 600 hours of theoretical-experiential studies, 350 of which are practical and begin in the first year. The number of study hours provides an optimum level of training and is in line with European directives for the recognition of courses leading to first degrees. At this level, different methods for the laying on of hands are studied as well as other healing systems, including Damanhurian Massage. At the end of the third year, work culminates in a presentation and discussion of a thesis. The successful submission of a thesis results in the conferral of the School Diploma.

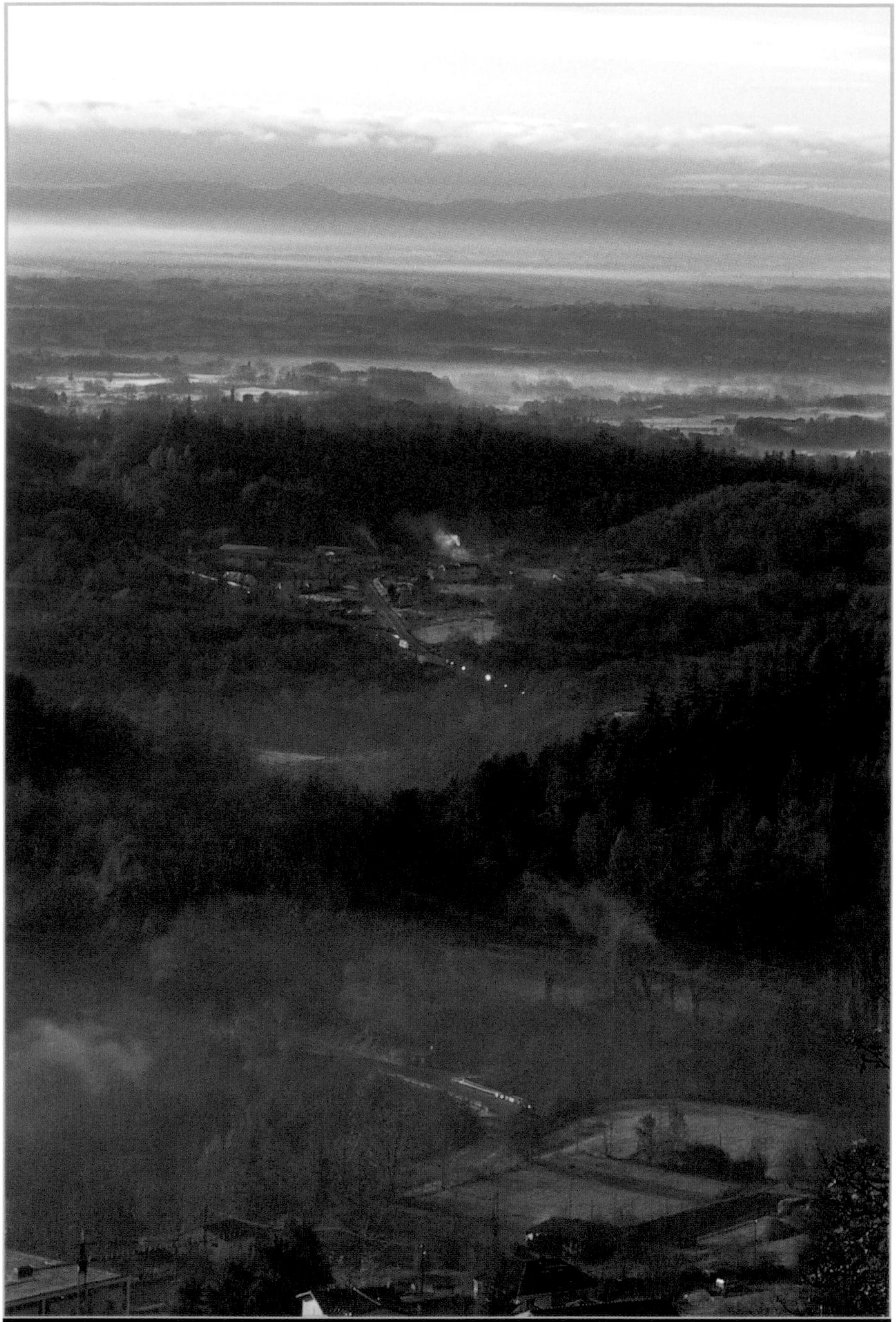

Piedmont Alps and valley of Turin seen from Ogni Dove at Damanhur

Travel Information

The Piedmont Region

Damanhur is located in the northern Italian region of Piedmont (Piemonte), which borders both France and Switzerland. Piedmont is celebrated for its food and wine, and is the headquarters of the international Slow Food movement, dedicated to promoting real cooking and fresh, locally produced ingredients. Sparkling white Asti and expensive red Barolo originate from towns in the region, and Piedmont's white truffles, hazelnuts, and chocolate are highly regarded.

The regional capital of Turin (Torino) is probably most famous for being the repository of Catholicism's greatest icon since 1578, the eponymous Turin shroud, but it has a busy contemporary profile as the second-largest industrial city in Italy after Milan. Turin hosted the 2006 Winter Olympics and is gradually shedding its old "city of industry" image.

In many ways, Damanhur is a reflection of the region's renewal and its emphasis on practical idealism, as well as older traditions of magic and mysticism.

Regional Attractions
Ivrea Historical Carnival *(Carnevale di Ivrea)*

This annual event, which traditionally starts on the Thursday before Lent, is not to be missed. Like other carnivals that revel in excess before the restrictions of Lent, the Ivrea carnival provides a weeklong celebration that is popular with both locals and tourists. Beginning with a masked ball and marked with reenactments of twelfth-century and Napoleonic era events and costumed processions through the town, the carnival reaches a climax with the Battle of the Oranges. For three consecutive days, nine teams of "Napoleonic revolutionaries" carry out a pitched battle in the town piazzas with over 400,000 kilograms (881,849 pounds) of oranges. Anyone venturing out onto the carpet of squashed oranges without some kind of red headgear is considered to be a fair target for the revolutionaries.

The pretty medieval town of Ivrea is just under 31.5 kilometers (20 miles) from Damanhur and a few miles east of the A5.

Web site: http://www.carnevalediivrea.com/inglese/carn_ing.htm

Pavone Medieval Fair

For thirteen years the historical/cultural association of Il Ruset has worked to promote the medieval fair in Pavone, right next to Ivrea, a short twenty-minute drive from Damanhur.

This event not to be missed, consisting of dinners with authentic flavors, historical costumes, music, dancing, and merriment, as well as medieval performances with duels and stage fights.

Groups from all over Europe are found throughout the village of Pavone, settled in encampments reliving the days of old.

Web site: http://feriemedievali@libero.it

Fortress of the Bard

The spectacular fortress of Bard and the Museum of the Alps are 40 minutes from Damjl. The highway exit points are at Pont-Saint-Martin to the south and Verres to the north (5 kilometers and 9 kilometers respectively from Bard).

Web site: http://www.fortedibard.it/home.php?fdb_lang=eng

The Magical City of Turin

Occult lore claims that Turin stands at a particularly powerful intersection of mystic energies, forming one of the corners of a white magic triangle together with the cities of Lyon and Prague, as well as being one of the points on a larger black magic triangle completed by London and San Francisco. Turin is also at the confluence of two major rivers: the Dora, identified with the female power of the moon, and the Po, which carries the male power of the sun.

The Egyptian Museum of Turin (http://www.museoegizio.it), established in 1824, has the most important collection of antiquities outside Egypt, including statues, papyri (a complete Book of the Dead), and the Tomb of Kha.

Tours to Turin to explore the Egyptian Museum and ancient mystical aspects of the city can be arranged through Damanhur's Welcome Center. ∎

Pavone Jazz Festival

National and international names in jazz and world music perform each year for three nights in Pavone and three nights in different towns close by, including in Vidracco at Damanhur Crea.

For more information, e-mail informazioni@music-studio.com

Getting There

Damanhur is located in the Valchiusella valley, 40 kilometers (25 miles) north of Turin. The closest town to Damanhur is Baldissero Canavese, near Castellamonte.

Driving to Damanhur: Ivrea is the closest exit on the A5 *autostrada* connecting Turin and Aosta. The journey to Damanhur from the exit takes about 20 minutes. Exit the autostrada and go toward Castellamonte for approximately 9 kilometers (5.5 miles). Take a right, still following signs for Castellamonte, and after just under a 1.5 kilometers (approximately 1 mile),

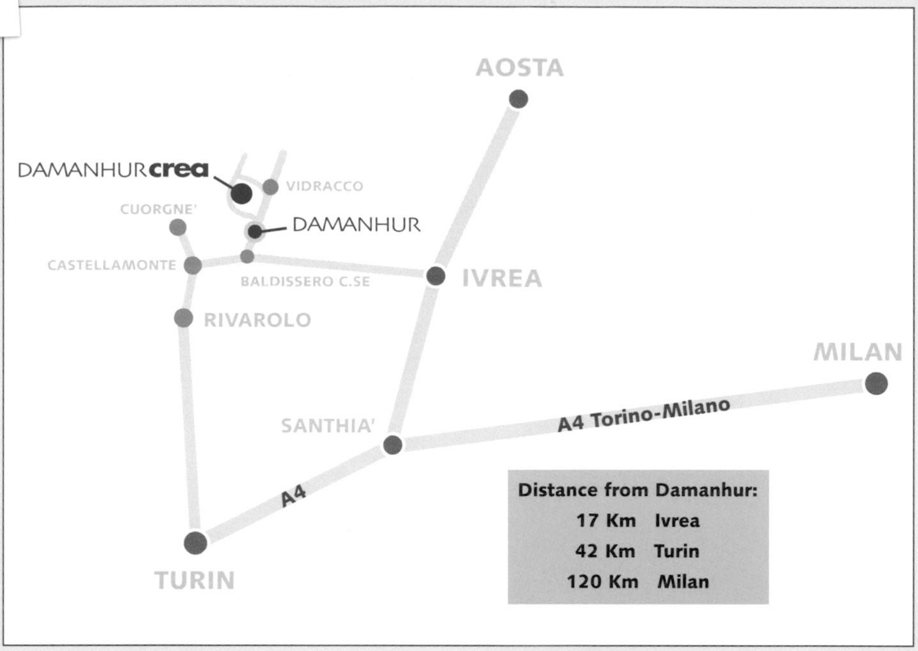
AOSTA
DAMANHURcrea
VIDRACCO
CUORGNE'
DAMANHUR
CASTELLAMONTE
BALDISSERO C.SE
IVREA
RIVAROLO
MILAN
A4 Torino-Milano
SANTHIA'
A4
TURIN
Distance from Damanhur:
17 Km Ivrea
42 Km Turin
120 Km Milan

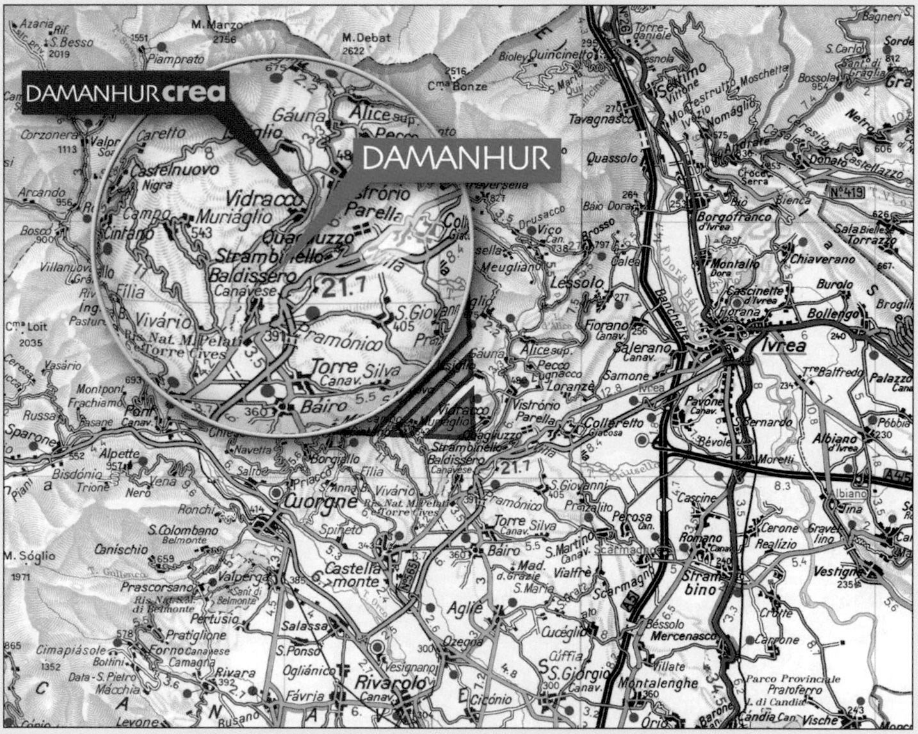
DAMANHURcrea
DAMANHUR
Ivrea
Cuorgnè
Rivarolo Canav.
Castellamonte
Vidracco
Baldissero Canavese

take a second right in the direction of Baldissero, Damanhur. After just over 2 kilometers (1 mile), you will see the entrance for Damanhur marked by a large yellow sign.

Local car rental agencies include Hertz Italiana in Ivrea (T [+39] 0125 251620) and several companies based at Turin airport, such as Tigercar Rental (http://www.tigercarrental.com/car-hire/turin-airport.htm).

Note: Be careful when driving on smaller rural roads in Italy. Drivers do not always stay in their lane, especially on winding country roads. Drivers also try to pass you even when there is oncoming traffic, so move to the right and let them pass.

Train: The closest train station to Damanhur is about 15 kilometers (9 miles) away in the town of Ivrea. Train travel in Italy is highly recommended; it is an eco-friendly and relaxing way to see the countryside. Please call the Welcome Center at Damanhur (T [+39] 0124 512205) a few days before your arrival to arrange a pickup.

The main train station in Turin is Porta Nuova in central Turin at the Piazza Carlo Felice. The Porta Susa Station is the main station for trains to and from Milan and is connected to central Turin and the main station by bus. A useful Internet resource is the Italian national railway's Web site Trenitalia (http://www.trenitalia.com), where you can plan train journeys, check timetables and prices, and book tickets.

Plane: Damanhur is a 40-minute drive from Turin airport (airport code TRN; T [+39] 011 5676361/2 for flight information; http://www.turin-airport.com), which is served by connections to European and national destinations. Please call the Welcome Center at Damanhur (T [+39] 0124 512205) at least a few days before your arrival and arrange a pickup. A Damanhurian will meet you in the downstairs arrivals area.

Facts for the Visitor

Information, Web Sites, and Maps

A wealth of information about Damanhur can be found on the official Damanhur Web site, http://www.damanhur.org.

Information on Italy and maps is available from the Italian National Tourist Office ([T] [39] 06 4 97 11; http://www.cnit.it and http://italian-tourism.com; Via Marghera 2, Rome 00185) and its branches abroad.

Communications

Telephone area codes all begin with 0 and can consist of up to four digits. The area code is followed by a number of anything from four to eight digits. Mobile phone numbers begin with a three-digit prefix such as 340.

To call Italy from abroad, dial the international access number (e.g. 011 in the USA), then Italy's country code (39), and then the telephone number, *including* the 0 in front of the area code.

Mail can be sent from post offices and post boxes. Stamps or *francobolli* are available at post offices and authorized tobacconists or *tabacchi*. The most reliable and commonly used mail service is *posta prioritaria* (priority mail).

Opening Hours and Public Holidays

Banks: 8:30 a.m.–1:30 p.m. and 3–4:30 p.m., Monday to Friday
Shops: 9 a.m.–1 p.m. and 3:30–7:30 p.m (or 4–8 p.m.), Monday to Saturday
Restaurants: noon–3 p.m. and 7:30–11 p.m.
National public holidays, in contrast to those of the US, often center on the Christian holy calendar:

New Year's Day (Capodanno or Anno Nuovo) January 1
Epiphany (Epifania or Befana) January 6

Easter Monday (Pasquetta) March/April

Liberation Day (Giorno della Liberazione) April 25, marking the
    Allied victory and the end of the German presence in 1945

Labor Day (Festa del Lavoro) May 1

Republic Day (Festa della Repubblica) June 2

Assumption (Assunzione) August 15

All Saints' Day (Ognissanti) November 1

Feast of the Immaculate Conception (Immaculata Concezione)
    December 8

Christmas Day (Natale) December 25

St. Stephen's Day or Boxing Day (Festa di Santo Stefano) December 26

Currency: Italian and Damanhurian

The unit of currency in Italy has been the euro since 2002. The seven euro notes come in denominations of 500, 200, 100, 50, 20, 10, and 5. The eight euro coins are in denominations of 2 and 1, and 50, 20, 10, 5, 2, and 1 cents. You can change money in banks, at the post office, or in a *cambio* (exchange office).

In Damanhur, you can exchange euros and other currencies for Damanhurian money, known as *creditos*.

1 Credito = 1 Euro

In 2006 the silver fifty-credito coin, equivalent to fifty euros, won the *Bulino d'Oro* (Golden Engraver) prize awarded by Red Exhibitions Italy and by the magazine *Graph Creative* for its design and the outstanding quality of workmanship.

The **credito** is the complementary monetary system of Damanhur. The credito has the aim of developing a new form of economy based on ethical values. The Damanhurian complementary monetary system has a high value and has been created to give back to money its original meaning: to be a means to facilitate change based upon an *agreement* between the parties. For this reason it is called the credito: to remind us that money is only a tool through which one gives, in fact, "credit"—that is to say, trust. Thanks to this monetary system, the Damanhurians want to elevate the concept of money, by not considering it an end in itself but only a functional tool for exchange between people who share ideals and values.

The use of the credito, in fact, allows all those who are part of this system to see themselves as part of the cultural, social, economic, and ethical values linked to the sustainability of the planet, including respect for human beings and every living creature, for quality of work and the added value of products thought of and realized with care and love.

A wide network of local producers and consumers—formed of around a hundred businesses and over 2,000 people—has chosen to use the credito through a system of agreements. In this way, the credito encourages the economic and social revitalization of Valchiusella because it facilitates keeping capital inside the area so that it can be re-invested to the benefit of the local economy, businesses, and activities.

Upon arriving in Damanhur, it is possible to convert one's money at the Welcome Center or at the special change machines located around the territory. Any unused creditos can be changed back into euros at any time.

One of the organizations that favors the use of the credito is the Damanhur Crea Consortium, to which the Damanhurian cooperatives belong. The Consortium guarantees the quality and ethics of their products and strengthens the network of trade and production.

Linked to the project of the credito and as a complement to it, there is the DES, a system of social loans which accepts deposits and issues financing both in euros and in creditos. DES arose from the idea of a finance service that serves the common good and makes use of the money to start up development projects with ethical and social aims (organic and GMO-free foods, eco-building, renewable energies, excellence in craftsmanship, art, culture, research). It is possible to participate in these projects by opening a savings account, available to members, with advantageous rates of interest.

First Aid and Health

All the activities of the Damanhurian health workers—doctors, healers, holistic practitioners, herbalists, obstetricians, physiotherapists, and other therapists—are coordinated by the association, Damanhur Health, which also operates the Center for Integrated Medicines open to the public at Damanhur Crea.

Damanhur Health

Center for Integrated Medicines

Damanhur Crea

10080 Vidracco (TO)

T (+39) 0125 7899

Places in the Valchiusella Valley

Where to Stay

To arrange accommodation in Damanhur, contact the Welcome Center T (+39) 0124 512205; e-mail welcome@damanhur.it. The Welcome Center can also provide assistance in booking local hotels, which sometimes offer discounted rates for Damanhur's guests.

There is a variety of different types of accommodation from camping to private bungalows, which the Welcome Center can arrange for you.

Hotels in the area include:

ALBERGO CENTRO in Vico Canavese, ⊤ (+39) 0125 74348

AGRITURISMO GARAVOT in Alice Superiore, ⊤ (+39) 0125 783143

ALBERGO ITALIA in Brosso, ⊤ (+39) 0125 795233

ALBERGO MINIERE in Traversella on the main village piazza, ⊤ (+39) 0125 749005; Web site http://www.albergominiere.com

CASTELLO DI PAVONE, hotel, four-star restaurant, and conference center in a stately castle, ⊤ (+39) 0125 672111; Web site http://www.castelladipavone.com

CASTELLO SAN GIUSEPPE, a romantic four-star hotel in Chiaverano d'Ivrea, ⊤ (+39) 0125 424370; Web site http://www.castellosan-giuseppe.it

FORESTERIA DEL CASTELLO, a former fortress turned into a charming hotel in San Giorgio San Canavese, ⊤ (+39) 0125 672111; Web site http://www.foresteriadelcastello.it

HOTEL AND RESTAURANT AQUILA NERA in Ivrea, in front of the train station, ⊤ (+39) 0125 641416; Web site http://www.aquilanera.it

HOTEL EUROPA in Rivarolo, ⊤ (+39) 0124 26097; Web site http://www.heuroparivarolo.it

HOTEL RITZ in Banchette d'Ivrea ⊤ (+39) 0125 611200; e-mail info-@hotelritzivrea.it

HOTEL TRE RE in Castellamonte, ⊤ (+39) 0125 515470; Web site http://www.trerecastellamonte.it

Recommended Restaurants

Many restaurants in the region accept creditos as payment. Most restaurants in the area are closed on Mondays for both lunch and dinner. Check with the restaurant or the Welcome Center for information Ⓣ (+39) 0124 512205.

Damjl

SOMACHANDRA CAFÉ: Serving world cuisine, this café is conveniently located on the patio of Rama in Damjl and is a meeting place of art, culture, and spirituality; it hosts themed events, evenings of dance, a library open to international community realities, and events for NGOs and ethical and spiritual networks. The café is run by the members of the Dendera nucleo, and its dishes reflect the diverse makeup of the nucleo; Dendera members are from Germany, Peru, Slovenia, and various regions of Italy, including the island of Sicily. Accepts creditos. Olami Welcome Center Ⓣ (+39) 0124 512205

Castellamonte

THE DREAMS PUB: An Irish pub with great beer and a friendly atmosphere. Ⓣ (+39) 333 5202635

FAST PIZZA AND LUNCH: The name says it all. Open during the week for lunch from noon to 2:30 p.m, and for dinner from 6 p.m. to midnight. Open for lunch only at weekends. Accepts creditos. Ⓣ (+39) 0124 582346

TRE RE: Known as one of the best restaurants in Piedmont. Traditional Italian cuisine and regional specialities with an excellent wine list. Ⓣ (+39) 0124 515470

Cuorgnè

MONSÙ BARBOT: Special wines and a very creative menu with local ingredients and old recipes. ⊤ (+39) 333 5202635; e-mail info@monsubarbot.it

Chiaverano d'Ivrea

CASTELLO SAN GIUSEPPE: A former seventeenth-century convent converted into a four-star restaurant and hotel with a spectacular view. Traditional Italian cuisine served with a selection of the best Piedmont wines. Closed on Sunday. ⊤ (+39) 0125 424370

Ivrea

AQUILA ANTICA: Regional seasonal cuisine. ⊤ (+39) 0124 641364

CERERE: Delicious macrobiotic vegetarian restaurant. ⊤ (+39) 0125 49349

VINERIA MORBELLI: Very creative cuisine in a romantic, informal but stylish atmosphere. ⊤ (+39) 0125 641675

Lake of Meugliano

RISTORANTE ALBERGO L'INCONTRO: Right on the beautiful Lake of Meugliano. Seasonal, regional specialties. ⊤ (+39) 0125 789920; e-mail incontro.lago@tiscali.net

Quagliuzzo

RISTORANTE MICHEL: A refined and creative seafood restaurant. ⊤ (+39) 0125 576204; Web site http://www.ristorantemichel.it

Trausella

TRATTORIA DA ANITA: A very traditional, quaint, and reasonably priced culinary experience. Ⓣ (+39) 0125 743311

Traversella

RISTORANTE LE MINIERE: Part of the Albergo Miniere hotel, serving traditional Piedmont cuisine. A favorite place for weddings and celebrations, with beautiful views of the Valchiusella valley. Ⓣ (+39) 0125 749005; Web site http://www.albergominiere.com

Vidracco

ARIELVO CAFÉ AND RESTAURANT: In the heart of Damanhur Crea, there is the Café Arielvo, a meeting place for drinks, a snack, a great coffee, or a steaming hot chocolate accompanied by delicious organic pastries baked every day in its own bakery. Next to the café, Arielvo also has a high quality, completely organic restaurant for lunches and dinners, characterized by its imaginative dishes.

Arielvo also offers tasting sessions of organically produced products of the region. Ⓣ (+39) 0125 789920

IL TIGLIO DI PAN: Organic restaurant with prix fixe menus in the evening and a self-service buffet at lunchtime. Farm-bottled Piedmont wine, river fish, and handmade pasta are features of the local, seasonal menu. Accepts creditos. Ⓣ (+39) 0125 789792

VAL DI KY: This café and pizzeria featuring organic Tuscan cuisine is a friendly place where Damanhurians love to hang out. Pizza is served in the evenings only. English is spoken. Open daily 7:30 a.m.–11 p.m. Closed Monday. Accepts creditos. Ⓣ (+39) 0125 791125

Shopping

Damjl

BOOKS: ValRa, the publishing house of Damanhur, has a bookstore selling Damanhurian literature in English, Italian, French, and German. Damanhurian CDs, DVDs, and postcards are also available, as well as a small selection of books by non-Damanhurian authors. The DVDs *Damanhur, for a Culture of Peace* (ValRa Damanhur, 30 minutes) and *Dreams of Damanhur* (Obscura Films, 1 hour) can be purchased from the store or its Web site. For more information about Obscura Films' DVD *Dreams of Damanhur,* visit http://www.dreams-ofdamanhur.com.

> Via Pramarzo, 3
> 10080 Baldissero Canavese
> Web site: http://www.valra.it

Damanhur Crea in Vidracco

Damanhur Crea presents an entirely new shopping experience, where shoppers may watch gifted artists at work and meet the Damanhurians who created the Temples of Humankind. On the upper floor, the reception area hosts a rich display of Damanhurian products, books, clothing, and artifacts, produced locally and by other Damanhur centers around the world. A beautiful jewelry workshop is located at the end of the exhibition area, where four master goldsmiths create unique selfic pieces in precious metals. You can order a custom piece of jewelry here, which will be ready for you in a day or two.

Tentaty—Organic and GMO-free Products

The first center in Valchiusella to promote ecologically sound trade and the culture of organic, genuine food, Tentaty offers the public over 3,000 articles, from food to herbal preparations and cosmetics, to products for the home and cleaning. Many of the foods on sale in Tentaty come from Damanhurian businesses, which guarantee the quality and the purity of all stages of production. Examples include the renowned cheeses from the cheese dairy La Buona Terra, the prestigious Aval, Erbaluce, red Anansal and white Setapta wines, and all the vegetables cultivated at Tiglio, Punto Verde, and the Fattoria. The food products on sale at Tentaty have a certificate of origin and are also tested by the analysis laboratory, Aset, which makes further checks that there are no traces of GMOs.

Tentaty is open Monday 8:30 a.m.–3:00 p.m., Tuesday to Friday 8:30 a.m.–8:30 p.m., Saturday and Sunday 8:30 a.m.–9:30 p.m.

T (+39) 0125 789729; e-mail tentaty@damanhur.com; Web site http://www.tentaty.it

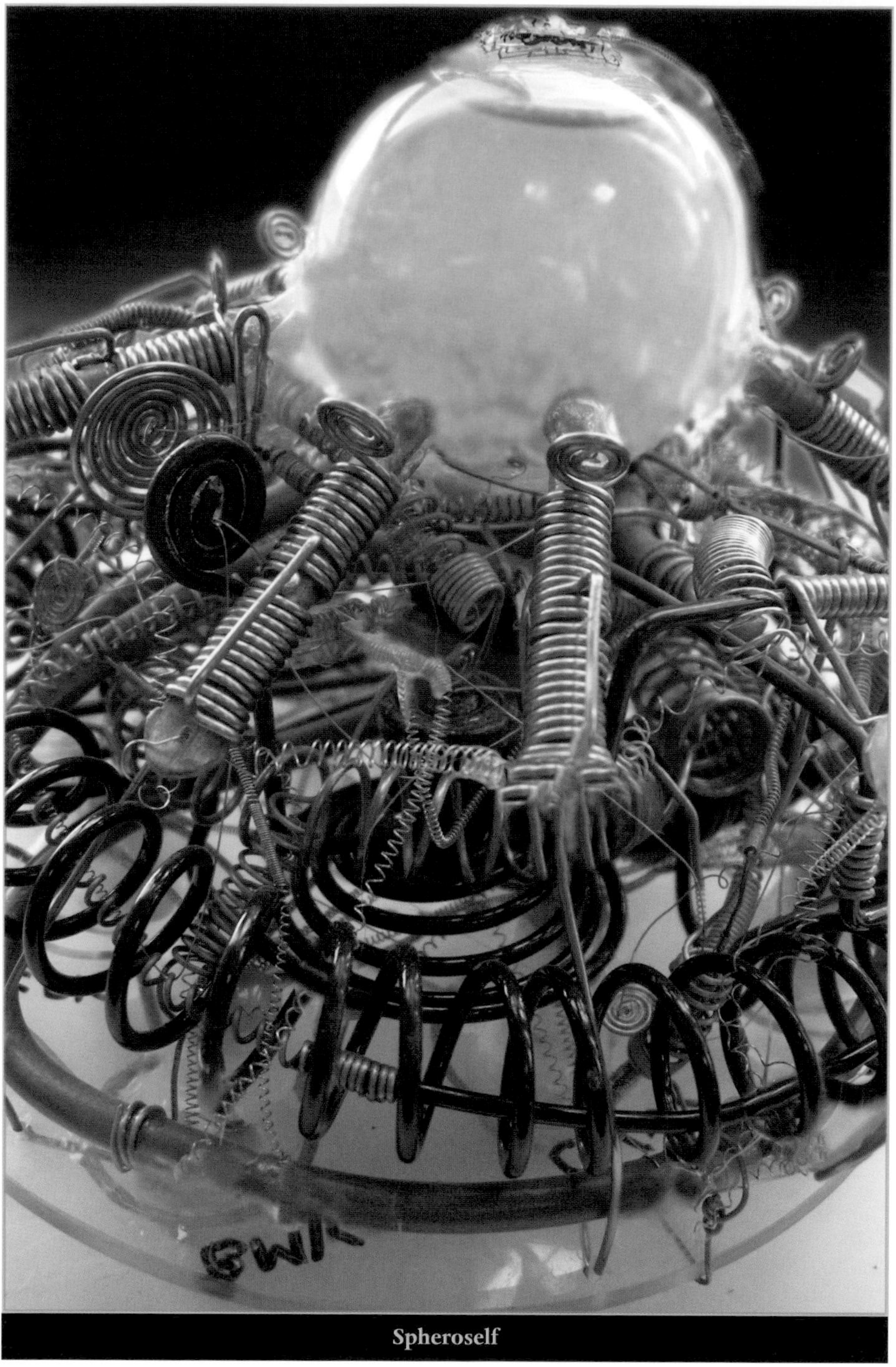

Spheroself

Visiting the Cosmic Machine on Earth

Pages from the Travel Journal of Richard Grossinger

Anthropologist and writer Richard Grossinger and his wife Lindy Hough traveled to Damanhur in September 2006.

SEPTEMBER 14, 2006: Lindy and I arrived at Damanhur knowing next to nothing about it except that it was a community involved in esoteric practices and that there were temples somewhere inside a mountain. I was vague on whether the members were resident or dispersed, autonomous practitioners or obedient devotees; to what degree their belief system was Buddhist, Hindu, Sufi, kabbalistic, Gnostic, New Age, eclectic, or completely idiosyncratic. I didn't know if they were authoritarian or democratic, sophisticated or credulous, devotional or millenary.

By late afternoon, I had experienced the rudiments of a far-flung intentional community, a federation with a thousand citizens, its own currency, schools, shops, social services, and a sacred art, architecture, and technology that rivals anything on the planet. I don't believe one could come here and see it with his or her own eyes and not be profoundly affected. Astonishing that such a thing exists and most people on Earth have no inkling of it!

Our guide was Esperide Ananas, a long-time Damanhur resident and author of a forthcoming book on the temples that our company was to distribute for artist Alex Grey under his CoSM (Chapel of Sacred Mirrors) imprint. She was prepared to conduct us through Damanhur, like Virgil, through wondrous and otherwordly tableaus; Dante couldn't have had a more enthusiastic and instructive chaperone.

It was raining very hard that morning, as it would all day, ranging from a steady downpour to sheets of windblown water. We were driven from the welcome center to Damanhur Crea, the old Olivetti factory that is now a multimedia studio and community hall. Esperide, (whose name I remembered to pronounce correctly by thinking "asparagus") met us inside the door. An advanced practitioner of Damanhurian sacred methods, she had attended NYU, so her English was excellent. After introductions, she led us at once into a gallery of Falco's paintings.

Falco, a.k.a. Oberto Airaudi, the founder of Damanhur, was traveling the month we visited so we didn't have a chance to meet him. An avatar who invented an entire culture and political system, he is an innovative painter as well as, for lack of a better title, an Atlantean alchemist. The gallery at Damanhur Crea consists entirely of his work, and was so unlike anything else I have ever seen that it is difficult to put into words.

The first impression, approaching the room at a distance, was of fluorescence. Esperide told us to experience the paintings energetically, characterizing the exhibit as a kind of intelligent transmission of metals, an alchemical message intended to impact our chakras and deep organs. The sigils hanging on the walls in the guise of paintings were essentially alchemical stations broadcasting singular and collective messages into our cells. Okay, here we go:

The lights are turned down and progressive floods falling on the paintings illuminate in detail colors as complex and wild in their own way as Jackson Pollack's works. As we enter, we are surrounded by their glow like an electric jungle. This illusion of abstract expressionism applies to many of the panels, but others are clearly figurative rebuses in inimitable Damanhurian ideographs; they throb like neon too. Some have a distinct Australian Aborigine look: dot-constructed roundish shapes inside soft, meandering borders inside an overall geography. Some look like "Picasso meets Bosch meets Escher," cubism overlapping moebius space. Others look like a combination of hermetic and Egyptian hieroglyphics mixed with complex meta-alphabetic characters not unlike what Pawnee Indians once inscribed on rocks and horsehide. Other paintings in the same genre tend toward a cross between a schematic for an electrical system (with pluses and minuses) and the sort of hieroglyphs that might be inscribed in colored paints on rocks from distant worlds with no connection at all to terrestrial calligraphy. Some look Mayan; some look Chaldean; some look Polynesian. Some resemble hypothetical Paul Klee astrological charts. Others could be Hubble telescope renderings of astral fields, galactic and bursting with primary colors. Some look like polarized images of planetary landscapes: river systems and lagoons in bright false colors. A few look like Lascaux cave creatures amid Greek trigonometry. Half a dozen or so are particularly reminiscent of Cocteau and Miro, especially those with hanging globes, partial globes, and sections of cones, with stars and glyphs painted on them. All of them, even the full abstracts, are under a kind of metaphysical regime, flirting at spots with traditional occult designs. Fluorescent paints shine from everywhere, creating the sensation of being in an aquarium of phosphorescent creatures, or floating in a space of moons, comets, and double stars.

Much of the art in the gallery draws explicitly from alchemy, tarot, and kabbalistic magic. In fact, probably a third of the paintings comprise more than one complete set of major and minor arcana. Several of the major trumps appear multiple times with wide ranging variations and occasional jokes; for instance, changing an "r" to a "p" in Italian makes the Emperor *(imperatore)* into the pepper-shaker *(impepatore)*. The Tower card depicts a millennial moment wherein old belief systems are shattered so that new ideas and knowledge can burst through, an interpretation that is not applied seriously enough to 9/11, in which a tower is likewise struck by a form of fire, as people fall through the heavens, and planetary consciousness shifts forever.

The works have "titles" that go on for paragraphs. Esperide handed us a book of with the titles in English translation, including "stories never told, dreams that were never lost, with those never dreamt . . . details that have not been told but intensely lived in the silence at the center of everyone . . . the ancient stellar message repeated by life itself . . ." and so on. She explained that the images also contained hidden stories at different esoteric levels, codes of Damanhurian philosophy and belief systems.

The images, it gradually became clear, are visionings as much as training manuals, actual communication devices to achieve direct knowledge from nonhuman intelligences. Their designs are links for sending and receiving information between dimensions. More than that, the paintings are precise wireless devices that can be accessed like ouija boards by tiny alchemical tools created by Falco to adjoin their edges.

The most distinctive feature of the exhibit, other than its luminosity, is the ubiquity of geometries, topographic outlines, crowns, and hand shapes applied in metallic overlay as though soldered onto the canvasses at the last phase of construction. Fields of raised gold leaf that form connected heraldic designs of glyphs and esoteric patternings are not so much orna-mental as what they look like: psychic paraphysical wiring that can be used to enter and receive information from the intelligence of the painting. We were not initiated to engage in this mode of dialogue with the networks, so we did not get to use the triangular devices fashioned for communica-tion through them.

Many of the canvasses could be thought of as the insides and outer matri-ces of a cell with bright shades of blue, yellow, purple, and orange, all rush-ing in intersecting fields. Some were biological, dense, and oozing; others were more astronomical and shimmering or radiating. I call them astronomical because Esperide described them as planetary landscapes. Their color fields, she said, include "patterns that come from extraterrestrial and cosmic transmission as well as past-life memories of Falco."

When I passed her again in front of a series of circular energy fields, I remarked that the paintings were very different from Alex Grey's work, yet I imagined he would appreciate them. I thought that if the imagistic energy within the atoms in Alex's sacred anatomies could be enlarged as through a microscope, they might look like Falco's whole paintings. Each was like an Alex Grey pixel blown up, operating at a related frequency.

"Ex-ac-tly," said Esperide. "Macrocosm and microcosm."

"It is not even quite that simple," I added; "Falco is the point at which the inside of the atom—"

"The quark," Esperide corrected, "meets the spiraling galaxies."

As the lights changed in the room, layers that had been invisible manifested such that the viewing began to have a profound psychedelic effect. Lindy and I wandered in this maze separately, gazing about, stopping to observe myriad details of bottomless landscapes. It was dizzying and transforming to occupy such a space. The luminosity and galactic qualities gave rise to sensations of trance and mystery.

After we had gazed for a half hour or so, Esperide sat us down in front of a canvas of a huge gleaming galactic corridor and instructed us in sounds to resonate with our chakras and massage our organs. We went sequentially through three counts each of a deep "ah" to "o" to "u" to "i," passing up from the solar plexus to the throat to the third eye and ending with one beat of a very high "i" through our crown chakras. A sound was initiated as classic inbreaths through the nose and outbreaths through the mouth and, during each of them, our thumb made a mudra circuit with a different finger from index to pinky to ultimately lie atop a closed fist.

The chanting complete, we spent another half hour walking the gallery again, as our internal experience of it should have deepened by the exercise. I began to have a nostalgic sense of a planetarium, imagining travel through starry clusters to exotic worlds. Only here it was seeping into my body on a subliminal level. Perhaps I was made receptive by jet lag, or perhaps we were being prepared and altered by the art—or maybe both.

From the gallery we were taken on a tour of the rest of the top floor of Damanhur Crea, which included a cafeteria, a Damanhurian supermarket, a sacred jeweler, an auditorium, and a school. The supermarket offers products manufactured by Damanhurians both here and in the Valchiusella Valley and elsewhere in Italy, from seed to plant to transformed product, including organic soaps and detergents, wines, cookies, oils, and biodynamic vegetables and fruits.

Damanhur educates its children within the community until they reach high school age. We visited a number of classrooms in session, all grade-school level, none with more than four very bright-looking Mediterranean children amid maps, posters, tools, and a teacher. They each stopped and welcomed us and then continued with their lessons as we observed. I felt energy, intelligence, and attention. The teachers were both formal and enthusiastic, and seemed very dedicated to their roles.. As we walked between classrooms, Esperide explained that the students also apprenticed in community foundries, agricultural plots, woodshops, bakeries, and wineries.

Mr. Olivetti built this factory himself in the 1960s to keep jobs in his home valley, but once he died, it was abandoned by his heirs as an idealistic and impractical folly. That left the Valchiusella community with high unemployment and poverty. When Damanhur colonized the valley, they tried to buy the building, but the Olivettis viewed the newcomers as cultists and pagans and refused to sell to them.

Valchiusella is a conservative valley in the most Catholic of countries, and the introduction of such a strange "religion" was fiercely resisted initially.

At some level, the whole movement is still resisted, particularly by the Church. Thus, for instance, local schoolchildren are not allowed to see the temples despite Damanhur's many invitations and offers of generous prizes for the best artistic work by a child reflecting the chambers.

Yet acceptance has come at other levels, for Damanhur has brought jobs to the area, erected new homes, and rebuilt the emergency systems. Now, twenty-five years or so after settlement, the mayor himself is a Damanhurian.

Eventually Damanhur swayed the Olivetti family by its good deeds for the whole community, non-Damanhurians as well, and the factory was sold to them. Damanhurians restored it in keeping with its history and architectural legacy. Part of the entry to the building celebrates Olivetti history in old black-and-white photographs blown up onto panels with accompanying text. The Olivettis were pleased enough by the result that they allowed their name to remain on the refurbished center.

The lower floor of the building contains a series of about twenty shops and businesses, all Damanhurian: solar and voltaic energy, fashion accessories, mosaic work, art restoration, selfic technology (which I will discuss later), painting, ceramic sculpture, baking, glass-blowing, green and alternative architecture, chocolate making, and computer training, all serving the community and beyond. For instance, art restorers from Damanhur work on churches and old statues and paintings throughout Europe. Mosaic artists prepare luxurious floors and walls for customers in many nations. This very day they are shipping finished tiles and mosaics to Israel and India. Silk painters are preparing exquisitely lovely high-end screens to go to Japan and Quebec.

As we walked through the building, Esperide narrated Damanhurian history and philosophy. The community is widespread, with families living in the valley and throughout Italy as well. All contribute to the community and participate in its industries. Some of the families farm; others operate factories, foundries, woodshops, bakeries, wineries, etc. Some live in apartments in cities, some in large communal houses locally; some even climb to their treehouse homes; all proudly fly the Damanhurian flag and use Damanhurian currency for their internal transactions.

After an hour's tour of the building and question-and-answer visits with a school teacher named Anaconda and a jeweler named Walrus (other Damanhurians we met were named Barracuda and Cobra), Esperide drove us to her communal family home for lunch, a house further up the mountain where we shared a buffet with the group: cheeses, pastas, tomatoes, and wonderfully irregular peaches and apples from local orchards. But before eating, we were asked to walk the labyrinth in final preparation for entering the temples.

Ordinarily those about to enter the temples are required to wander and meditate for at least an hour in the labyrinth. Its basic grid surrounds the house with many intricate branches defined by paths of yellow and blue and unpainted stones leading to dead ends or spiraling into and out of centers. The entire geometry, Esperide told us, was laid out by Falco spontaneously, and it stretches, unseen from the alcove, for miles through the woods and includes nodes for healing and esoteric transmissions of knowledge. Falco had no prior map for this megacircuitry. He apparently saw an energy field that was already there and had someone follow him with string, tracing lines as he pointed out its path.

Because it was pouring rain, we were only expected to stay in the grid briefly at our discretion. Pendants with wooden glyph-inscribed rhomboids were hung about our necks to activate the circuits and we were dispatched into the downpour, babes in the woods. Esperide said not to get lost or to cross a line of stones after activation by our entry.

I had long had a desire to walk a labyrinth, so I stayed in for about twenty minutes in the heavy rain, eventually taking off my shoes and socks and walking barefoot, carrying them in each hand, as they had become soaked. My pants and shirt were also sopping wet and dripping where my rain jacket didn't protect me.

Strange and forgotten feelings arose, and I made space for them in my heart. I walked in sometimes dizzying courses, corkscrewed into three tight centers to avoid crossing stones. Tiny, thin Italian grasshoppers reminiscent of *Pinocchio's* Jiminy Cricket hopped out of the way as I walked along, trying to avoid them. I meandered, or was led by the labyrinth, behind the house and to its side and might have traveled longer; instead I was relieved to find myself in a yellow exit branch, so I took it straight to the door where I joined the meal in progress.

After lunch Lindy and I were given blankets and sent to an upstairs studio to take a half-hour siesta before entering the most sacred space.

How to characterize the temples? My images beforehand were vague and inaccurate, a textbook instance of misplaced concreteness. Without realizing it, I had pictured a sort of sci-fi B-movie : a giant mountain, a secret society carving out its inside and creating a temple with Alex Grey genre sacred anatomies, hiding the whole affair from the government, then having it discovered and almost destroyed by the authorities before it was accepted. I understood that the Italian judiciary and constabulary were outraged when they had first learned of this megalith and wanted it eradicated as an illegal structure, a heathen worship site for, god forbid, a cult.

From Esperide we heard a more nuanced version: Falco and his colleagues had searched the world from Japan to Africa to Peru looking for a place where the planet's four main synchronic ley lines come together and would allow him to tap into their energy field and implement a vision he was incarnated with from another time and place in the universe ("Falco brought the basic plan of the temples with him here," she explained). He came to this world to give the human race a device for a different form of communication, energy, and healing, and for getting back in touch with the cosmos, but he needed to plug it in somewhere.

Not entirely coincidentally after all this journeying, he found himself back in his native Italy, where he discovered one of the two places on the planet where four synchronic lines cross deep under the earth (that's too long a story to recount here). For the place he would build on the spot, he took an Egyptian name, Damanhur, City of Light, an ancient temple and metropolis apparently also constructed partly underground and lit alchemically.

In 1978 the Damanhurians started digging into the mountain, hauling out the rock bucket by bucket, using only hand drills and picks to carve their way in. The point was not merely to create an architectural *tour de force* but to be altered by the process, to be transformed by the elements, spirits, and energies in the mountain, to engage them slowly and be exposed to their intrinsic qualities and ancient messages. Once they hollowed out spaces inside, they sculpted pillars and painted walls for the first of the temples. By the time the government discovered the existence of this catacomb in 1992, there was already a huge underground temple complex in place, a virtual city.

When the *carabinieri* couldn't figure out how to enter through the hidden doors and tunnels, a judge threatened to have the whole mountain dynamited unless they were shown the way in—the Papal authorities wanted the abomination blown up regardless. Falco is said to have gone into deep meditation to consult with the assembly of higher intelligences who surround and supervise the Earth. He asked for permission to open the structure to the secular world. The various mages and spirit beings debated, some of them opining that the Earth was hopeless and headed for disaster anyway, so the temples should be destroyed before the idiots who run things got their hands on sacred technology; others averring that the chambers hold the key to cultural transformation and are the only way to lead human-ity on another path. Like Moses, Falco came down from the intergalactic council and, on majority cosmic vote, let the authorities into Damanhur.

Even then, it took a four-year campaign with international signature gathering and a grueling court battle before the Italian government changed the law to legitimize the structures and rescue the Temples of Humankind from the danger of destruction and the long arm of the Vatican.

The world at large has yet to understand or discover this situation or place. That is, the world has yet to understand that a second Atlantis has already been built.

In appearance, the mountain is a large wooded hill, pretty much out of the way and obscure. A house sits up against it, an ordinary residential villa, a bit run-down in appearance, though on its far side beautifully stylized, photorealistic sunflowers are depicted, arising from a wild garden. There is nothing unusual or promising about either the house or the hill. The hill is just a big mound in one of many valleys, in no way centrally located or obvious. You'd walk right by it, and soon you'd pass bigger hills and similar houses with lovely art (this kind of decoration is not uncommon in Italy on otherwise unspectacular outer walls).

Once you enter through the tunnel, everything changes.

Before seeing legendary landscapes, there is a tendency in the mind to minimize their complexity and vastness or inaccurately exaggerate them along the wrong parameters. Damanhur cannot be foreseen. Inside the hill is an architecture and series of rooms that defies description. Imagine New York City's entire Metropolitan Museum of Art taken apart and then reassembled in underground chambers leading up through a mountain. It is not, of course, that immense, but unless you think in that scale, you don't get the vastness. It may not be that vast in terms of pure space, but the Met-ropolitan Museum is a tomb of cultures, a repository for tridents, prayer sticks, and chalices that were once powerful. The temples at Damanhur are a living organism that is so massive on an astral plane that it dwarfs the Metropolitan or any other terrestrial museum. The temples are quite colossal and complicated in an ordinary sense, too.

Picture the imaginary inside of the Face on Mars, in which the legacy of a whole Martian civilization is preserved room by room. That is what a journey through the temples feels like. You are viewing the entire Earth, an Earth you know in your heart but have never actually seen, an extraterrestrial planet. It is our world not as historians and scientists depict it but as a spiritual karmic event on a cosmic plane. Damanhur is a gallery meant for visitors five hundred thousand years in the future or from other solar systems and time-space continua.

Yet one never has the sense of visiting a mere museum, even a transgalactic one. Imagine instead being in a time machine in which past and future take on different meanings, and nonverbal communication throughout the creationary whorl, independent of temporal or spatial location, is possible through sacred structure and active code.

The temples at Damanhur are more than a gallery or an exotic sculpture garden; they are a message from humankind to the galaxy, to the future—a direct calling card to ET and to diverse intelligences wherever in space and time. The complete Buddhist canon or the annals of physics and biology might also be such calling cards, but they require syntax of one sort or another. The temples are more like a transcultural time capsule, a glyphic and geometric compilation of the cumulative wisdom and memory of humanity.

Here is the key fact: The entire complex is linked by nine hundred tons of intricately and carefully laid copper wiring plus large amounts of gold and silver, a mostly camouflaged circuitry that can be viewed in some of the chambers as golden metal filaments and knotty assemblages. With its magically connected independent radionic rooms, the whole is a vast sending and receiving device, like a radio telescope or activated crop circle.

The temples are also networked by "wireless" globes of alchemical salts in fluids set into nodes cut in walls, culminating with an array in the Hall of Waters, each glowing with a different spagyric color. In addition, many designs and shapes at sites throughout the catacomb carry instructions or transmit information in a secret language. These receive transgalactic and interdimensional messages, heal body-minds, and transform consciousness.

The cumulative feeling is of walking through the etheric body of a crop circle, instructions engraved on and into its morphology. The very structure and shape of the machine are queuing one constantly to the higher dimensional space and time through which it is passing.

A superalchemy runs this complex, Falco's selfic technology, culminating in an operating hermetic city as might have been pictured by Pico della Mirandola or Robert Fludd. Falco uses the word "selfic" instead of "radionic." Radionics is a discredited nineteenth-century metascience for transmitting energies through grids and geometries to heal at a distance. It generates a kind of metaphysical electricity that does not require direct contact. Falco intends something slightly more discrete: the release of the intelligent alchemical properties of metals for transmission of energies across dimensions without reference to limitations of relativity, ordinary terrestrial language, or the speed of light. In this cosmology metals are given to humans primordially and archetypally as devices that can be converted to spiritual transmission, but thus far have been used at large only to imbed a lesser secular technology into the molecular memory provided by each distinct metal's intrinsic shape—that is, its capacity to hold form and transmit primitive kinetics in the form of electricity and magnetism. What is crucial to the Damanhurian belief system is that all metals are also individually intelligent in another, more animistic way, at a level that has

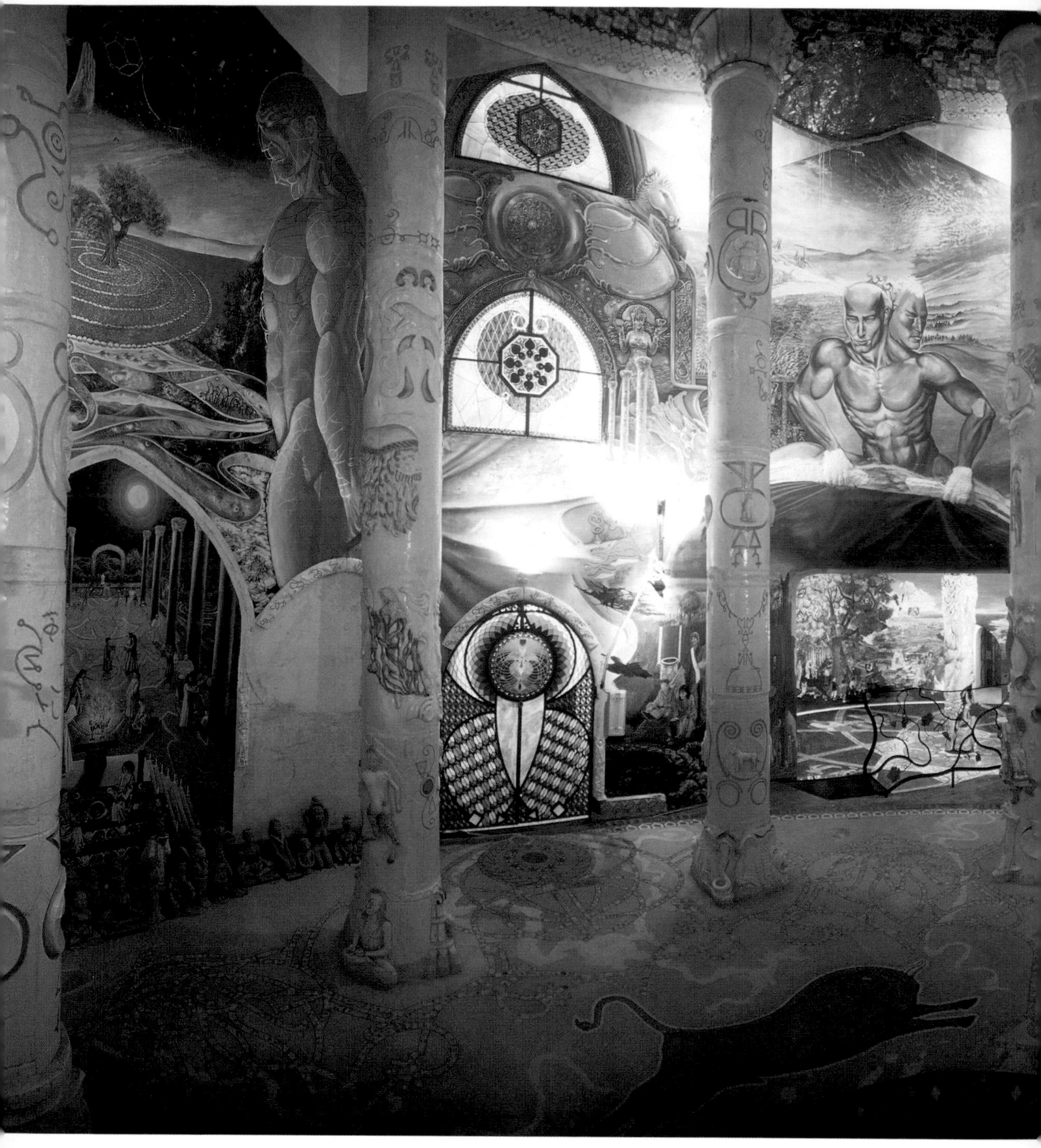

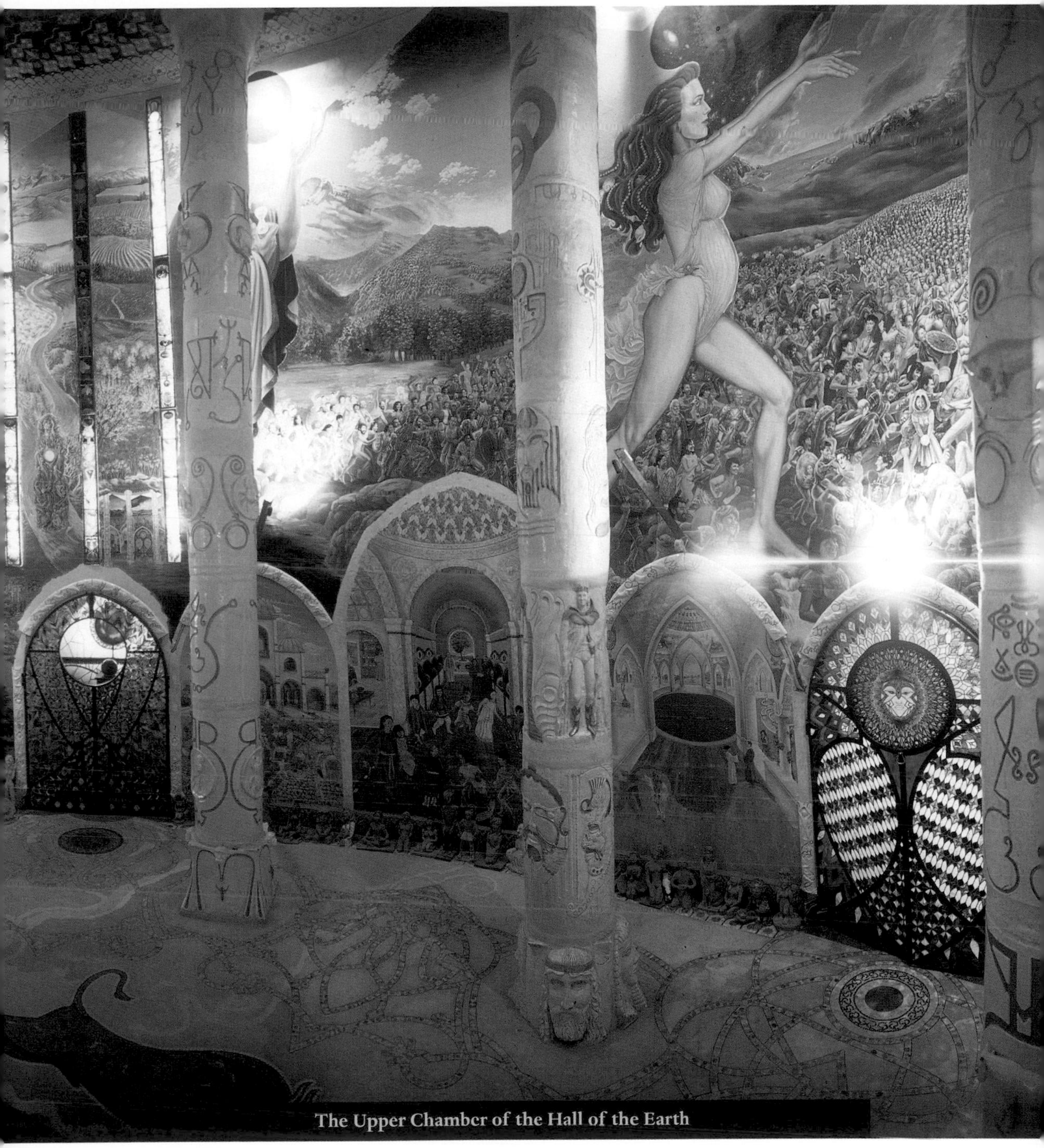

The Upper Chamber of the Hall of the Earth

not yet been discovered by humankind as a whole. One does not have to run voltage through metals to get them to transmit information and force. We as a civilization and a world among many worlds have missed the point; we have lost the operating manual for our own planet inside our beings. We are running a gas station when living alchemical theater and free-energy technology are at hand.

There happens, in fact, to be an actual alchemical laboratory in the temples, just off the Hall of Spheres, with thousands of minerals, compounds, chemical solutions, and ancient liquids and salts. We had to stand in the room in darkness because of the sensitivity of some of these elements to light, but the space resonated and smelled of John Dee and Paracelsus—an indefinable, musty pungency.

Near the laboratory is one of many zones within the structure where the intricate selfic wiring comes together visibly in big golden copper tangles and octopuses that look as complex as the circuitry for an oil refinery or the electric power plant for a city.

The original paraphysical charge for this grid comes off the synchronic intersection of the four ley lines drawing on Gaia's energy and transfusing it in concentrated form from the black asteroidal mylonites inside the mountain. Government geologists visiting Damanhur to check its stability reported that these temple-girding bedrocks are among the oldest formations on the planet, created when the earth's original mantle congealed.

In principle, everything esoteric in the temples runs through the radionic wiring and alchemical globes. All the site's devices except the lights, the elevator, and the drawbridge and moving panels are proposed as selfic, employing circuits of sacred geometry rather than electromagnetism or radiation. What enterprises or functions these machineries activate or release an outsider can only guess, but (for instance) I later heard a rumor that the reason no one knows where Falco is presently is that he likes to time-travel. That, however, could be the Damanhurian equivalent of an urban legend.

One temple in the Hall of Water is covered from ceiling to floor on every wall with symbols and ideograms in Damanhurian, written by Falco not only to provide the history and esoteric science of the human race to date, but to offer numerous alternate outcomes for our species. Esperide describes it as "ancient alphabets, ancestral symbols, signs from the future, and selfic patterns." These flow together in an unbroken diagram-like drawing that blankets the entire room. It looks like a zany gameboard for something far more complex than Chutes and Ladders or even chess or tarot, and it also suggests a hermetic circuit board, the kind of thing that might be the control panel for a Martian, if not an Egyptian, pyramid. This secret library was inscribed in a time of peril as the memory of the entire alchemical system, set deep within a chamber in case the outer temple was obliterated.

Adjoining the laboratory is a room where the illusion of an apartment has been created, as though this were merely a room with a table and chairs someone might live in. A giant selfic machine looking like an MRI device from the 1930s, a virtual ball of copper wiring entangling and falling from it like Medusa's hair, hangs over a bed from which Dracula might arise. It is "electric" without electricity. Esperide says that it is a prototype healing device of a sort that has since been vastly improved upon, so is used now only for experimentation and archiving.

Imagine entering one of the Egyptian pyramids and finding laboratories and giant murals with mathematical formulas that go on and on beyond a seeming plausible scale of human endeavor (let alone of a mere thousand people—maximum—over two and a half decades).

I am not saying that I know the machine at Damanhur works. I am simply saying that it has been built comprehensively, piece by complicated piece, and tattooed meticulously and confidently *as if it absolutely works.*

There is no escaping the fact that everything in the temples is devoted to the faith that this proposition is *real*. An unbelievable amount of work went into building a replica of a time machine, an imago of a cosmic transmission device, and making it look and track like exactly that rather than just the most ambitious and heroically illustrated New Age temple on Earth. (Even as a science-fiction set, Damanhur is stunningly convincing, at no point lapsing into mere decoration or genre.)

The experience of walking through the complex gives the flat-out sense that Damanhur's builders were confident that a functional astral temple could be erected and were preparing formal metaphysical conditions for it. The temples thus are actualized on a scale grand enough and meticulous enough to allow interdimensional transmissions—interstellar, intergalactic, transpersonal, and transtemporal flows of intelligence—if in fact there are such things under any heaven and earth. Falco made the presumption of such a reality his context for the entire assemblage, and his boldness and surety (sustained apparently by his memory of other such cities on other worlds) rings from every quarter of every chamber.

The primary impact of Damanhur is, "This machine is somehow alive and operating," but more than that: "We are men and women willing to place our lives and our deaths at its service and conveyance." That is why the various temples are populated by little clay replicas of every Damanhurian, his *lares* or *wairua* (to cite Latin and Maori) set in mysterious portals and strewn willy-nilly along the floors like voodoo dolls. Each Damanhurian has a clay statue of him- or herself and a handprint somewhere in the temples, and these are used in death ceremonies to guide passed ones through zones of the afterlife.

The temples are also a sarcophagus behind whose walls the ashes of the Damanhurian dead are stored and in whose galleries photographs of the dead sit in unlikely places as if spontaneous shrines, "to keep their images before us," Esperide says, "to remind us that those who have passed are still part of the community."

Every Damanhurian is additionally painted into the grand murals photographically, so that each actor represented in the landscapes is a real person, with some blanks to be filled in with new members. That is, the paintings are inhabited not by idealized or composite humans but actual, picture-perfect humans, much as the Face of Mars might, hypothetically, contain a face-by-face census of the citizens of the last Martian city or as the temples of Atlantis, somewhere beneath the water, might show the faded priests and officials of that kingdom in its last months.

Imagine going through the Metropolitan Museum and seeing your friends and neighbors and various storekeepers, bus drivers, and assembly-line workers in various giant artworks at epic, religious, historical, and symbolic scale.

The physical temples at Damanhur comprise maybe a dozen separate, gigantic rooms with mazes of hallways connecting them. If they were just halls of a museum, they should at very least be honored and admired for their elaborate and magnificent artwork, a stunning realization of sacred architecture. Yet each specific temple serves a different esoteric purpose, and each one is entirely different from all the others—different in shape, different in mood, different in hue, different in energy, different in light and vibration, but most of all, different so absolutely as to seem to be part of an entirely different culture and conceptual scheme. In passing from room to room, one changes planets, suns, cosmological dimensions, and root languages. Meaning begins utterly anew at each portal.

The rooms are connected to each other by a kind of Egyptian magic amplified by ordinary but complexly employed electronics. Sections of seamless wall suddenly part to allow you through. A drawbridge uncoils like a moebius snake and, after seeming to be a staircase up or down, ultimately settles into a bridge leading to the next room. Wherever there is an exit and entrance, a clue is painted into the artwork, a child pushing in the right direction, or Egyptian figures with hands against the panel on the wall.

The art in the temples of Damanhur is as epic and detailed as in great Medieval and Renaissance cathedrals and mosques. It is painted on all the walls of immense rooms and includes sculptures, pottery, mosaic work, inlaid marble, terra-cotta, and abundant stained glass. The Hall of Mirrors is capped by the world's largest Tiffany dome. Other temples have stained glass, ornately carved pillars, and three-dimensional inlays in the walls. Still others mix selfic circuitry and artwork. It is beyond my capacity and the scope of a travel journal to give a sense of what we saw in our three hours in the temple complex, but here is a brief summary:

We come first through a tunnel and a secret door. We descend for about ten seconds in tight little elevator, the only part of the edifice not created by Damanhurians. Then we enter at the bottom, the newest temple, with a plan to work our way up and around the structure. In our journey we are accompanied by not only "Virgil" but "Beatrice," one of the keepers of the temples, who graciously carries Lindy's coat and later assists Esperide in changing conditions of light from control rooms in each chamber and, when appropriate, providing sounds.

We step into the lower chamber of the Hall of Earth where the species, tribes, geographies, and habitats of Earth, including the ocean floor and sky, are represented. We see exquisite depictions of forests, mountains, volcanoes, rivers, and savannas. Among the leaves of large painted trees, hundred of the creatures of the Earth are realistically portrayed, with an emphasis on endangered species as a reminder of our responsibility to the planet.

A central marble column in the room has been sculpted into a man and a woman emerging out of each other and holding up the heavens. Above the marble, an illuminated stained-glass capital unites the column to the night sky of the ceiling. This rainbowlike abstraction, distending to meet the dome, represents, Esperide says, "the Big Bang." When the lights are turned off, the room becomes a planetarium, its dome lit by the complete summer sky over Damanhur twenty-two thousand years ago (a millennial pivot point). All the zodiac signs and myths are elegantly drawn with constellations fleshed out to the point of appearing three-dimensional.

Intricate floor mosaics show the various games and talents of humankind, ranging from a baby and a child in separate play, to jazz musicians in dynamic motion on drums and saxophone, to a communications satellite beside a flying woman with a camera around her neck, to a crone using her wisdom to defeat her younger self in a chess match. The latter is Falco's mother pictured as a young lady playing chess against herself as an old woman, with wisdom triumphing over youth. The stand under the chessboard is a clock, for time is a critical aspect of this room. The woman's wrinkled hand is in the process of reaching to a castle or knight while her younger self looks on, worried.

Eight steps up from the lower chamber one enters the totally different upper chamber. Eight white ceramic columns highlight the room. Somewhat resembling Falco's paintings and also quite Egyptian, they are embossed with high-relief glyphs in gold leaf, depicting in sacred Damanhurian language the religious and philosophical doctrines and philosophies of the planet. At either side of the room are alcoves with Gothic arches and intricate stained-glass doors with complex mandalalike designs. The Sun Door is orange-red, with feather and sunburst motifs referencing the subtle metamorphic interaction between the Solar disc and the Earth's physical atmosphere. The Moon Door has a silver-lavender, slightly yellowed glow with crescent motifs; it embodies the divine feminine radiance dissipating into the blue of night.

On the ceiling seven childlike, wide-eyed male and female masks form a circular mandala within a dozen or more complex wheeled designs that comprise a kind of giant Persian metaphysical rose with white snowflakes and gold photon droplets (among other motifs) within it. Esperide says, "The Sapphire Masks represent the hidden memories of every human being."

The paintings on the wall of the Hall of Earth's upper room celebrate the masculine principle in both men and women. This concept segues into a history of the divine embodied in humanity, which morphs over the wall into the internal battle over our divine origin as it has been lost and regained throughout civilizations. In one zone, the war between the our spiritual side and the side that denies the spiritual is vividly represented in murals showing, among other things, a battlefield in which each individual skirmishes with a mirror image—that is, with his or her own limitations—like something out of Hieronymus Bosch. Men and women of all ages, though at war, show joy and laughter as well as grim determination.

Giant naked figures of men and androgynes dominate the hall's vistas like gods on Olympus. One huge warrior treads a cosmic landscape of planets and quasi-stellar objects, a bird with active wings on his right shoulder, his left hand extended in a mudra. This is the pure Androgyne, but his superimposed female aspect is visible only in ultraviolet light. Out of his torso and upraised hand, a demiurge with galaxies for glowing hair blows the light of the universe into existence out of her illuminated palms. Heavenly bodies from comets to suns and quasars emerge out of a floating white-hot disk in the upper fold of one cupped hand, while tresses of cosmic energy spill below both hands, the energy collecting in a luminous shell forming an occult, quasiastrological sign across a gap beneath it.

Around the curve is a huge robotic figure embodying denial of our divine origin and devoted to scientism; it is caged in Damanhurian ideograms (to indicate that its damage is inherently limited), and it is fused in dynamic duality with the androgyne of humanity. Included within this section of the mural is an esoterically configured history of the universe, imbedding the Earth within worlds across the galaxies and joining humanity by a DNA ribbon to entities and landscapes of other dimensions and planets of the cosmos. These remote cultures are depicted ideogrammatically and energetically as tiny landscape sectors.

On the other side of a stained-glass alcove, duality in the form of a muscular two-headed being lifts the sheets off a beautiful garden entangled with esoteric symbols and vines that represent the essence of creation.

Next comes the Hall of Metals, an entire temple dedicated to the metals, their astrology and alchemy, their metallurgy and atomic states, and their relationships to the different stages of human existence, such as the esoteric seasons of life from conception to death. The ambiance of the entire room is golden and copper with a kind of solar light. This comes simultaneously from ceiling, columns, and stained-glass windows.

Each of the eight metals has its own deep-set stained-glass window shaped like a Gothic arch and divided into three sections. Each individual shrine incorporates a metal's entire alchemical, chemico-physical, and astrological spectrum. The windows are: iron (early childhood), lead (late childhood), sulfur (adolescence and early adulthood), copper (prime of life), mercury (middle age), tin (transition between middle age and old age), silver (old age), and gold (over eighty years old). Each of these generates landscapes of flowers and meadows, woods and springs in ancient lands, as depicted luxuriously in the stained glass. The panoramas are lyrical and nostalgic and draw me into a richness of the milieus of life, so that I feel young and then adolescent again while staring at successive windows. Memories and actual states of being flood back.

Between the windows are stained-glass doors in Gothic arches representing the meeting zones between two metals and the alchemical element in which they are linked (as copper and iron in water).

The Hall of Metals is highlighted by an embossed central copper column culminating in a lit capital. Representative of living fire, it is carved with two masculine and two feminine naked figures amid vines, depicting a human tree. Four outer embellished columns indicate aspects of the greater Tree of Immortality. The polished floor has a solar corona near the central column with anticlockwise spiraling figures orbiting it. Reflecting symbolic sunlight from the ceiling, it transmits a cold nocturnal fire. The gold ceiling is illustrated with elaborate terra-cotta knights and dancers in a clockwise solar spiral of humankind's evolution.

As Esperide narrates the particulars of this room, it is clear that it has esoteric aspects beyond the scope of our tour. The most I can grasp is that the metals represent their divine potential as alchemical portals and signaling devices at a higher level of intelligence as well as their more secular uses in the creation of objects that preserve civilization beyond human lifetimes in memory-shapes of utensils and cities.

The room also is a symbolic door to the afterlife. The outer rim of its floor under the stained-glass windows is populated with motley throngs of clay figurines of Damanhurians and the recessed windows hold photos of passed Damanhurians.

We pass from the Hall of Metals through hidden panels into the labyrinth, a great hall of three principle naves connected to each other by corridors in such a way to create a baffling maze of multiple pathways. Along all three of the naves is represented the union of divine forces, the gods and goddesses of forty-two different traditions, each with its own elaborate stained-glass window, ranging from Egyptian to Celtic, Hawaiian to Australian Aboriginal, Ainu to Sumerian, Norse to Sumerian, Zulu to Aztec, and so on, including Hebrew and Arabic ones in which no god or goddess is shown but the tradition is represented in symbols and glyphs. Giant divine figures are carved into the wall between the arched niches of the windows and curve with the rounded nave, seemingly bending down from another realm. Going one by one, we stand before images of Astarte, Balder, Athena, Cybel, Ganesh, Huehetecotl, Osiris, Mithra, Pan, Ra, Sin, Poseidon, Tengri, Thoth, Bran, and so on, each god with his or her own window. It takes at least five minutes to appreciate all the details in each window, to do them even minimal justice.

Paintings on the walls depict civilization after the destruction of Atlantis, with masculine and feminine principles getting more and more out of balance.

On one wall is the history of Europe, from the Crusades through the industrial revolution, Communism, Guernica, the Berlin Wall, and culminating with a suit-wearing globalized businessman trampling on life, carrying his briefcase with money and gold spilling out. On the opposite wall is the New World with the ships of Columbus, slaves, conquistadors, and various Indian shamans, sand-painters, and indigenous families being trampled in the foreground. These vast, complicated murals morph from vista to vista through history.

Across a hallway a separate alcove depicts the future. On the side corresponding to the New World, you see blue sky blending into night; spaceships are ascending, fuel shooting out of them in white streams; men are walking on the Moon; others are orbiting a space station, and so on. At the base are biotech tubes and clones of babies in flasks. The opposite wall is unpainted and will eventually be imprinted with the unknown future of humanity. This sector shows the Damanhurian belief that Atlantean and Western science are branches of a greater cosmic system.

As we pass from chamber to chamber, the message Esperide gives is: "We don't want tourists trampling through here, but we mean to draw people from all over the world to come, prepare spiritually, and experience it. This is a hope for mankind, that a small group of people with intention could create something like this. We want people to have hope."

After about four rooms, we felt that we had seen a tour de force and were astonished when she said there were many more temples to go and we had just begun. If those four rooms had been the whole thing, it would have been remarkable enough, but the tour went on another hour and a half. As we viewed each room, Esperide would narrate its symbols, tell the stories pictured on the wall, allude to many more, esoteric ones that we did not have time to hear or were not ready to understand, then change to alternate lighting and/or make the sound appropriate to the sacred shape and acoustics of the room.

Most rooms had a gong or a drum or chimes, and a vibration was released that filled its shape with mind-altering resonance. In the Hall of Mirrors the noise from a hanging gong grew so loud as Esperide drummed that it sounded at once like the dawn of creation and the din of destruction, reaching a terrifying crescendo.

Following the labyrinth was the Blue Temple, historically the first room of the edifice with its huge mosaic of the Star tarot on the floor and color allegories of the five alchemical elements on the walls. Then came the Hall of Water with the selfic healing structure at its center and on whose walls Falco painted the whole system and the future Earth. Next was the Hall of Spheres with the aforementioned transparent balls functioning as alchemical nodes in the greater selfic mechanism, the chamber itself covered in gold leaf and dark-red marble, glowing with a kind of ruby alchemical luminosity. "Four times a year," Esperide explained, "the Hall of Spheres is activated to contact different parts of the Galaxy through the mylonite network of the Synchronic Lines. Actual extraplanetary conduits of paraphysical energy and intelligence link the entire universe and all its populated worlds." The Hall of Spheres is thus Damanhur's answer to NASA: you can use its selfic technology to go inward into astral space and meet intelligent life in the universe; you don't need futuristic rockets to travel light years.

After the Hall of Spheres comes the alchemical laboratory adjoining it; then the stage set of the "normal" apartment room with its machine, the so-called selfic cabin; and, last, the Hall of Mirrors with its gigantic cathedral cupola, making it almost a traditional temple. Light through the crown of stained glass is dispersed among the mirroring surfaces to produce an endlessly re-emanating kaleidoscope of effects, a holographic rendering of divine fragments shattering in order to enter the material world.

As you might guess, in the Hall of Mirrors, you see mainly yourself under the great Tiffany dome. Because the room is holographic like a blastula, you are depicted in many sizes in blocks of polished volcanic rock, caught by mirrors. Just as every shard of divinity contains the absolute nature of its source, so every cell in you holds the genetic possibility of your entire being.

The Hall of Mirrors, at least compared to the other temples, is simple, representing the fragmentation of light and divinity from moment to moment. Holographically reflected as we pass through this chamber, we see our own present being at last within the pantheon of the temples. We look at ourselves in black stone. Then our mind is cleansed and transmuted by the gong, which harmonizes the hall's geometry and activates its esoteric aspects.

We sit there exhausted. The myriad complications of the journey have been sublimated and transmuted into singleness— one deafening roar, one clonal image of ourselves and our lineage. We are made pure, single and whole, before being released into the Italian rain.

You can look at photographs of paintings, marblework, stained glass, exotic pottery and sculptures, inlaid landscapes in various mediums, terracotta eaves, and carved columns in the book we are distributing for CoSM. Those are pretty wonderful, and you get a faint sense of Damanhur from them. The art alone would have been worth the effort, but add the selfic technology and the overall intention to communicate with higher intelligences and other races through the cosmos, and you have something more than your New Age Italian cathedral.

What is harder to convey, as I indicated earlier, is the sense of being inside a crop circle, inside a living temple of Giza, of having flown in a UFO, of having visited an alchemical laboratory, of having participated in a séance, of having shared a funerary ceremony on a community scale, of having walked through an underground basilica of seemingly limitless dimensions. And even this does not bespeak the aura of promise, the feeling that humankind could build different things than it has, *entirely different,* not as "maybe" idealisms but in actuality, in full understanding of the duality of our existence, representing suppressed parts of ourselves in creative irres-olution with other parts, all in process toward a new awakening.

Damanhur is an alchemical, selfic laboratory, perhaps the only one on the planet. It is an intentional transmission of the Earth to the galaxy, not from without, like SETI's mindless beeps through the external circuitry of radio telescopes aimed at the sky, but from within, as an expression of human essence into the microcosm. It is a reception point for the galaxy to the Earth.

At the same time, you realize that so few people on Earth have been here, and hardly anyone knows of the temples' existence. Even the art crit-ics of Italy have not come flocking, though I would put Damanhur up against the churches or galleries of Rome or Florence. It is a different kind of thing, but its scope and ambition are equivalent.

There is an experience awaiting each Terran here, for you cannot go through these temples without being changed forever. I defy you. They alter the shape and meaning of the planet we dwell on and the life suit in which we each dwell. The temples at Damanhur intimate a "possible" that explodes so far beyond George W. Bush and jihad, beyond computers and cloning and cyclotrons, in fact beyond the entire history, philosophy, and technology of Western civilization, that we become a mere interlude between one Atlantis and another.

I keep returning to the notion that the temples are the proposition of another order, another science, another planet, constructed with something more committed than mere hope or idealized archetypal representation. The commitment is a demonstration of man and woman as divine beings with infinite compassion and capacity, with membership in a cosmic community, whether they know it or not.

When you walk through the temples, you feel as though you are released from the confines of terrestrial culture and transposed into a fraternity and sorority of creatures and entities everywhere, imaginable and unimaginable, now and forever. And here is the strange sense: in the Temples of Humankind, you *know* both that they exist whether they exist or not and that you are on an open-ended journey to find out whether they exist or not and who you are among them. The visit to Damanhur establishes this one thing absolutely and irrefutably: this proposition is the central mission of our existence on this planet, of life in this benighted civilization. We don't know it, but it is. We are in touch with millions of other creatures and sentiences through creation, but we don't know how to tell ourselves this is true or to make it real. The temples at Damanhur first and foremost remedy that problem, at least in intention, at least in commitment and spirit. Whether the telephone system operates literally, and how its transmissions are decoded, are other matters.

Yes, the temples could have been dynamited and could still be dynamited. Look at what is presently happening to Mesopotamia, to Babylonia. Look at what happened to Atlantis. Look at North Korea, at Darfur, at the Pentagon, what elapses when the purpose of existence is lost, betrayed, and perverted beyond recognition—when we forget who we are. The temples at Damanhur are proof that you can blow the universe up, obliterate any trace of life or matter, and it will come back, somewhere, somehow, pure and perfect. They are a demonstration that ordinary people carry the entire cosmic plan, the soul-map inside themselves, and, if they are willing and committed, they can enact it from a single stone or molecule into an entire flower, a mandala containing hundreds of diverse flowers inside it, millions of others emerging inside those. They can engrave the mute, dark inside of a mountain with the inner history of a planet and the cosmos. The journey through the temples is a lesson in this ineffable, unerasable deed. Once you have walked them, however desultorily, however distractedly, however imperfectly, you will not forget the singlemost fact: man and woman could not have made such an edifice without cosmic collaboration and a divine origin.

By the time you have passed through this cinema, you are in a waking dream. In fact, when Esperide roused us for our tour, she said, "Wake up, but don't wake up, for it will be a continuation of your loveliest dreams."

I usually get tired after half an hour in an art museum; yet traveling through these temples, my interest was held by a cliffhanger of a plot, by the sense that there is cruciality here, that everything is being put on the line for all of us, is hanging by a delicate and exquisite thread. And that's not only a dream; that's every dream, remembered and forgotten, dreamed and transmuted together.

This epistle is meant, yes biblically, to be "good news." If Damanhur isn't for real, it sure looks like what the real thing would be if it ever happened. If this isn't Atlantean technology rediscovered and reconstructed on the modern Earth, what is? Whether this vast machine and library, plugged into synchronic ley lines and packed with magical wiring and ideograms worthy of Ficino and Bruno, actually works, I can't tell you, obviously. Yet I don't believe that Falco and crew would have dug such a gigantic hole and carved and embossed such an elaborate edifice and machinery to plug it into a mere alchemical metaphor or affectation and perpetrate a fantastic hoax. People don't invest that sort of time wiring a Trojan horse. We are talking about almost thirty years of intense labor to assemble a paraphysical laboratory, to build a time machine, to write an ideographic code in the form of an entire language, to wire an intelligent device, to hollow out an underground palace wherein the divine origin of humanity could be reclaimed, to establish communication with other dimensions and extraterrestrial beings in this dimension. There are plenty of New Age hoaxes, frauds, and self-delusions, none at this scale. It is either a singular living manifestation of the possible, or it is collective madness and betrayal in the form of a hermetic theater, a ruse the size of a small city.

I believe in what I saw and felt. Damanhur was elating and overwhelming but, most of all, after an exhausting day, it gave me hope for our species, the kind of brave hope that cannot be dashed by anything short of what swallowed Atlantis, another mythic or real federation that is probably the best model for what Damanhur is or might be. Even assuming that Atlantis once was, and now is gone without a trace, Damanhur exists as proof that the Atlantean proposition remains—another science, another wisdom, another fundamental human identity, another journey through space and time that does not end in towering machines, casual armies, and worship of a golden calf. It will probably remain or be recovered on this planet as long as beings are incarnated here.

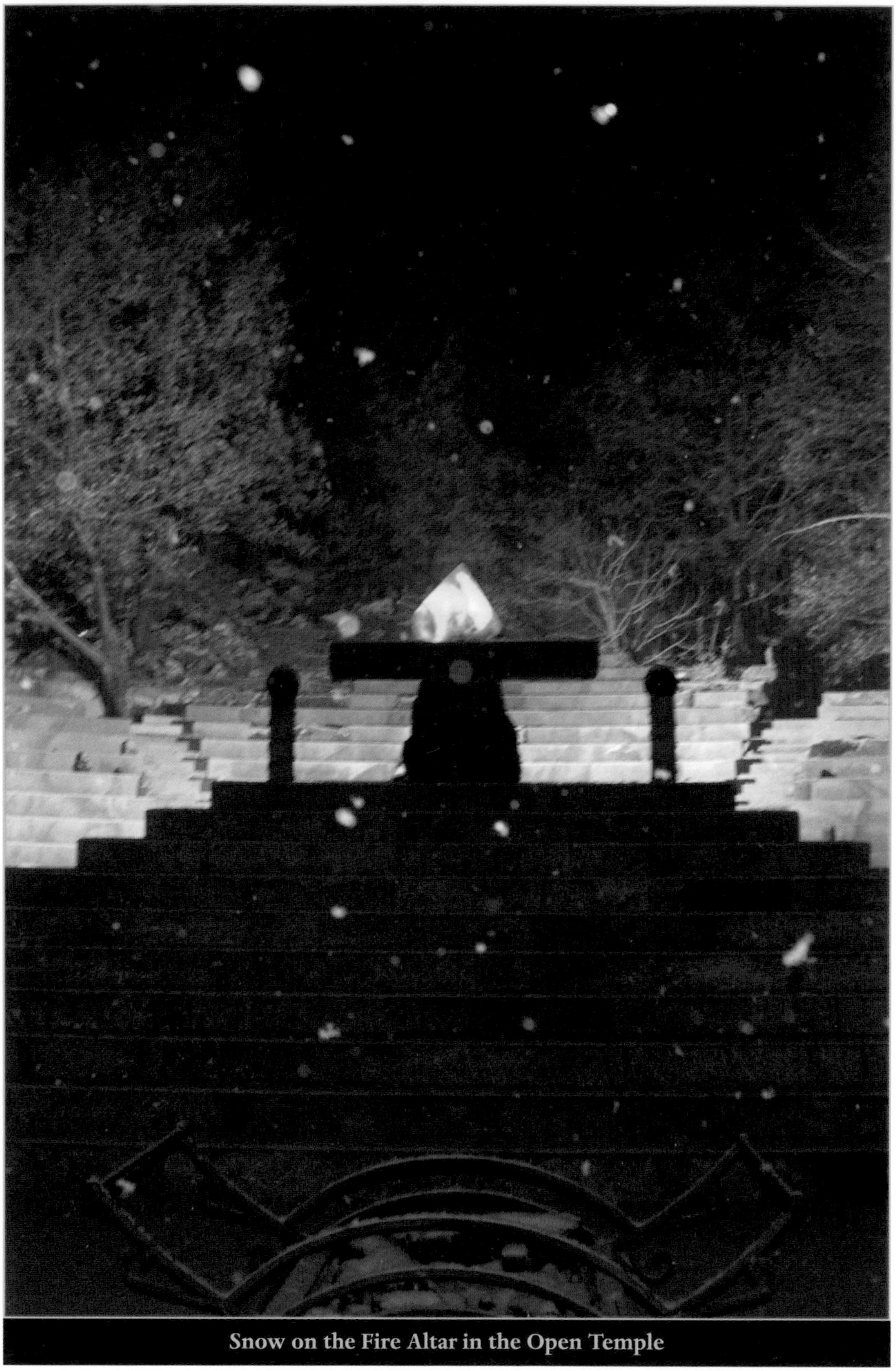
Snow on the Fire Altar in the Open Temple

PART TWO

A History of Damanhur

My Story of Damanhur

An Introduction to the Comic Book *Checkmate to Time*

Stambecco Pesco is the editor in chief of ValRa, the Damanhurian publishing house. He has been a citizen of Damanhur since 1981.

We were wrapping up the last details of the Damanhur comic book *Checkmate to Time* when it occurred to us that readers might think the whole story was a fantasy. We wondered, "Isn't this story so dreamlike that nobody will believe it?" In fact, this story contains nothing but the truth—except, of course, for a little poetic license. It is important that readers realize that the story of Damanhur is real and not a science-fiction fantasy, otherwise they would miss out on half the fun. To cut a long story short, we decided to write a brief introduction to Damanhur in order to tell people about the real experience that inspired this story, which seems so incredible when you read it.

Esperide Ananas, my partner in the adventure of writing this book, suggested that we include some autobiographical notes drawing on the memories of someone who had been there from the very beginning; this would make the story come alive. "Good idea," I said, rather naively.

Immediately, everyone present turned to me and said, smiling, "That's a really good idea: Damanhur introduced by a personal story. Why, you could write it!" It was as if they had already planned it—and I bet they had!

After a moment of confusion, I remembered that, a long time ago, I had actually begun to write my story. Perhaps those sheets were still lying in one of my drawers—then all I had to do was to add the last twenty years of events! So I accepted the proposal and here is my story: the fabulous adventure of Stambecco Pesco.

I've been living in Damanhur for over twenty-five years. When I first arrived I was finishing my studies in high school and I starting to plan my future.

Everything began for me in 1978, but Damanhur's story began a little earlier, in 1975. At that time, Oberto and his friends were focused on the Horus Center in Turin; nobody was thinking about living in community yet. The Center had been created to encourage research about ESP phenomena, esotericism, and natural medicines. These are now considered to be different branches of knowledge, but at the time they were often linked together as part of a "new" culture. This was a quest for the ultimate meaning of life, for finding spiritual and social answers in those aspects of the human being which are still largely unknown: our psychic powers, our need for a balance with nature, our sensitivity.

The Horus Center gradually opened different branches, first in northern Italy, and then in several towns throughout the country. Those were difficult years for Italy. It was the time of terrorist attacks by the "Red Brigades" and of the new fascist movements, a time in which revolution seemed possible—and not a peaceful one.

In those years everything was expected to express a political "commitment."—the music you listened to, the course of study you chose, the clothes you wore, the places you went in the evenings. Everything was saturated with a feeling of political and social activism. Everything had to be discussed very seriously and then executed as rigorously as it had been planned.

Despite the fact that all my friends were politically involved, I was not attracted to that way of living. I always thought there should be another way to make the world a better place, a way not based upon the separation between ideas and how people lived.

In 1978 my parents attended the Horus Center in Grosseto, our home town, where they regularly received *prana*-therapy treatments. One night, I met a few healers who were visiting with my parents. Among them was the young Oberto Airaudi, whom my family had spoken of before. Perhaps I greeted him, or perhaps I didn't even do that, but during the days and weeks after that very short first meeting, I thought about him very often. So often, in fact, that I finally realized I was very curious to know more about him and the other healers. Oberto—or "Falco" as he is known today in accordance with the habit of the citizens of the Federation to use animal names— is the one who planned Damanhur and built it with a group of friends.

At the very beginning, I wasn't able to understand why I was so struck by his character. As time passed, I understood that I had met someone I would define as "a magician," because of his ability to unite, transform, and make vital everything he touched. Moreover, he is a painter, a writer, an extraordinary healer, and the author of many fascinating projects—Damanhur, for example. More than a charismatic character, he is someone who stimulates others, whose words always give you food for thought. His ideas and suggestions never obstruct your own ability to judge and elaborate.

Today, after twenty-five years, I still hold the same opinion. Even though I usually prefer quiet people, and Falco is a volcano of ideas and always in a hurry, my esteem for him has never faded. Falco is a constant source of inspiration, with the extraordinary ability of keeping everybody's dreams alive.

I began to attend the Horus Center in my town, secure knowing that I was finally taking part in a project wider and more positive than political activism; a project that would really contribute to changing society. Those were the years that Damanhur was beginning to be built. At first there was only the big white house of Damjl, the one you can see today all painted with flowers and butterflies. There were eleven apartments, all on the same floor, with an unusual serpentine plan, strictly seismically reinforced and, even in those days, already outfitted with ecological sanitation systems.

In December 1979 the community of Damanhur officially opened, but some of the pioneers had already been living there for years. They had the task of supervising and checking the phases of construction, which were full of obstacles, to say the least. Damanhur was born as a social experiment based on action-meditation, productive self-sufficiency, respect for the environment, and the discovery of a real connection with the "divine" both inside and outside oneself.

In those years there were a lot of communities and spiritual movements, but few of them still exist today. I think this Damanhur has survived because it grew from a model not limited to a specific time frame. For sure, there was in Damanhur—and still is—a very unusual way forward, through interpreting the word "medit-a(c)tion." From the beginning, we studied the esoteric and spiritual traditions of humankind, and there were moments of mystic self-communion and moments of communion with others and the environment, but above all, we worked on projects and thought about how to develop the community. We were convinced that a good philosophy is one that is manifest in practical works, not just in matters of the heart.

I was fascinated by Damanhur, and when, in the summer of 1981, I heard it was possible to become a citizen of the community, I submitted my request without a second thought. The answer arrived immediately that I was accepted.within a week I was awaited in Valchiusella to start my period of "probation" as a citizen.

My mother didn't welcome this news. She broke a couple of doors of our house by slamming them, which, of course, could also be attributed to the lamentable quality of the fittings of our flat, built in accordance with the rules of government housing. There was almost nothing she didn't say, but in the end she hugged me with love when I left. So my journey started on a warm August morning when I got into a friend's small green Fiat 126 and we drove north for five hundred kilometers, where I entered what I think of as "the great game."

What was I attracted by? It is not so easy to explain. Many things about Damanhur impressed me, and one above all others: the completeness of its vision, which called to me as a spiritual being, and also as a worker, as a philosopher, as an artist, as a nature lover. That to me was the flavor of the Renaissance—the vision of a new human being, eclectic rather than specialized. This resounded deeply in me, as I was born and raised in Tuscany, the land of Lorenzo the Magnificent, the early Renaissance patron of the arts and sciences.

I arrived in Damanhur when nature was in its full glory and I was feeling "in bloom" inside. For me, living in the community was not a continuation of my previous life in a different context, but rather was a bet with myself. I told myself that victory would be represented by fully living this experience, and I would decide later if I really wanted to make this my life. Now I'm convinced I won that bet. I have grown as a person, making my ideals stronger—for example, I serve as a volunteer more today than in the past—and the range of my interests and actions has become wider. The community is a place to be and participate in the world around, not to be apart.

I had received a Catholic education and I identified with it for many years. I served as a volunteer in the poor areas of my town, I sang and served Mass, until the the feeling that those liturgical and political systems were consuming my every spiritual longing became so strong it alienated me from that world.

Damanhur wasn't asking me to have faith. Of course, faith played a part: there is divine nature in every human being, and an entire spiritual ecosystem around us; when God reawakens "inside" we come to understand the divine nature "outside," all around us.

The focus, however, was on my role in the universe: my duties toward and expectations of myself and others. Damanhur was offering something that gave me responsibility and made me feel like an active participant. My relatives said, "You can find these things here [in the world outside Damanhur]!" They were really saying: "Let others look for those sorts of things. What do you have to do with this?" But why should I limit my research field to what my family traditions had established? I didn't really expect to be encouraged, but I was hoping they would be a little more open.

So, in spite of my family's negative opinion, I left my known world, my traditions, my *petit bourgeois* certainties, and moved to a community with a name hard to understand, but with very intriguing features. My mother, little by little, agreed that her son had the right to choose his own life, and that the life he was choosing was animated by profound ideals, shared by people who were serious and generous. She knew some of them personally. She repaired the broken doors and she became a good friend of Damanhur.

But let's go back to that summer of 1981. There were only about forty people living in the community itself, but there were many more friends in the surrounding area. When on Sunday afternoons all the active members came to Damanhur, there were a few hundred of us. A few terraces had been built around the great white house with good dirt brought there by truck, but all the rest of the land was made of mud, hectares and hectares of mud. The myth has it that hundreds of boots and tools lie hidden under the ground, lost during the building work.

The first Damanhurians were from the middle class, more bourgeois than proletarian, more used to good books than to street slogans, but as time passed by, people of every social, cultural, and economic extraction joined the community. When I arrived in Damanhur almost every component of Italian society at that time was present, all of them moved by a shared aspiration of a better and more concrete society. Eleven "community families" were living there, together forming the Damanhur community.

At the beginning I lived with Angela, one of the founders, whose flat still had a vacant place. The real master of the house was the cat Tric Trac. During the day he seemed not at all interested in me, but every night he showed me who the boss was by generously wetting my bed. Tric Trac cost me a lot of money in sheets. Angela, who always defended him, was an intelligent and sensitive woman indeed, and she helped me a lot in learning about Damanhur. To live in a community is neither easy nor difficult, but to succeed you need to learn a specific alphabet for living together, different from the one you can use in a single family home. With humor and a sense of complicity, she taught me to find a point of balance between my personal needs and everybody's rhythms, between my points of view and shared choices.

Damanhur at the time printed a monthly bulletin, the *Notiziario Horus*. It was distributed to all the centers' members. Damanhur also produced leaflets and newsletters on its various research activities. I asked to work in the pressroom and I learned typewriting, proofreading, cyclostyling (thanks to that tremendous Gestetner!); and I learned how to do all the things that are needed in any big or small editorial office.

(And in the evenings, all was silent—that's why I put this in parentheses—we went to the temples and dug. In case you imagine that we used electric hammers, concrete mixers, and trucks, I should clarify what I mean by "silent." The building of the temples always put us in a happy mood; we usually shared plenty of songs and laughs while forming long chains to transport the buckets of earth. At that time, we wanted the temples to remain our big secret, so we were silent in our thoughts. Since "thought creates everything," the temples have been unknown to most people for many years. The temples are mine, ours, a signature on the great "Book of Humankind.")

Damanhur grew up day after day. At the beginning of 1983, the well-established community was preparing for a jump in development. As many centers had been opened in Italy, even in Rome, a lot of new citizens were knocking on our doors because the first national meetings we organized attracted a lot of attention. Activities were also growing and with them our houses and land increased. The temples, of course, were also expanding.

But perhaps something was still missing. . . . In February the "French Revolution" began. I call it that because, if the real French Revolution of the 14th of July 1789 was the beginning of the modern world, then the Game of Life, our "French Revolution," was the sign of Damanhur's having reached maturity. There is a difference, however: our revolution was joyful, everybody had the opportunity to be protagonists, and there was nothing to fight but our old habits.

This happened due to Falco's initiative to completely change the Damanhurian way of life in one month. We had to totally redo all our structures, from social rules to physical spaces in the houses; we were to move in the direction of a more shared life. Dozens and dozens of new people arrived, making a journey to Damanhur with tents, trailers, and camping stuff; weeks and weeks moving across Italy, in shifts, to leave behind old habits, to experiment with new ways to be, to choose an animal name, to do, act, live, change ourselves. Fears, prejudices, and habits were destroyed.

After months of transforming ourselves—the first scheduled month had been extended—at the end of the uproar and the confusion of those who still thought Damanhur was as it had been before, we found ourselves in a new reality. There were no longer eleven community families each living in its own space, but a sole big collective body in which everybody's time and rhythm harmonized. Many of the inner walls had been demolished in order to obtain big, shared spaces where we could meet, talk, and work together. We created ateliers and workshops so that we could create, and then told people about Damanhur using objects, paintings, and music. After, when we looked back, we wondered why we hadn't done all that before.

Today, with its thirty years of history, Damanhur is a movement that includes a Federation of communities; the Horus centers became branches of the Damanhur Association and there are centers throughout Italy, from Turin to Palermo. Some of these centers, like the one in Florence, offer lectures, speeches, therapies, arts and crafts courses, and lessons in bioagriculture research. And why should we only talk about Italy? Today there are Damanhurian centers in many European countries, Japan, and the U.S.A.

"Damanhur" as a brand has become synonymous with "biobusiness," from the production of organic food to ecofriendly building companies. A huge building in Vidracco that had previously been an Olivetti factory was purchased by the community and transformed into a cultural center for the creative and healing arts.

The political movement *Con te, per il paese* ("With you, for the country") also comes out of Damanhur. At present, this movement boasts a town council with twenty-two town councilors in different towns of the Piedmont area. It is even possible that by the time this book will be reprinted for the tenth time that the President of the Republic of Italy will come out with "Con te, per il paese."

Damanhur has hundreds of people serving as volunteers for the Red Cross, the AIB (forest fire–fighting squads), and Civil Protection. Our community is a research and application center working in the fields of conventional, natural, and energetic medicine.

My personal story is intertwined with those of all the other citizens. I never left the pressroom where the *Notiziario Horus* was printed, but today we bring out a bilingual quarterly issue, in full color. We also have a multimedia publishing house and graphic and photographic studios! I've been married twice, to two Damanhurians. The first time, we were both young people and when we reached maturity we decided to continue as very good friends but not as a couple anymore. Then I married Furetto Oliva (Ferret Olive), a very sensitive woman full of energy. We married many years ago, but to me it seems that it was just yesterday afternoon. We didn't have children, but my wife and I are both active collaborators with the Damanhur education association, so our lives are enriched by relationships with young children and teenagers.

I do have some regrets, sometimes. Damanhur is a very fast-growing creature, while I'm like a tree that tends to bloom at the end of the season. I have held many different offices of responsibility in Damanhur and sometimes I was faced with internal struggles because of these roles, as they tried my abilities and patience. So I've chosen in recent years to dedicate most of my energy to my job. I still think that going fast is not always the best way, but I have become more dynamic.

I read in our daily journal, *Qui Damanhur Quotidiano,* about all the things that happen each day here in Damanhur, and, if I think back to what I used to know, I am astonished at how much we have grown. I get astonished and excited, and I write; primarily I write for the theater. Together with other enthusiasts, I founded a company that organizes performances, shows, concerts, and a summer festival as well.

Today Damanhur is all the things I wrote about and more. Not wanting to seem boastful, there are so many things I didn't mention. As soon as this book is printed I'm sure I'll regret the things I didn't mention.

And this is obviously only the beginning. . . . That's the most interesting characteristic of Damanhur: it's always the beginning of something new, without being the end of anything.

In the following pages you will read about what we are today and you will understand our dream of the future of the planet and humankind.

Now, you only have to come and meet us. Don't worry, Tric Trac, the cat, is no longer here.

We've had a lot of fun writing this story. And it has also been quite a challenge. How could we condense so many years of real history, so many adventures, choices, and directions into a story with the mind-opening effect of science fiction, which also represents the Damanhur of today?

We chose to play. To play with dimensions and time; with what is real and what could be; with what has been a reality and what is maybe just a dream. A dream that moves events and pushes you to overcome all obstacles.

The dates indicated in the story—from 1950 to 1996—are the real ones of the described events. They mark the borders of the narration on our plane of time, as the calendar indicates.

The behind-the-scenes glances at cosmic events represent possible causes and effects of, and correspondences with, what was being created by our hands here in our time to build and then to defend the Temples.

The figure of Falco—to those of us who have spent a long time with him—provides constant stimuli for all possible flights of imagination; this time too we have stretched the limits of our fantasy. We cannot exclude though, that reality is even more fantastic.

The events, as well as the characters, are real. Often they concentrate on themselves also actions, ideas and effects of others. Damanhur's history is truly a collective one, and it would have been impossible to narrate it including all the protagonists who created it. We therefore present our apologies to all the Damanhurians who are not presented here: It is certainly not because of a lack of merit on their part, but a mere necessity of the script.

the Authors

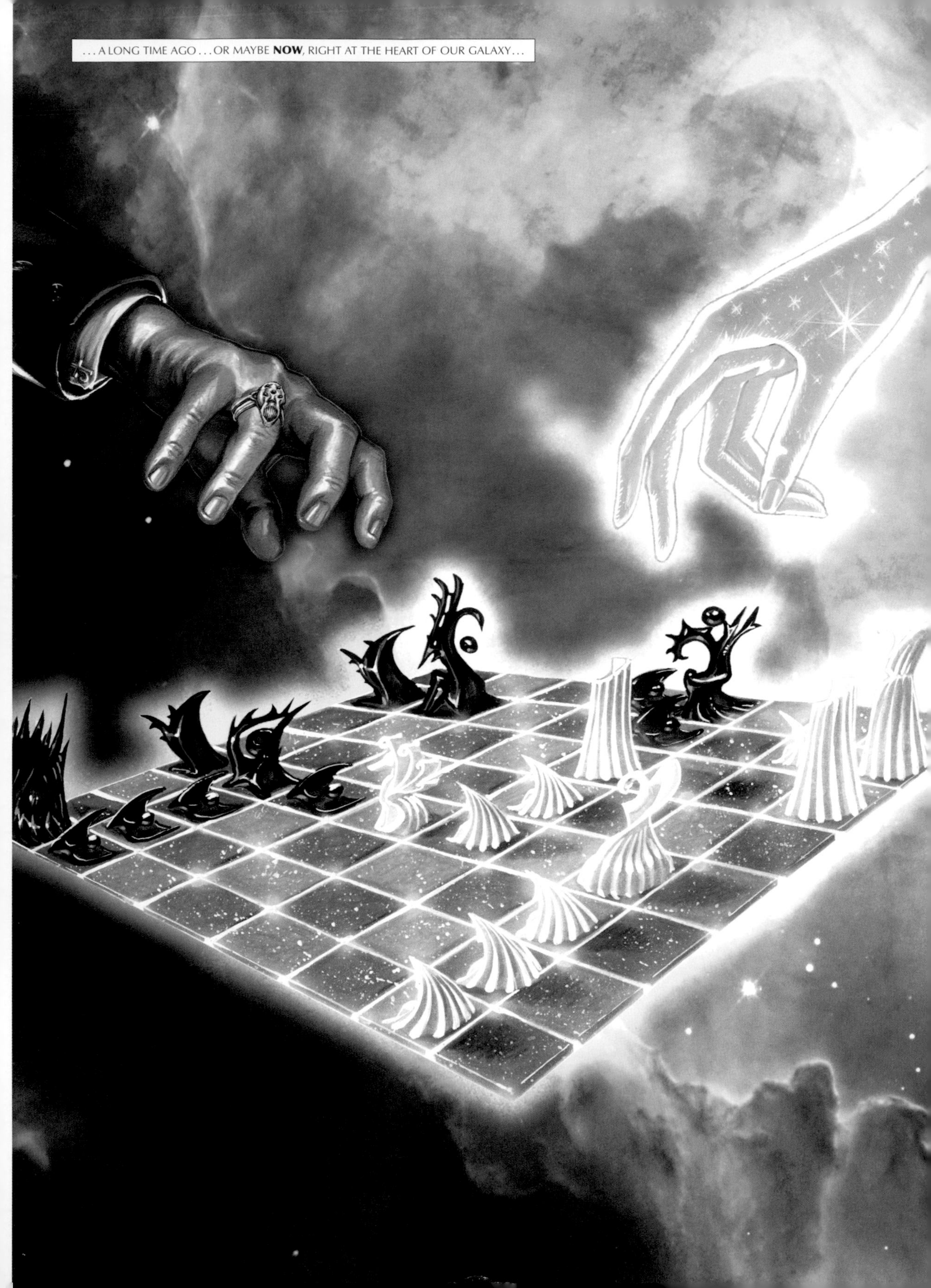
. . . A LONG TIME AGO . . . OR MAYBE **NOW**, RIGHT AT THE HEART OF OUR GALAXY . . .

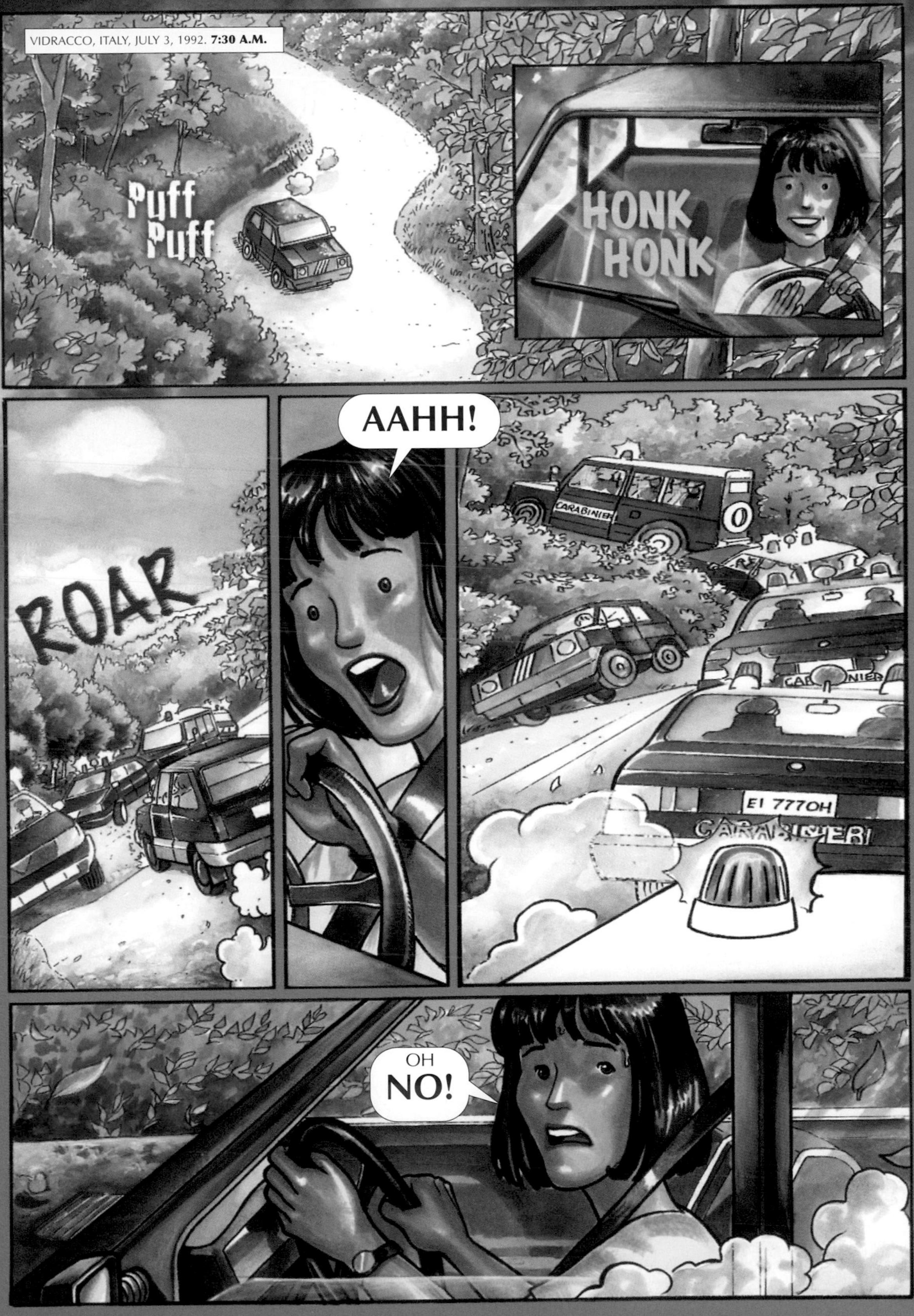
VIDRACCO, ITALY, JULY 3, 1992. **7:30 A.M.**
Puff
Puff
HONK
HONK
ROAR
AAHH!
CARABINIERI
EI 7770H
OH
NO!

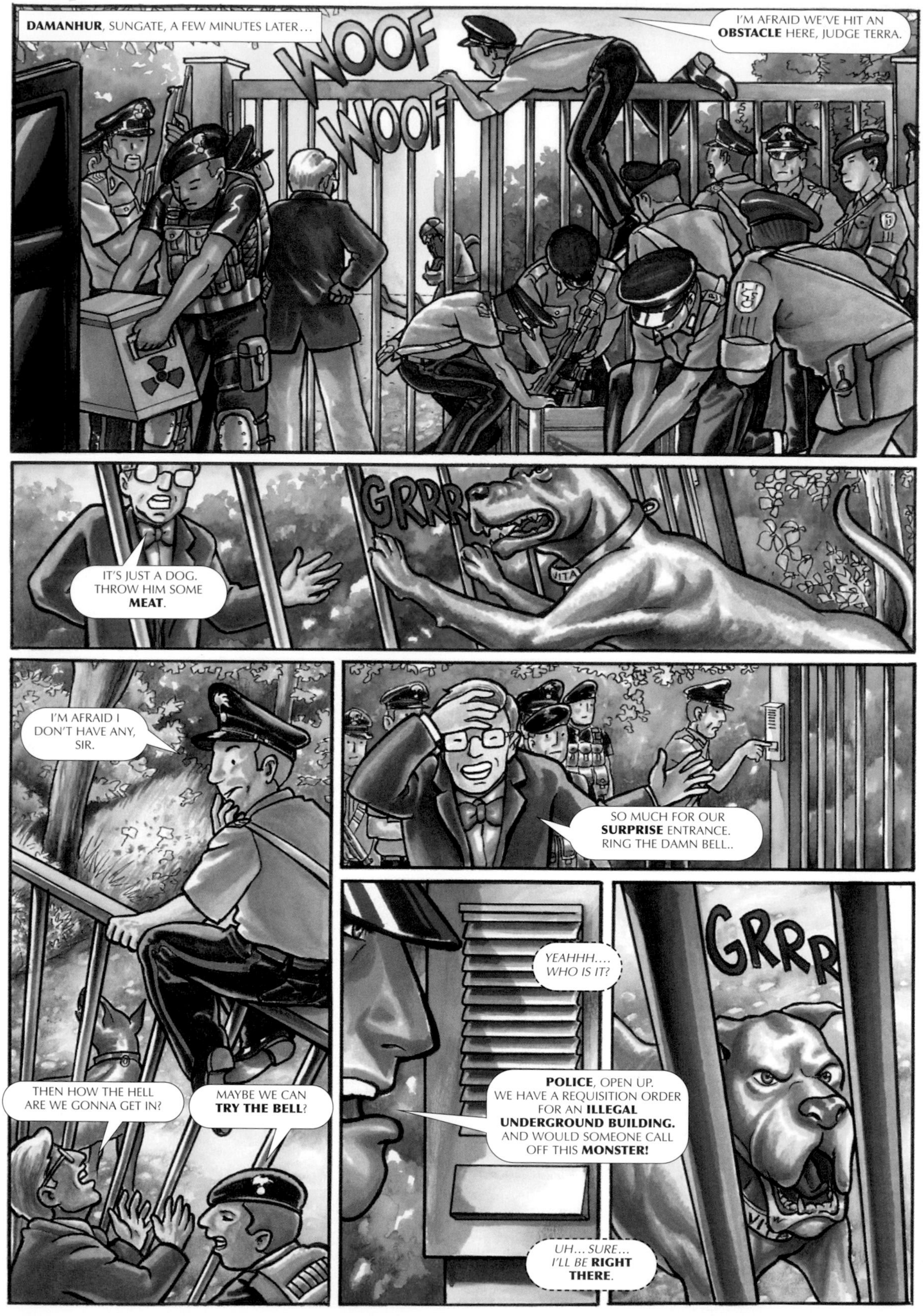
DAMANHUR, SUNGATE, A FEW MINUTES LATER…
WOOF
WOOF
I'M AFRAID WE'VE HIT AN OBSTACLE HERE, JUDGE TERRA.
IT'S JUST A DOG. THROW HIM SOME MEAT.
GRRR
I'M AFRAID I DON'T HAVE ANY, SIR.
THEN HOW THE HELL ARE WE GONNA GET IN?
MAYBE WE CAN TRY THE BELL?
SO MUCH FOR OUR SURPRISE ENTRANCE. RING THE DAMN BELL..
YEAHHH…. WHO IS IT?
POLICE, OPEN UP. WE HAVE A REQUISITION ORDER FOR AN ILLEGAL UNDERGROUND BUILDING. AND WOULD SOMEONE CALL OFF THIS MONSTER!
UH… SURE… I'LL BE RIGHT THERE.
GRRR

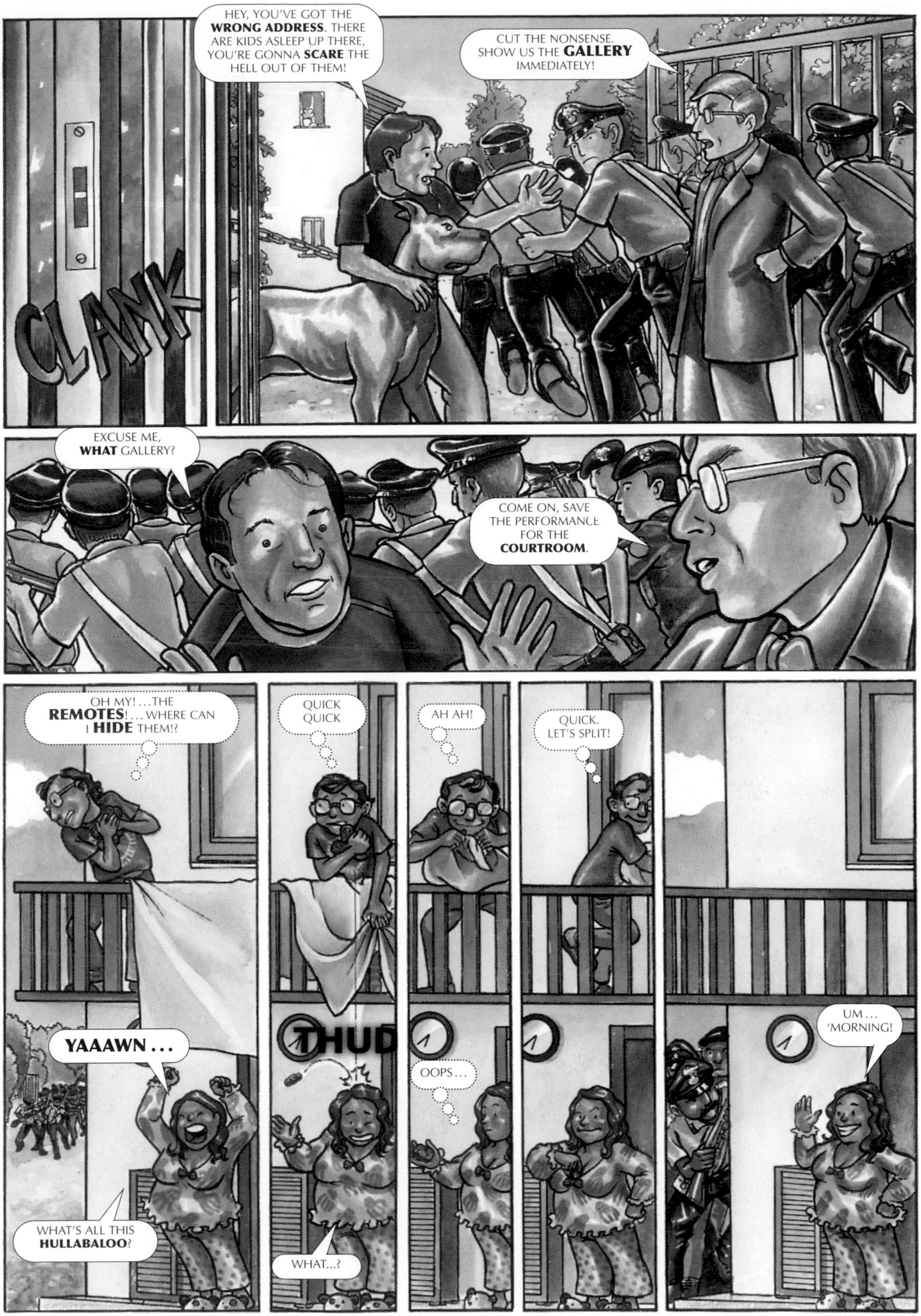
HEY, YOU'VE GOT THE WRONG ADDRESS. THERE ARE KIDS ASLEEP UP THERE, YOU'RE GONNA SCARE THE HELL OUT OF THEM!
CUT THE NONSENSE. SHOW US THE GALLERY IMMEDIATELY!
CLANK
EXCUSE ME, WHAT GALLERY?
COME ON, SAVE THE PERFORMANCE FOR THE COURTROOM.
OH MY! . . . THE REMOTES! . . . WHERE CAN I HIDE THEM!?
YAAAWN . . .
WHAT'S ALL THIS HULLABALOO?
QUICK QUICK
THUD
WHAT...?
AH AH!
OOPS . . .
QUICK. LET'S SPLIT!
UM . . . 'MORNING!

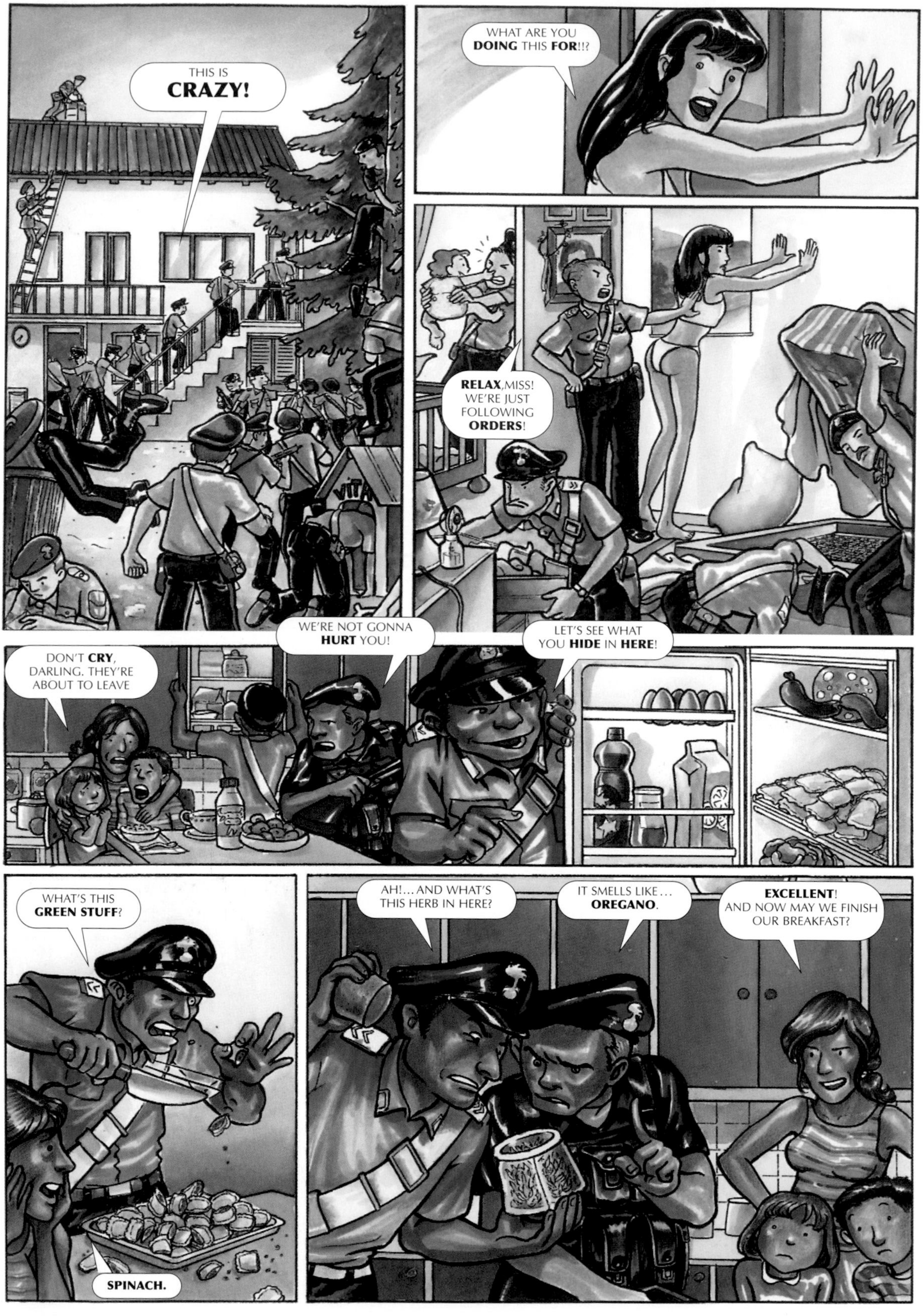
THIS IS CRAZY!
WHAT ARE YOU DOING THIS FOR!!?
RELAX, MISS! WE'RE JUST FOLLOWING ORDERS!
DON'T CRY, DARLING. THEY'RE ABOUT TO LEAVE
WE'RE NOT GONNA HURT YOU!
LET'S SEE WHAT YOU HIDE IN HERE!
WHAT'S THIS GREEN STUFF?
SPINACH.
AH!... AND WHAT'S THIS HERB IN HERE?
IT SMELLS LIKE... OREGANO.
EXCELLENT! AND NOW MAY WE FINISH OUR BREAKFAST?

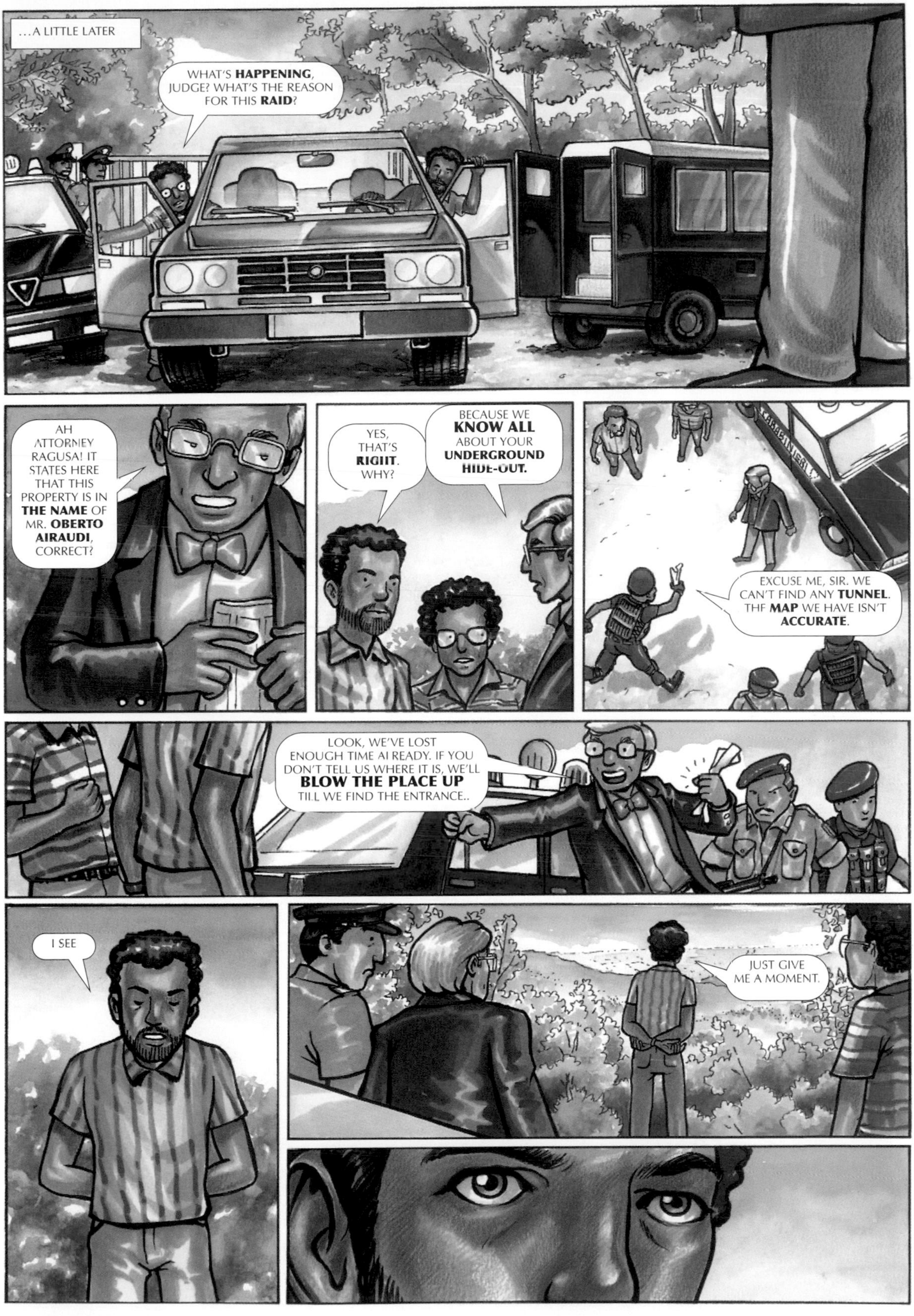
…A LITTLE LATER
WHAT'S **HAPPENING**, JUDGE? WHAT'S THE REASON FOR THIS **RAID**?
AH ATTORNEY RAGUSA! IT STATES HERE THAT THIS PROPERTY IS IN **THE NAME** OF MR. **OBERTO AIRAUDI**, CORRECT?
YES, THAT'S **RIGHT**. WHY?
BECAUSE WE **KNOW ALL** ABOUT YOUR **UNDERGROUND HIDE-OUT.**
EXCUSE ME, SIR. WE CAN'T FIND ANY **TUNNEL**. THE **MAP** WE HAVE ISN'T **ACCURATE**.
LOOK, WE'VE LOST ENOUGH TIME ALREADY. IF YOU DON'T TELL US WHERE IT IS, WE'LL **BLOW THE PLACE UP** TILL WE FIND THE ENTRANCE..
I SEE
JUST GIVE ME A MOMENT.

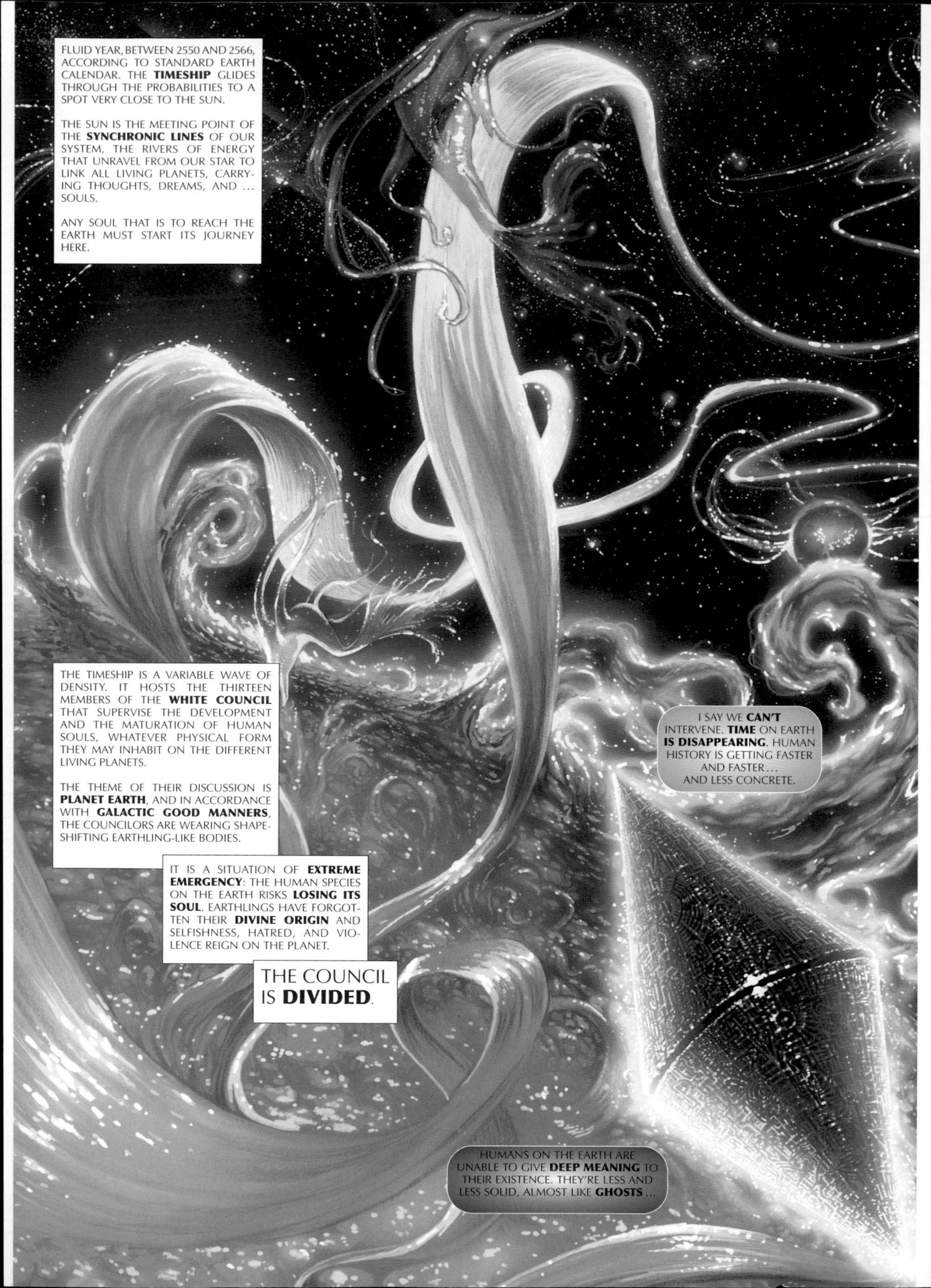
FLUID YEAR, BETWEEN 2550 AND 2566, ACCORDING TO STANDARD EARTH CALENDAR. THE **TIMESHIP** GLIDES THROUGH THE PROBABILITIES TO A SPOT VERY CLOSE TO THE SUN.
THE SUN IS THE MEETING POINT OF THE **SYNCHRONIC LINES** OF OUR SYSTEM, THE RIVERS OF ENERGY THAT UNRAVEL FROM OUR STAR TO LINK ALL LIVING PLANETS, CARRYING THOUGHTS, DREAMS, AND ... SOULS.
ANY SOUL THAT IS TO REACH THE EARTH MUST START ITS JOURNEY HERE.
THE TIMESHIP IS A VARIABLE WAVE OF DENSITY. IT HOSTS THE THIRTEEN MEMBERS OF THE **WHITE COUNCIL** THAT SUPERVISE THE DEVELOPMENT AND THE MATURATION OF HUMAN SOULS, WHATEVER PHYSICAL FORM THEY MAY INHABIT ON THE DIFFERENT LIVING PLANETS.
THE THEME OF THEIR DISCUSSION IS **PLANET EARTH**, AND IN ACCORDANCE WITH **GALACTIC GOOD MANNERS**, THE COUNCILORS ARE WEARING SHAPE-SHIFTING EARTHLING-LIKE BODIES.
IT IS A SITUATION OF **EXTREME EMERGENCY**: THE HUMAN SPECIES ON THE EARTH RISKS **LOSING ITS SOUL**. EARTHLINGS HAVE FORGOTTEN THEIR **DIVINE ORIGIN** AND SELFISHNESS, HATRED, AND VIOLENCE REIGN ON THE PLANET.
THE COUNCIL IS **DIVIDED**.
I SAY WE **CAN'T** INTERVENE. **TIME** ON EARTH **IS DISAPPEARING**. HUMAN HISTORY IS GETTING FASTER AND FASTER… AND LESS CONCRETE.
HUMANS ON THE EARTH ARE UNABLE TO GIVE **DEEP MEANING** TO THEIR EXISTENCE. THEY'RE LESS AND LESS SOLID, ALMOST LIKE **GHOSTS**…

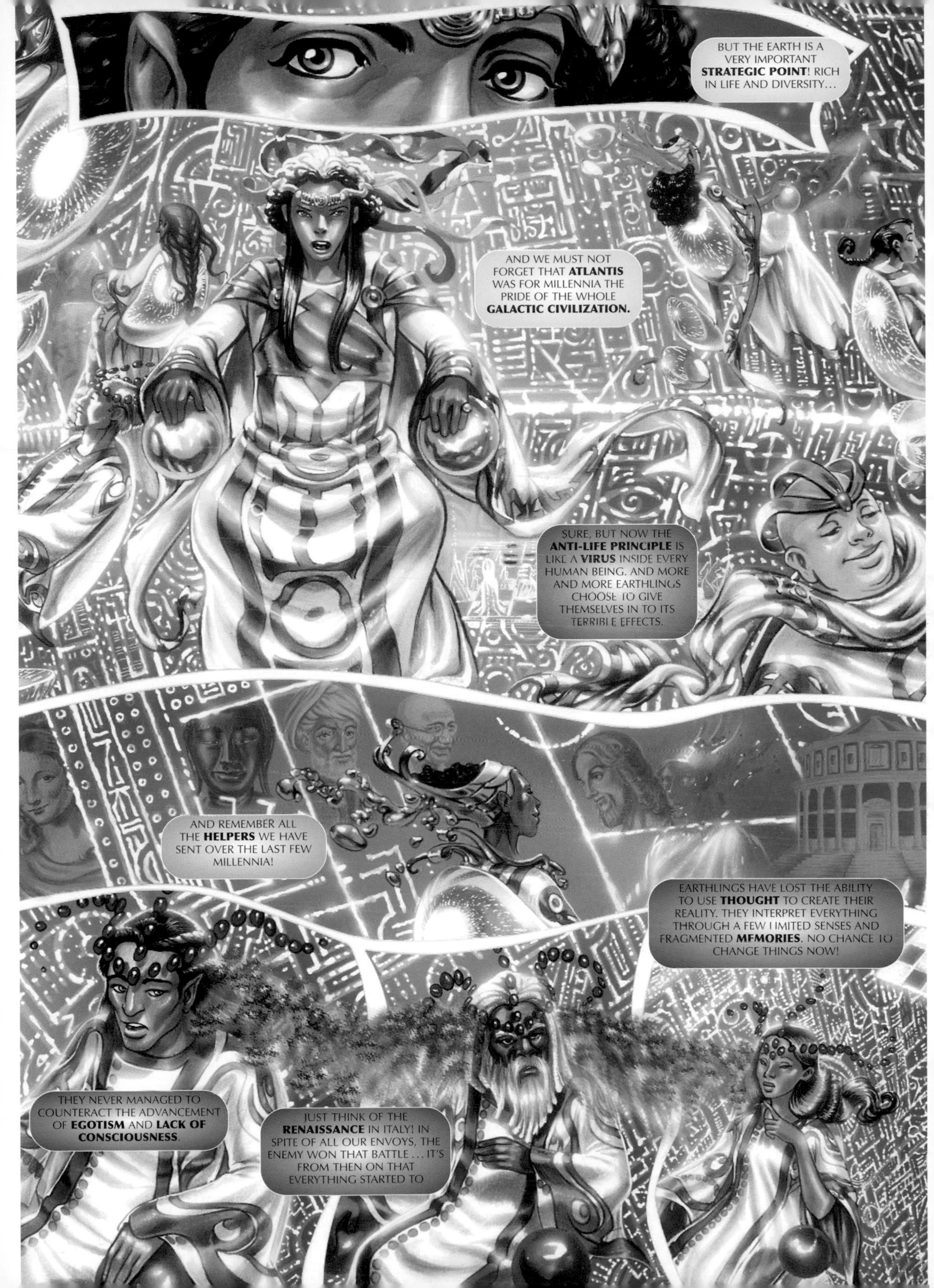
BUT THE EARTH IS A VERY IMPORTANT **STRATEGIC POINT**! RICH IN LIFE AND DIVERSITY…
AND WE MUST NOT FORGET THAT **ATLANTIS** WAS FOR MILLENNIA THE PRIDE OF THE WHOLE **GALACTIC CIVILIZATION.**
SURE, BUT NOW THE **ANTI-LIFE PRINCIPLE** IS LIKE A **VIRUS** INSIDE EVERY HUMAN BEING. AND MORE AND MORE EARTHLINGS CHOOSE TO GIVE THEMSELVES IN TO ITS TERRIBLE EFFECTS.
AND REMEMBER ALL THE **HELPERS** WE HAVE SENT OVER THE LAST FEW MILLENNIA!
EARTHLINGS HAVE LOST THE ABILITY TO USE **THOUGHT** TO CREATE THEIR REALITY. THEY INTERPRET EVERYTHING THROUGH A FEW LIMITED SENSES AND FRAGMENTED **MEMORIES**. NO CHANCE TO CHANGE THINGS NOW!
THEY NEVER MANAGED TO COUNTERACT THE ADVANCEMENT OF **EGOTISM** AND **LACK OF CONSCIOUSNESS**.
JUST THINK OF THE **RENAISSANCE** IN ITALY! IN SPITE OF ALL OUR ENVOYS, THE ENEMY WON THAT BATTLE . . . IT'S FROM THEN ON THAT EVERYTHING STARTED TO

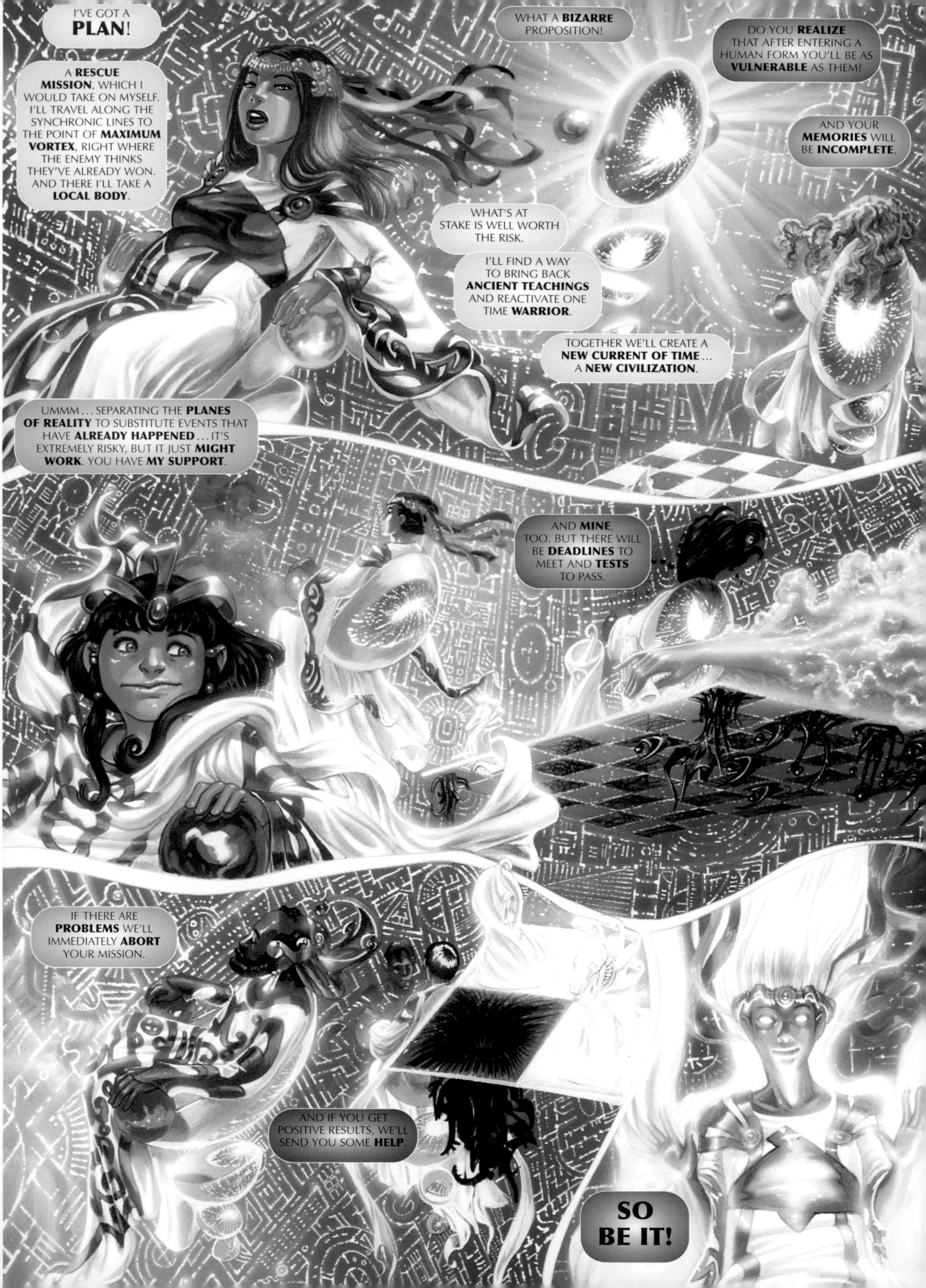

I'VE GOT A **PLAN**!
A **RESCUE MISSION**, WHICH I WOULD TAKE ON MYSELF. I'LL TRAVEL ALONG THE SYNCHRONIC LINES TO THE POINT OF **MAXIMUM VORTEX**, RIGHT WHERE THE ENEMY THINKS THEY'VE ALREADY WON. AND THERE I'LL TAKE A **LOCAL BODY**.
WHAT A **BIZARRE** PROPOSITION!
DO YOU **REALIZE** THAT AFTER ENTERING A HUMAN FORM YOU'LL BE AS **VULNERABLE** AS THEM?
AND YOUR **MEMORIES** WILL BE **INCOMPLETE**.
WHAT'S AT STAKE IS WELL WORTH THE RISK.
I'LL FIND A WAY TO BRING BACK **ANCIENT TEACHINGS** AND REACTIVATE ONE TIME **WARRIOR**.
TOGETHER WE'LL CREATE A **NEW CURRENT OF TIME** ... A **NEW CIVILIZATION**.
UMMM ... SEPARATING THE **PLANES OF REALITY** TO SUBSTITUTE EVENTS THAT HAVE **ALREADY HAPPENED** ... IT'S EXTREMELY RISKY, BUT IT JUST **MIGHT WORK**. YOU HAVE **MY SUPPORT**.
AND **MINE**, TOO. BUT THERE WILL BE **DEADLINES** TO MEET AND **TESTS** TO PASS.
IF THERE ARE **PROBLEMS** WE'LL IMMEDIATELY **ABORT** YOUR MISSION.
AND IF YOU GET POSITIVE RESULTS, WE'LL SEND YOU SOME **HELP**.
SO BE IT!

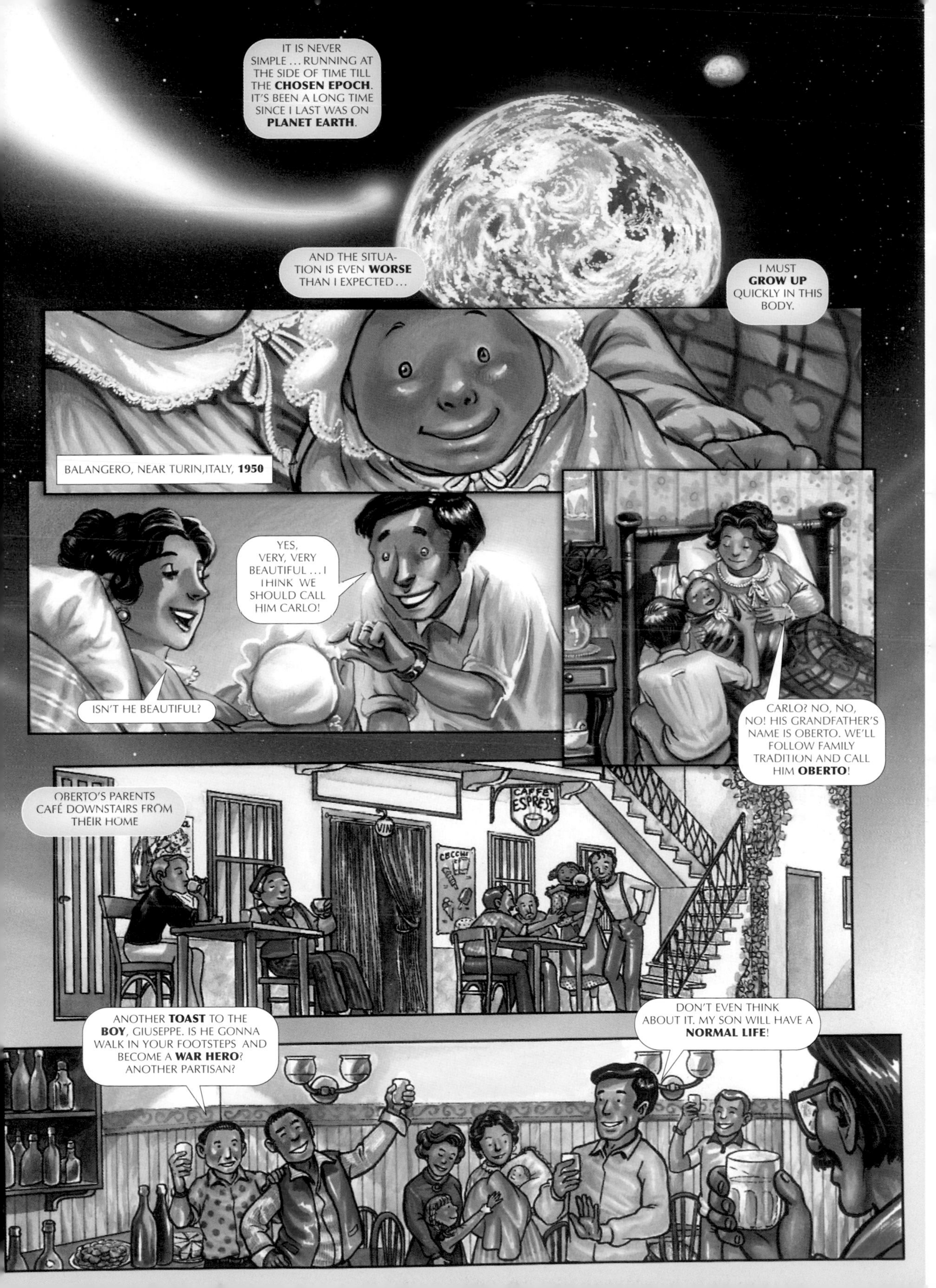

IT IS NEVER SIMPLE … RUNNING AT THE SIDE OF TIME TILL THE **CHOSEN EPOCH**. IT'S BEEN A LONG TIME SINCE I LAST WAS ON **PLANET EARTH**.
AND THE SITUA-TION IS EVEN **WORSE** THAN I EXPECTED …
I MUST **GROW UP** QUICKLY IN THIS BODY.
BALANGERO, NEAR TURIN,ITALY, **1950**
ISN'T HE BEAUTIFUL?
YES, VERY, VERY BEAUTIFUL … I THINK WE SHOULD CALL HIM CARLO!
CARLO? NO, NO, NO! HIS GRANDFATHER'S NAME IS OBERTO. WE'LL FOLLOW FAMILY TRADITION AND CALL HIM **OBERTO**!
OBERTO'S PARENTS CAFÉ DOWNSTAIRS FROM THEIR HOME
CAFFE' ESPRESSO
VINI
ANOTHER **TOAST** TO THE **BOY**, GIUSEPPE. IS HE GONNA WALK IN YOUR FOOTSTEPS AND BECOME A **WAR HERO**? ANOTHER PARTISAN?
DON'T EVEN THINK ABOUT IT. MY SON WILL HAVE A **NORMAL LIFE**!

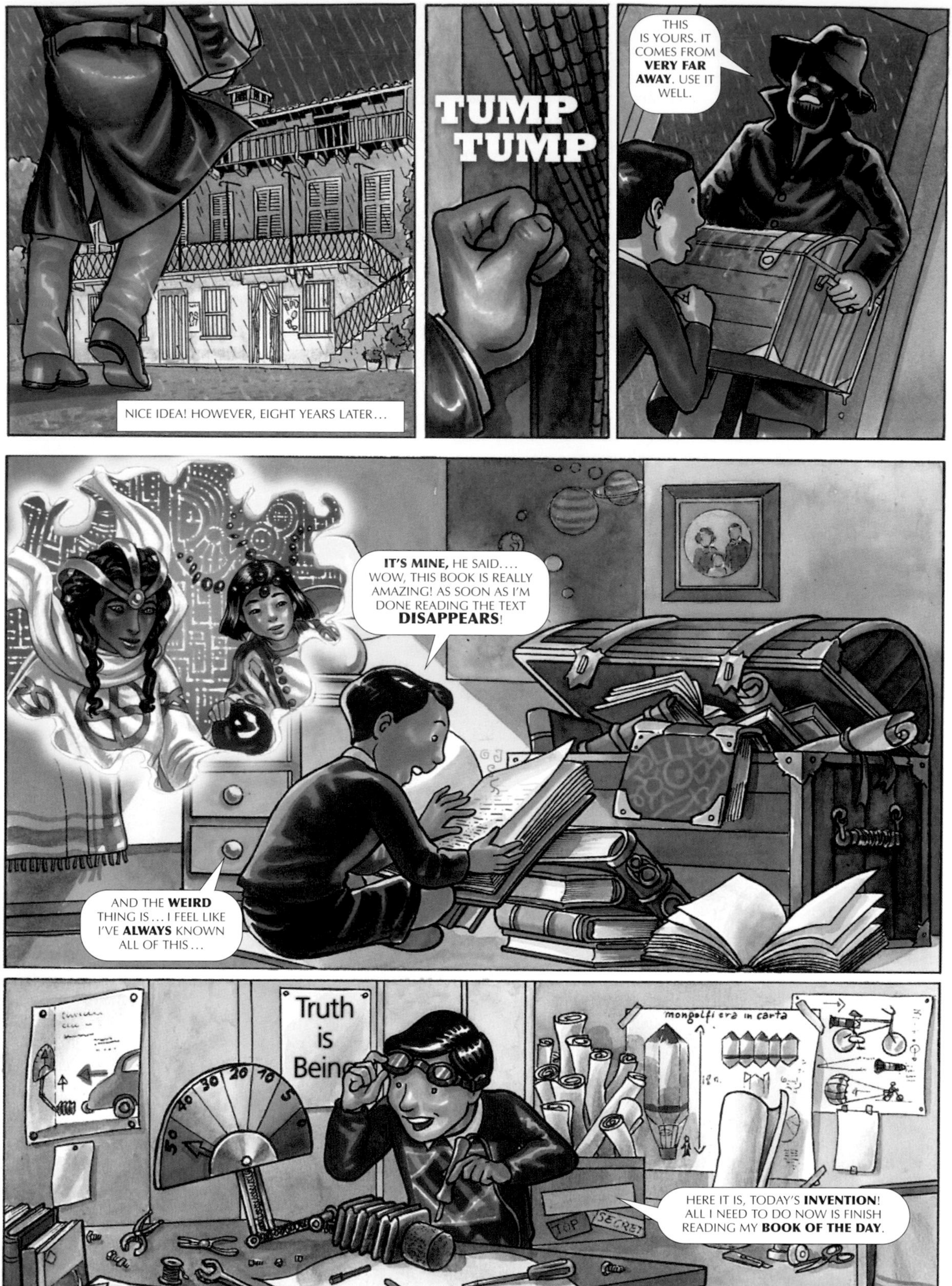
NICE IDEA! HOWEVER, EIGHT YEARS LATER...
TUMP TUMP
THIS IS YOURS. IT COMES FROM **VERY FAR AWAY**. USE IT WELL.
IT'S MINE, HE SAID.... WOW, THIS BOOK IS REALLY AMAZING! AS SOON AS I'M DONE READING THE TEXT **DISAPPEARS**!
AND THE **WEIRD** THING IS... I FEEL LIKE I'VE **ALWAYS** KNOWN ALL OF THIS...
Truth is Bein
mongolfiera in carta
TOP SECRET
HERE IT IS, TODAY'S **INVENTION**! ALL I NEED TO DO NOW IS FINISH READING MY **BOOK OF THE DAY**.
GRADUALLY AWAKENING HIS **MEMORIES**, OBERTO GREW UP EXPERIMENTING WITH ALL SORT OF THINGS.

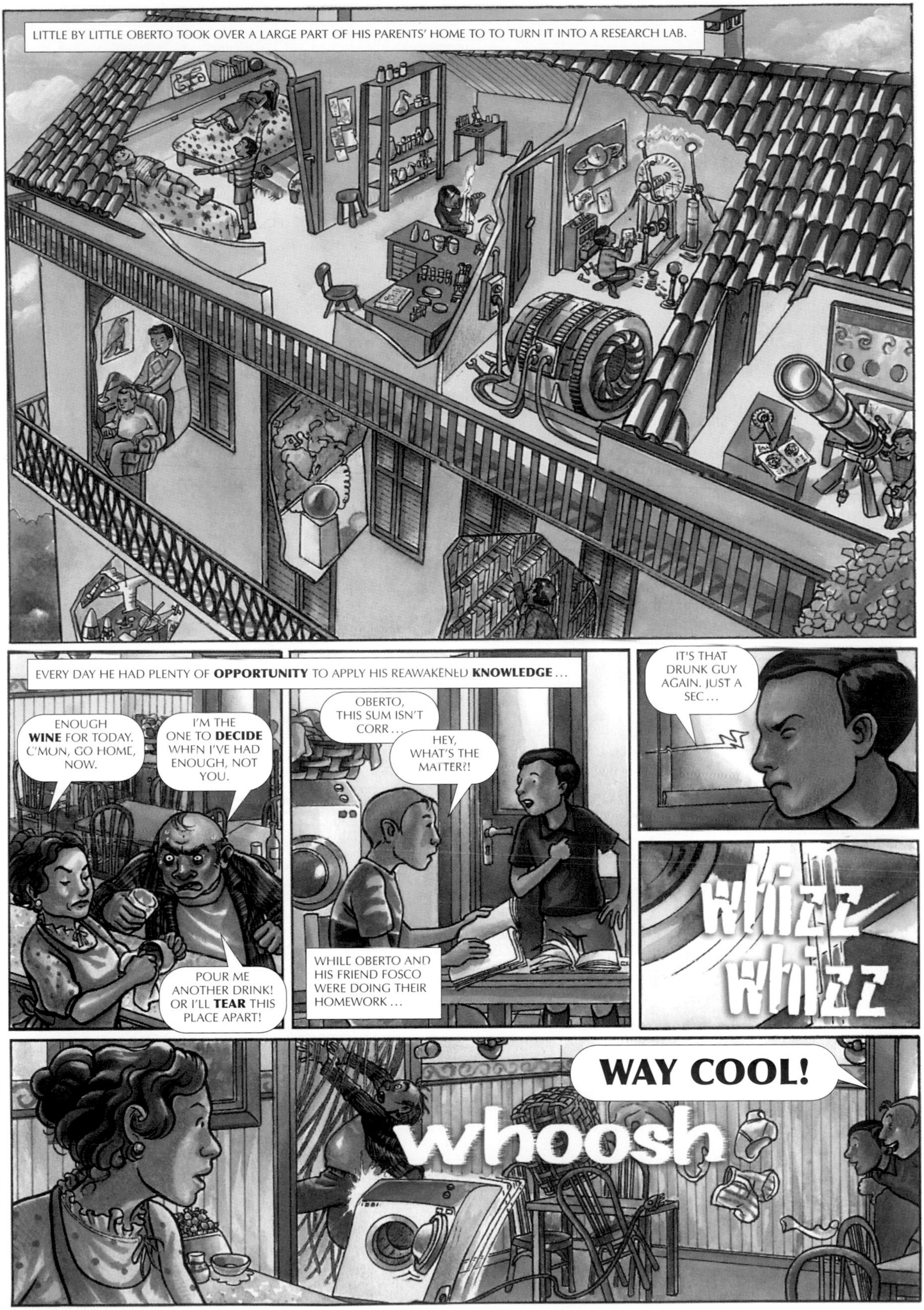
LITTLE BY LITTLE OBERTO TOOK OVER A LARGE PART OF HIS PARENTS' HOME TO TO TURN IT INTO A RESEARCH LAB.
EVERY DAY HE HAD PLENTY OF **OPPORTUNITY** TO APPLY HIS REAWAKENED **KNOWLEDGE** …
ENOUGH **WINE** FOR TODAY. C'MON, GO HOME, NOW.
I'M THE ONE TO **DECIDE** WHEN I'VE HAD ENOUGH, NOT YOU.
POUR ME ANOTHER DRINK! OR I'LL **TEAR** THIS PLACE APART!
OBERTO, THIS SUM ISN'T CORR …
HEY, WHAT'S THE MATTER?!
WHILE OBERTO AND HIS FRIEND FOSCO WERE DOING THEIR HOMEWORK …
IT'S THAT DRUNK GUY AGAIN. JUST A SEC …
whizz whizz
WAY COOL!
whoosh

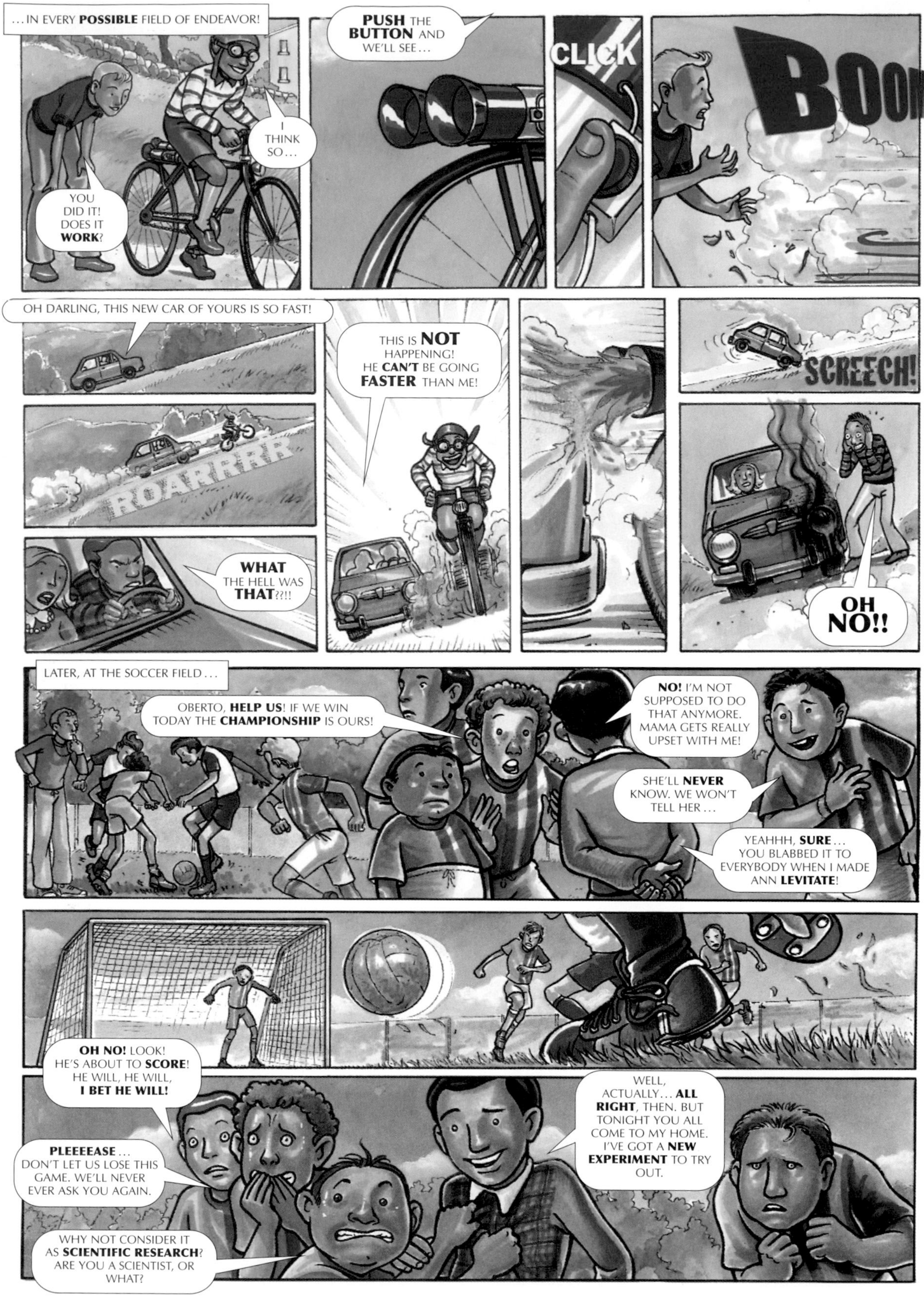

. . . IN EVERY **POSSIBLE** FIELD OF ENDEAVOR!
YOU DID IT! DOES IT **WORK**?
I THINK SO . . .
PUSH THE **BUTTON** AND WE'LL SEE . . .
CLICK
BOOM!
OH DARLING, THIS NEW CAR OF YOURS IS SO FAST!
ROARRRR
WHAT THE HELL WAS **THAT**??!!
THIS IS **NOT** HAPPENING! HE **CAN'T** BE GOING **FASTER** THAN ME!
SCREECH!
OH NO!!
LATER, AT THE SOCCER FIELD . . .
OBERTO, **HELP US**! IF WE WIN TODAY THE **CHAMPIONSHIP** IS OURS!
NO! I'M NOT SUPPOSED TO DO THAT ANYMORE. MAMA GETS REALLY UPSET WITH ME!
SHE'LL **NEVER** KNOW. WE WON'T TELL HER . . .
YEAHHH, **SURE** . . . YOU BLABBED IT TO EVERYBODY WHEN I MADE ANN **LEVITATE**!
OH NO! LOOK! HE'S ABOUT TO **SCORE**! HE WILL, HE WILL, **I BET HE WILL!**
PLEEEEASE . . . DON'T LET US LOSE THIS GAME. WE'LL NEVER EVER ASK YOU AGAIN.
WHY NOT CONSIDER IT AS **SCIENTIFIC RESEARCH**? ARE YOU A SCIENTIST, OR WHAT?
WELL, ACTUALLY . . . **ALL RIGHT**, THEN. BUT TONIGHT YOU ALL COME TO MY HOME. I'VE GOT A **NEW EXPERIMENT** TO TRY OUT.

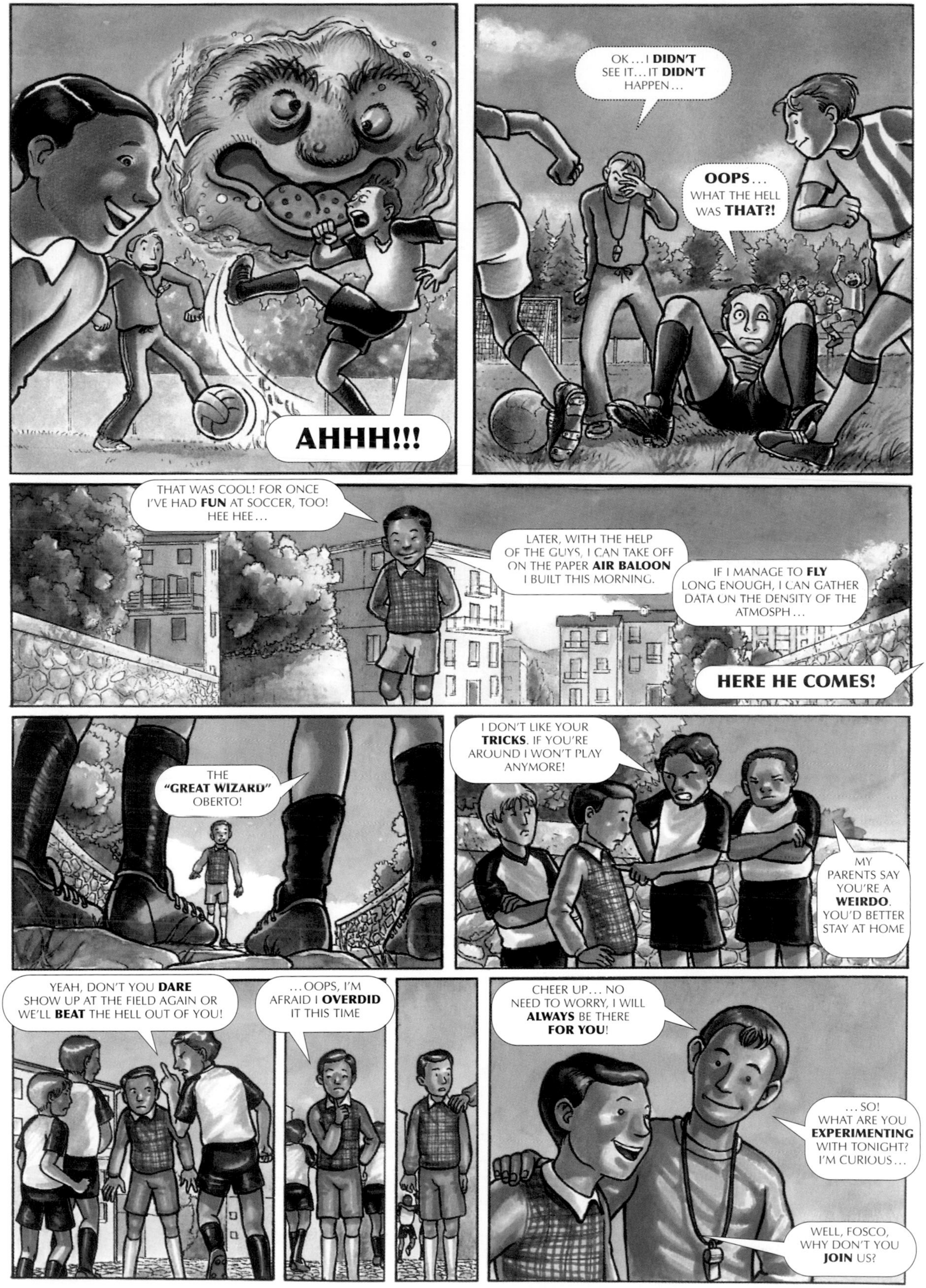
AHHH!!!
OK... I DIDN'T SEE IT... IT DIDN'T HAPPEN...
OOPS... WHAT THE HELL WAS THAT?!
THAT WAS COOL! FOR ONCE I'VE HAD FUN AT SOCCER, TOO! HEE HEE...
LATER, WITH THE HELP OF THE GUYS, I CAN TAKE OFF ON THE PAPER AIR BALOON I BUILT THIS MORNING.
IF I MANAGE TO FLY LONG ENOUGH, I CAN GATHER DATA ON THE DENSITY OF THE ATMOSPH...
HERE HE COMES!
THE "GREAT WIZARD" OBERTO!
I DON'T LIKE YOUR TRICKS. IF YOU'RE AROUND I WON'T PLAY ANYMORE!
MY PARENTS SAY YOU'RE A WEIRDO. YOU'D BETTER STAY AT HOME
YEAH, DON'T YOU DARE SHOW UP AT THE FIELD AGAIN OR WE'LL BEAT THE HELL OUT OF YOU!
...OOPS, I'M AFRAID I OVERDID IT THIS TIME
CHEER UP... NO NEED TO WORRY, I WILL ALWAYS BE THERE FOR YOU!
...SO! WHAT ARE YOU EXPERIMENTING WITH TONIGHT? I'M CURIOUS...
WELL, FOSCO, WHY DON'T YOU JOIN US?

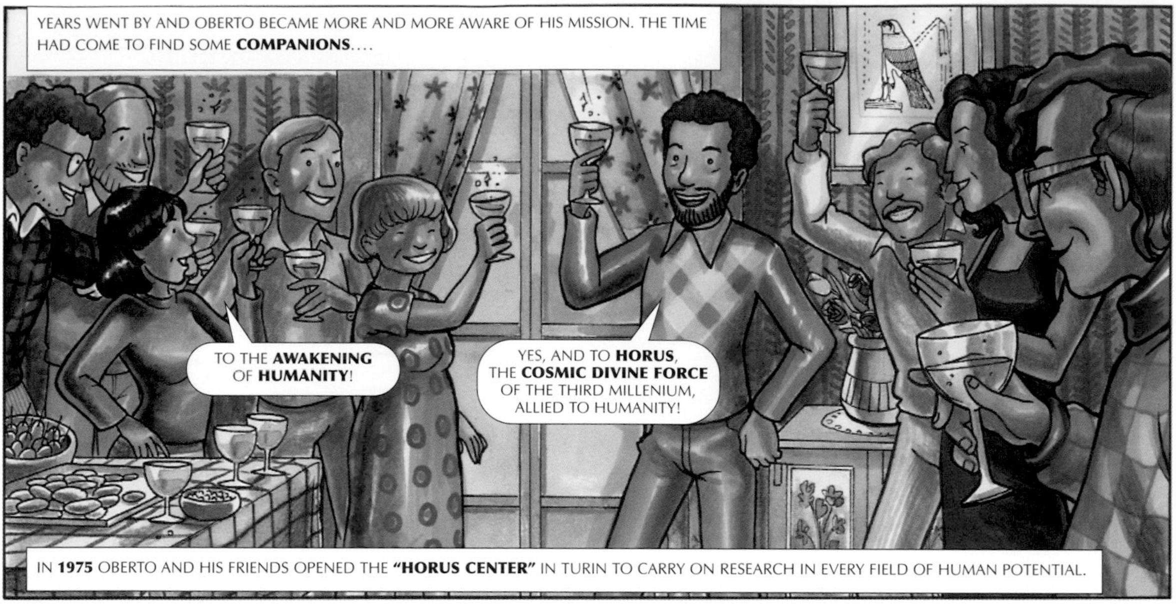
YEARS WENT BY AND OBERTO BECAME MORE AND MORE AWARE OF HIS MISSION. THE TIME HAD COME TO FIND SOME **COMPANIONS**....
TO THE **AWAKENING** OF **HUMANITY**!
YES, AND TO **HORUS**, THE **COSMIC DIVINE FORCE** OF THE THIRD MILLENIUM, ALLIED TO HUMANITY!
IN **1975** OBERTO AND HIS FRIENDS OPENED THE **"HORUS CENTER"** IN TURIN TO CARRY ON RESEARCH IN EVERY FIELD OF HUMAN POTENTIAL.

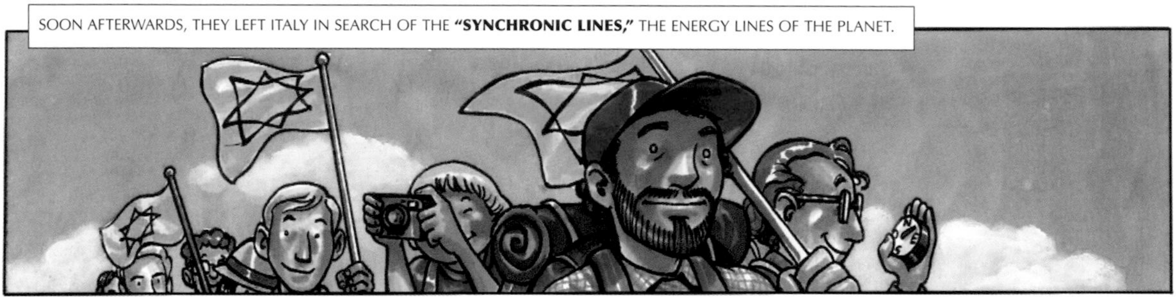
SOON AFTERWARDS, THEY LEFT ITALY IN SEARCH OF THE **"SYNCHRONIC LINES,"** THE ENERGY LINES OF THE PLANET.

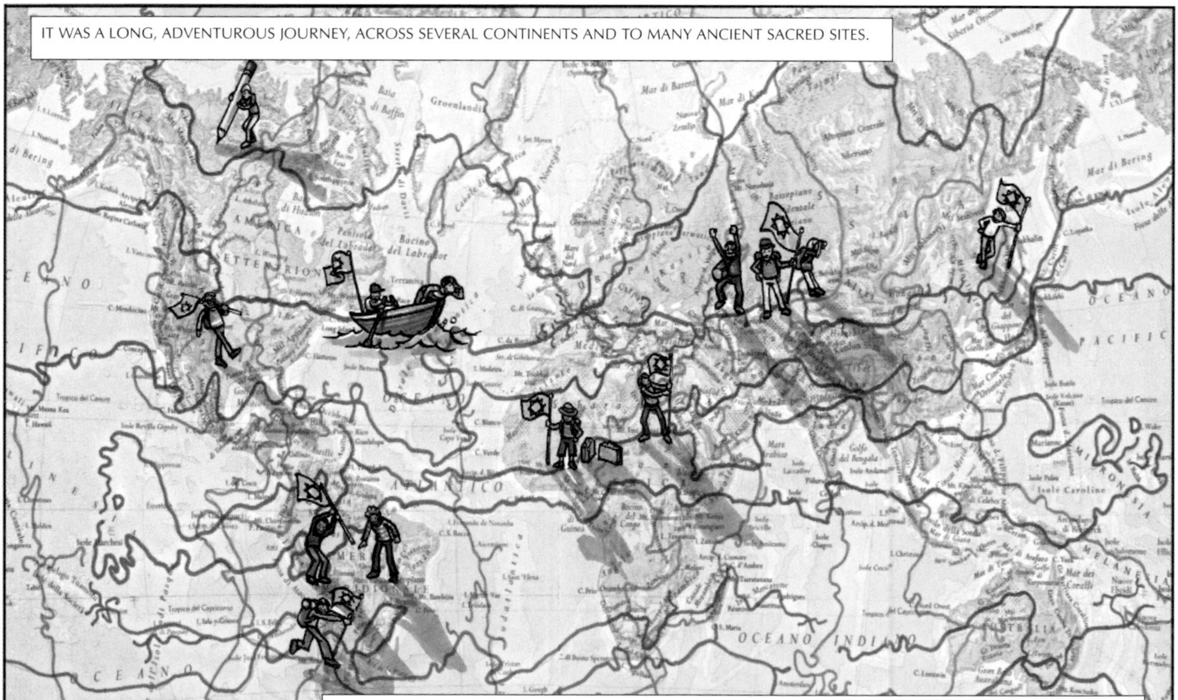
IT WAS A LONG, ADVENTUROUS JOURNEY, ACROSS SEVERAL CONTINENTS AND TO MANY ANCIENT SACRED SITES.
...TO FIND THE PLACE WHERE THE PLANET'S ENERGIES ARE STRONGEST AND THERE BUILD A **NEW SOCIETY**.

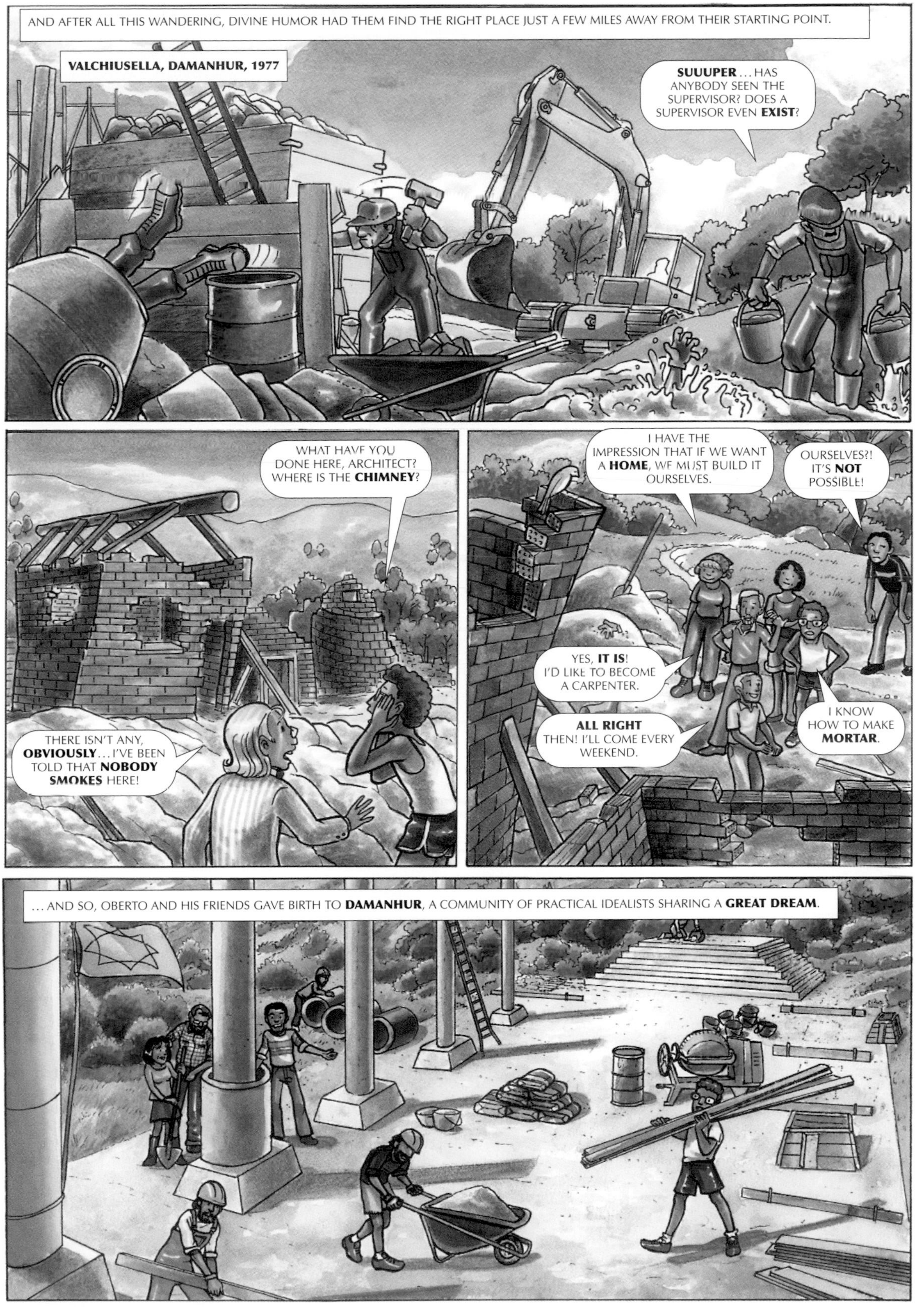
AND AFTER ALL THIS WANDERING, DIVINE HUMOR HAD THEM FIND THE RIGHT PLACE JUST A FEW MILES AWAY FROM THEIR STARTING POINT.
VALCHIUSELLA, DAMANHUR, 1977
SUUUPER . . . HAS ANYBODY SEEN THE SUPERVISOR? DOES A SUPERVISOR EVEN **EXIST**?
WHAT HAVE YOU DONE HERE, ARCHITECT? WHERE IS THE **CHIMNEY**?
THERE ISN'T ANY, **OBVIOUSLY** . . . I'VE BEEN TOLD THAT **NOBODY SMOKES** HERE!
I HAVE THE IMPRESSION THAT IF WE WANT A **HOME**, WE MUST BUILD IT OURSELVES.
OURSELVES?! IT'S **NOT** POSSIBLE!
YES, **IT IS**! I'D LIKE TO BECOME A CARPENTER.
ALL RIGHT THEN! I'LL COME EVERY WEEKEND.
I KNOW HOW TO MAKE **MORTAR**.
. . . AND SO, OBERTO AND HIS FRIENDS GAVE BIRTH TO **DAMANHUR**, A COMMUNITY OF PRACTICAL IDEALISTS SHARING A **GREAT DREAM**.

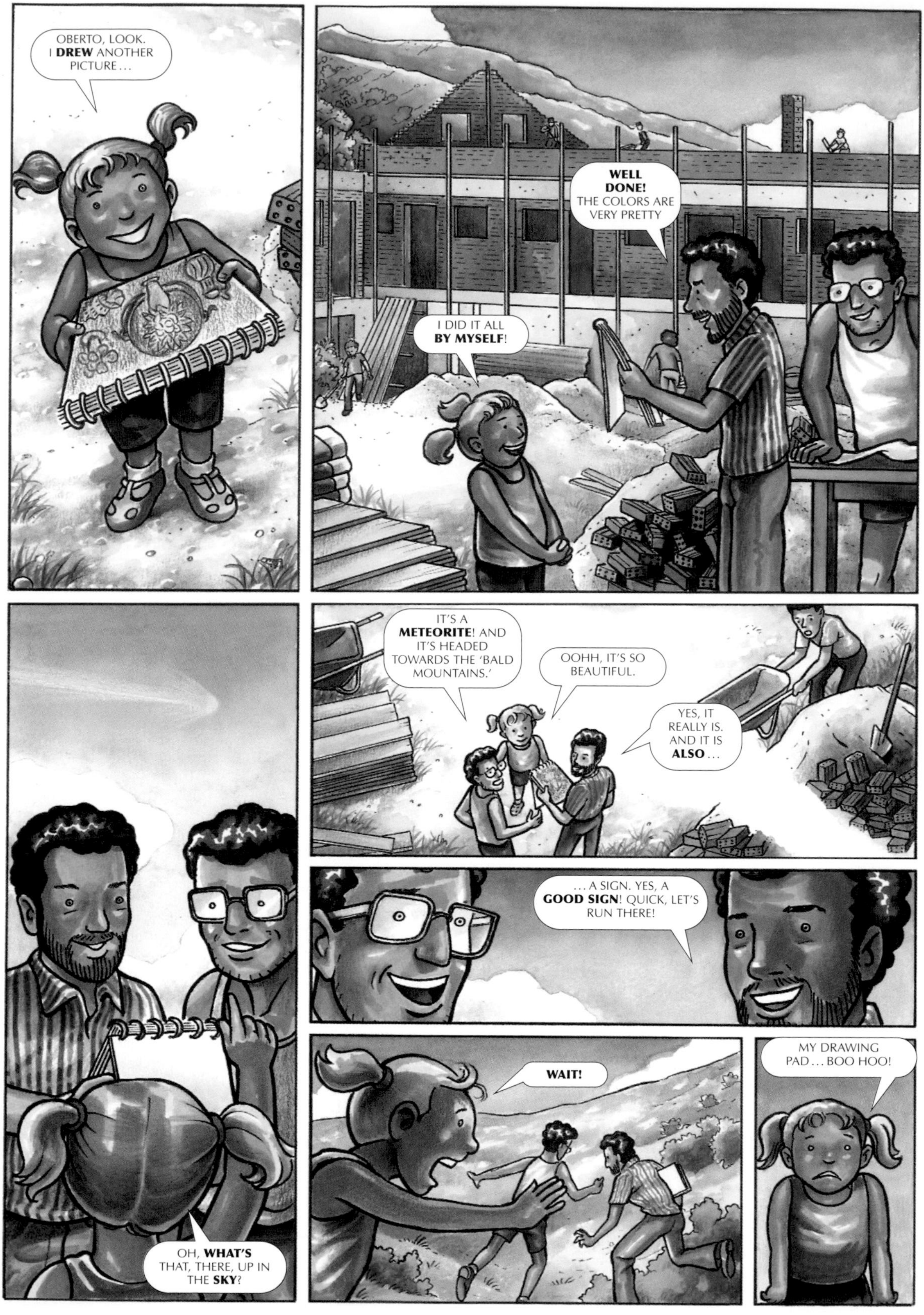
OBERTO, LOOK. I **DREW** ANOTHER PICTURE…
WELL DONE! THE COLORS ARE VERY PRETTY
I DID IT ALL **BY MYSELF**!
OH, **WHAT'S** THAT, THERE, UP IN THE **SKY**?
IT'S A **METEORITE**! AND IT'S HEADED TOWARDS THE 'BALD MOUNTAINS.'
OOHH, IT'S SO BEAUTIFUL.
YES, IT REALLY IS. AND IT IS **ALSO**…
… A SIGN. YES, A **GOOD SIGN**! QUICK, LET'S RUN THERE!
WAIT!
MY DRAWING PAD… BOO HOO!

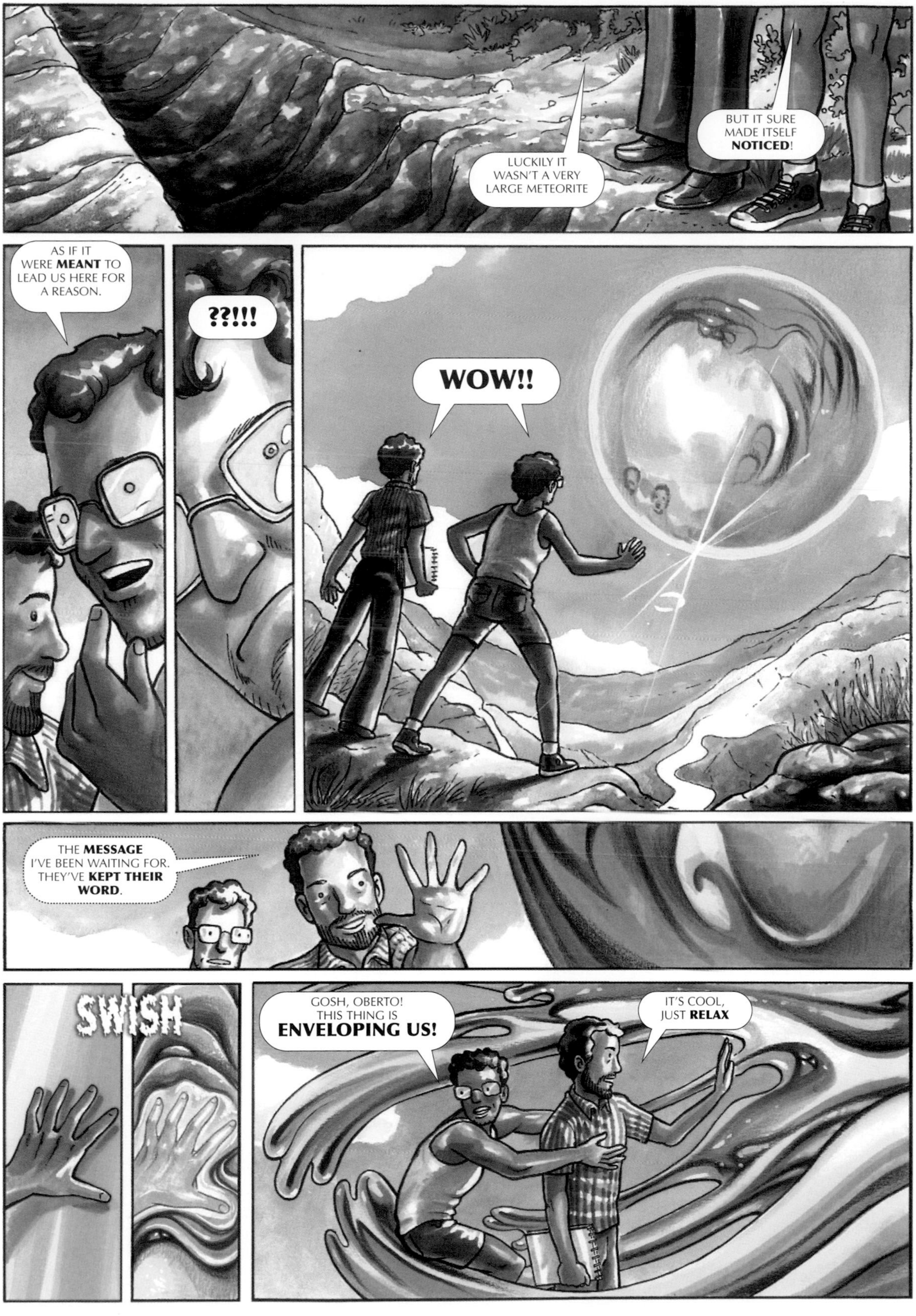
LUCKILY IT WASN'T A VERY LARGE METEORITE
BUT IT SURE MADE ITSELF NOTICED!
AS IF IT WERE MEANT TO LEAD US HERE FOR A REASON.
??!!!
WOW!!
THE MESSAGE I'VE BEEN WAITING FOR. THEY'VE KEPT THEIR WORD.
SWISH
GOSH, OBERTO! THIS THING IS ENVELOPING US!
IT'S COOL, JUST RELAX

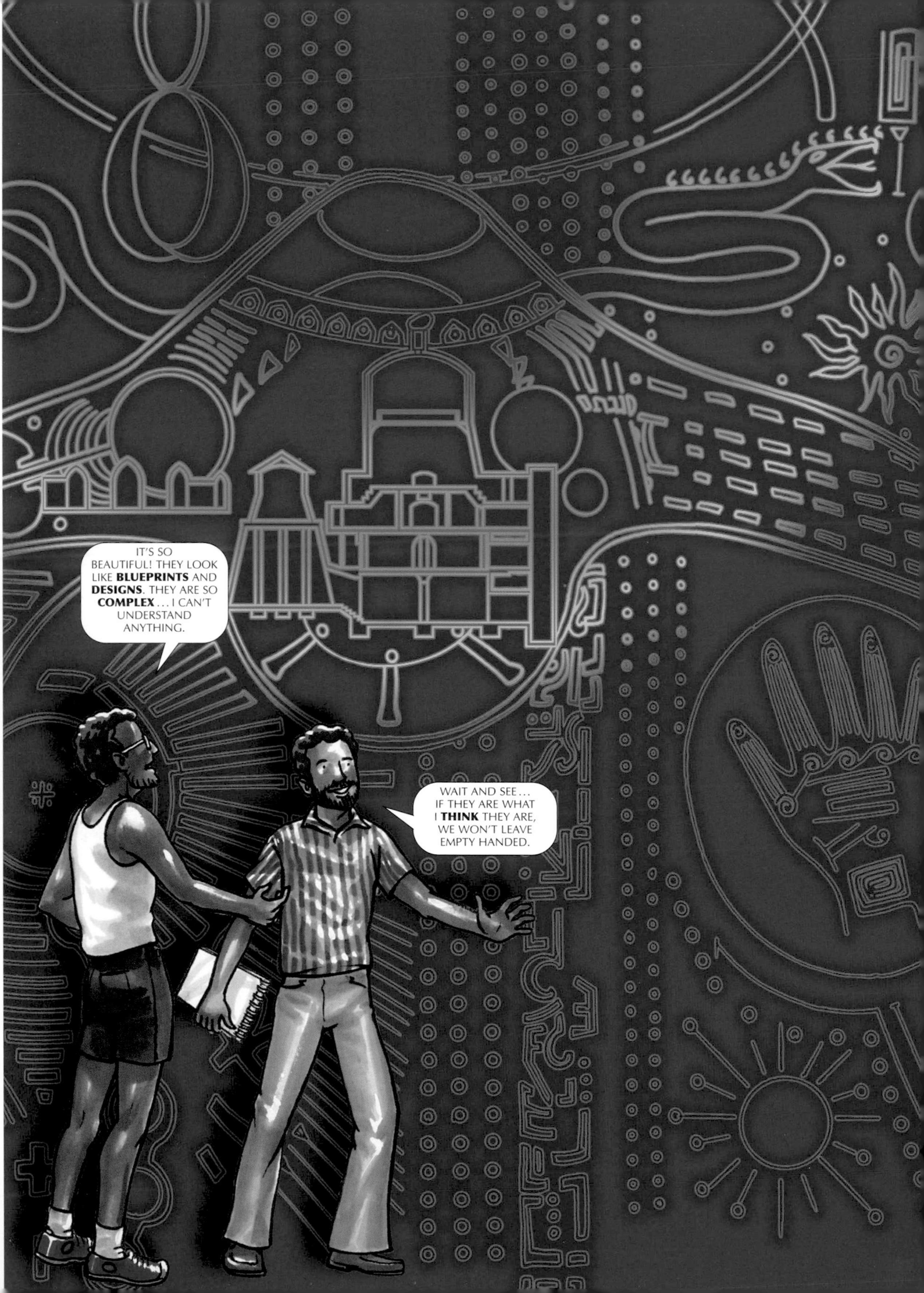
IT'S SO BEAUTIFUL! THEY LOOK LIKE **BLUEPRINTS** AND **DESIGNS**. THEY ARE SO **COMPLEX** . . . I CAN'T UNDERSTAND ANYTHING.
WAIT AND SEE . . . IF THEY ARE WHAT I **THINK** THEY ARE, WE WON'T LEAVE EMPTY HANDED.

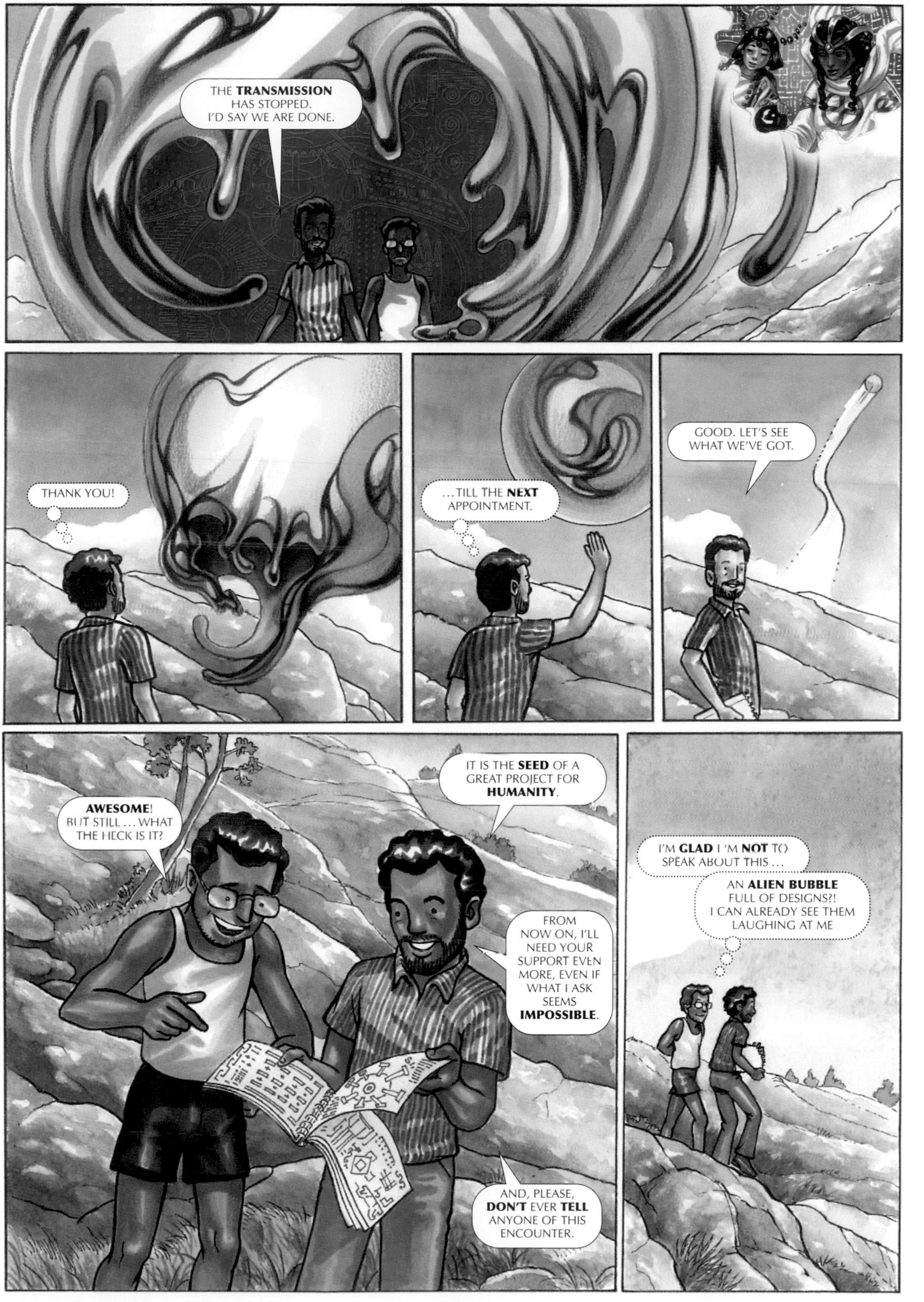
THE TRANSMISSION HAS STOPPED. I'D SAY WE ARE DONE.
THANK YOU!
...TILL THE NEXT APPOINTMENT.
GOOD. LET'S SEE WHAT WE'VE GOT.
AWESOME! BUT STILL ... WHAT THE HECK IS IT?
IT IS THE SEED OF A GREAT PROJECT FOR HUMANITY.
FROM NOW ON, I'LL NEED YOUR SUPPORT EVEN MORE, EVEN IF WHAT I ASK SEEMS IMPOSSIBLE.
AND, PLEASE, DON'T EVER TELL ANYONE OF THIS ENCOUNTER.
I'M GLAD I'M NOT TO SPEAK ABOUT THIS ...
AN ALIEN BUBBLE FULL OF DESIGNS?! I CAN ALREADY SEE THEM LAUGHING AT ME

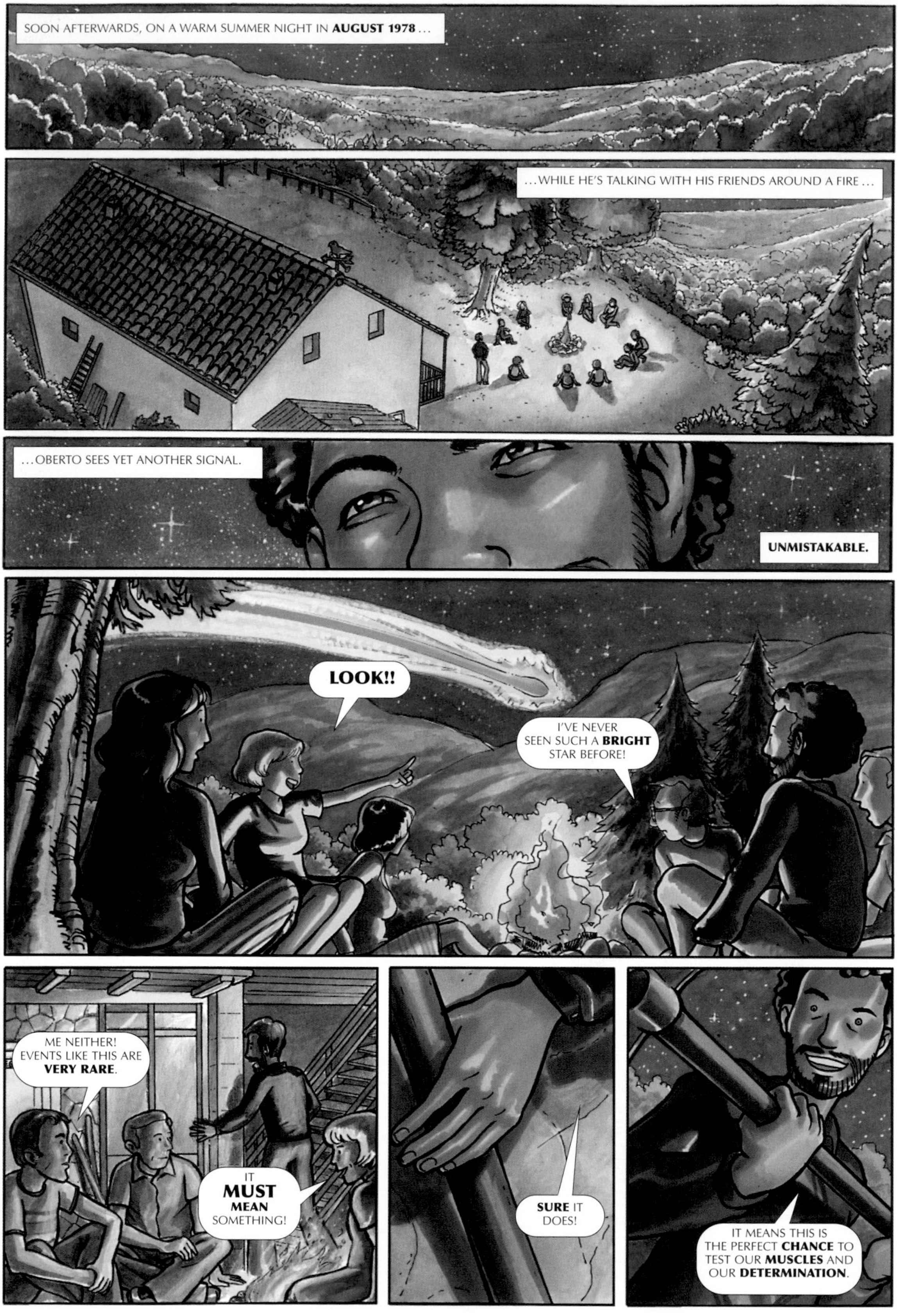
SOON AFTERWARDS, ON A WARM SUMMER NIGHT IN **AUGUST 1978** . . .
. . . WHILE HE'S TALKING WITH HIS FRIENDS AROUND A FIRE . . .
. . . OBERTO SEES YET ANOTHER SIGNAL.
UNMISTAKABLE.
LOOK!!
I'VE NEVER SEEN SUCH A **BRIGHT** STAR BEFORE!
ME NEITHER! EVENTS LIKE THIS ARE **VERY RARE**.
IT **MUST MEAN** SOMETHING!
SURE IT DOES!
IT MEANS THIS IS THE PERFECT **CHANCE** TO TEST OUR **MUSCLES** AND OUR **DETERMINATION**.

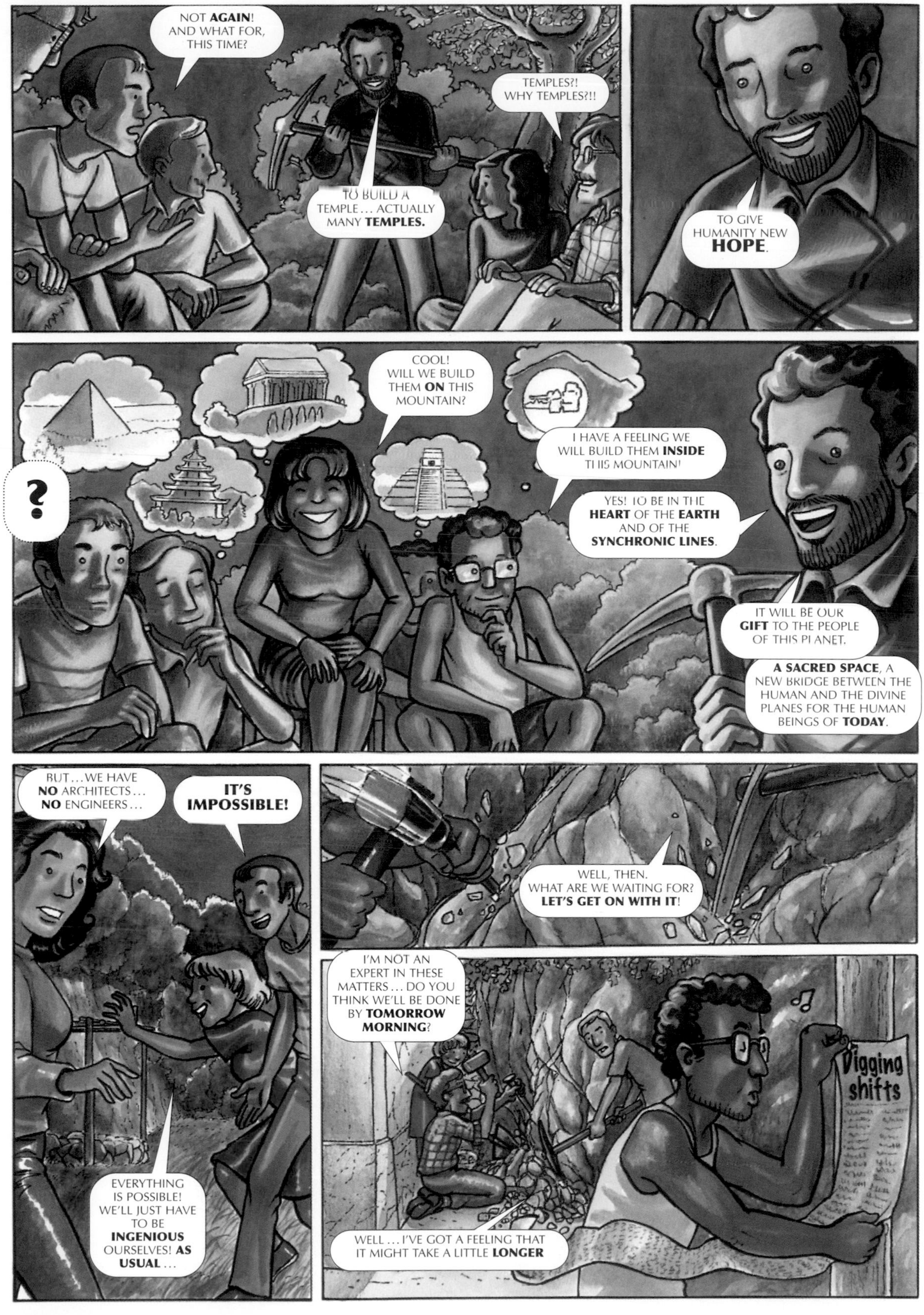
NOT AGAIN! AND WHAT FOR, THIS TIME?
TO BUILD A TEMPLE... ACTUALLY MANY TEMPLES.
TEMPLES?! WHY TEMPLES?!!
TO GIVE HUMANITY NEW HOPE.
?
COOL! WILL WE BUILD THEM ON THIS MOUNTAIN?
I HAVE A FEELING WE WILL BUILD THEM INSIDE THIS MOUNTAIN!
YES! TO BE IN THE HEART OF THE EARTH AND OF THE SYNCHRONIC LINES.
IT WILL BE OUR GIFT TO THE PEOPLE OF THIS PLANET.
A SACRED SPACE, A NEW BRIDGE BETWEEN THE HUMAN AND THE DIVINE PLANES FOR THE HUMAN BEINGS OF TODAY.
BUT... WE HAVE NO ARCHITECTS... NO ENGINEERS...
IT'S IMPOSSIBLE!
EVERYTHING IS POSSIBLE! WE'LL JUST HAVE TO BE INGENIOUS OURSELVES! AS USUAL...
WELL, THEN. WHAT ARE WE WAITING FOR? LET'S GET ON WITH IT!
I'M NOT AN EXPERT IN THESE MATTERS... DO YOU THINK WE'LL BE DONE BY TOMORROW MORNING?
Digging shifts
WELL... I'VE GOT A FEELING THAT IT MIGHT TAKE A LITTLE LONGER

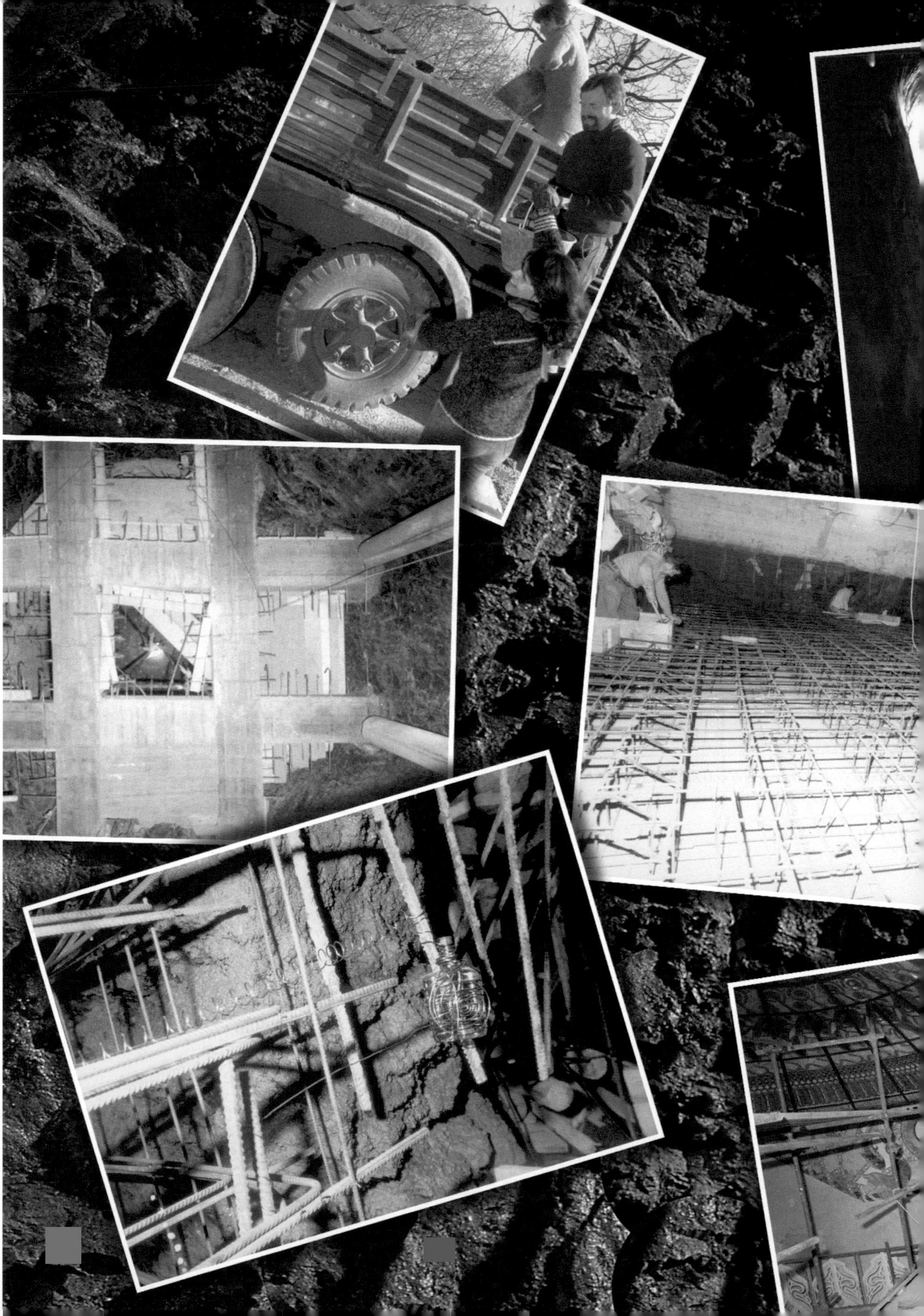

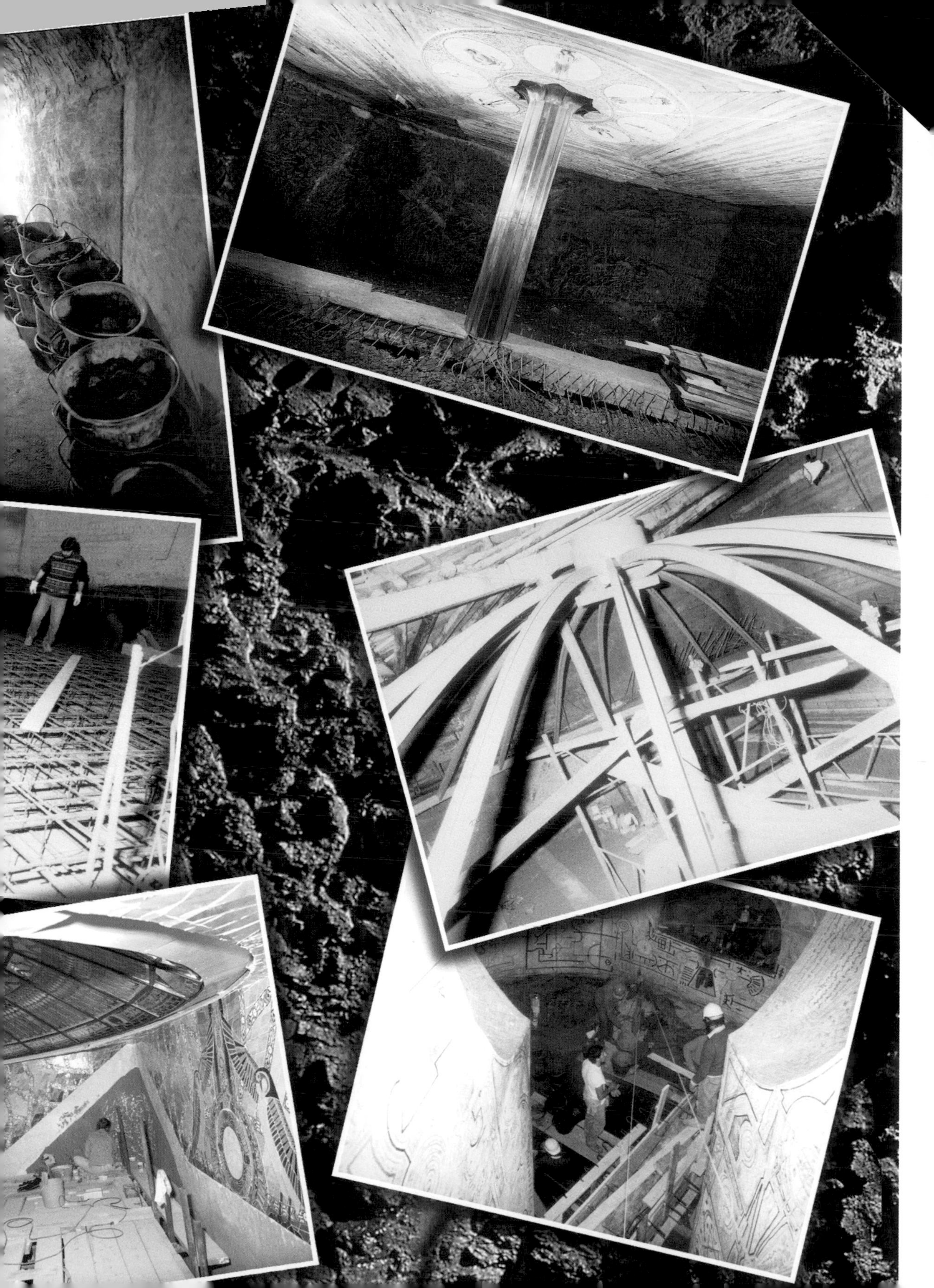

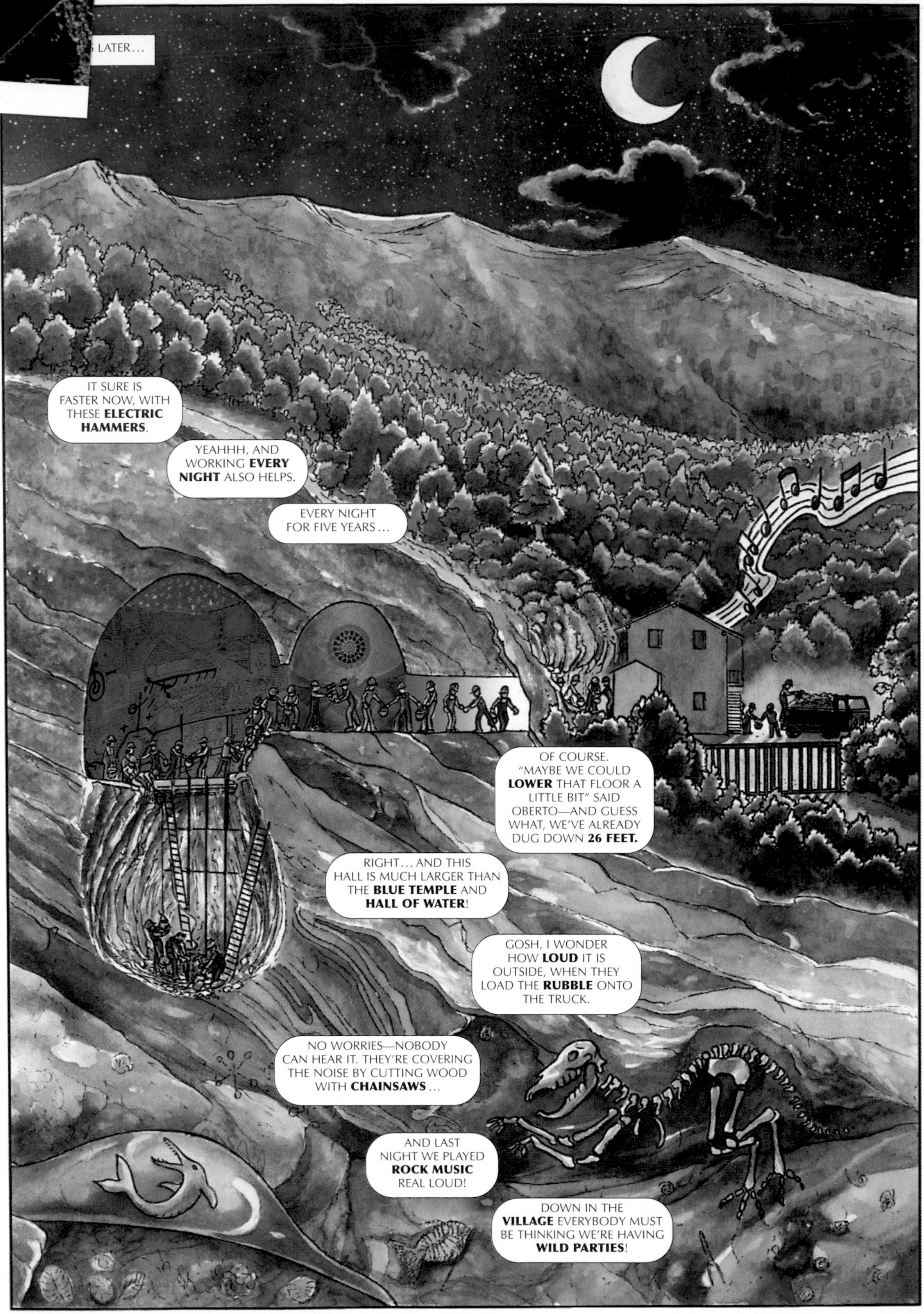
LATER…
IT SURE IS FASTER NOW, WITH THESE **ELECTRIC HAMMERS**.
YEAHHH, AND WORKING **EVERY NIGHT** ALSO HELPS.
EVERY NIGHT FOR FIVE YEARS…
OF COURSE. "MAYBE WE COULD **LOWER** THAT FLOOR A LITTLE BIT" SAID OBERTO—AND GUESS WHAT, WE'VE ALREADY DUG DOWN **26 FEET.**
RIGHT… AND THIS HALL IS MUCH LARGER THAN THE **BLUE TEMPLE** AND **HALL OF WATER**!
GOSH, I WONDER HOW **LOUD** IT IS OUTSIDE, WHEN THEY LOAD THE **RUBBLE** ONTO THE TRUCK.
NO WORRIES—NOBODY CAN HEAR IT. THEY'RE COVERING THE NOISE BY CUTTING WOOD WITH **CHAINSAWS**…
AND LAST NIGHT WE PLAYED **ROCK MUSIC** REAL LOUD!
DOWN IN THE **VILLAGE** EVERYBODY MUST BE THINKING WE'RE HAVING **WILD PARTIES**!

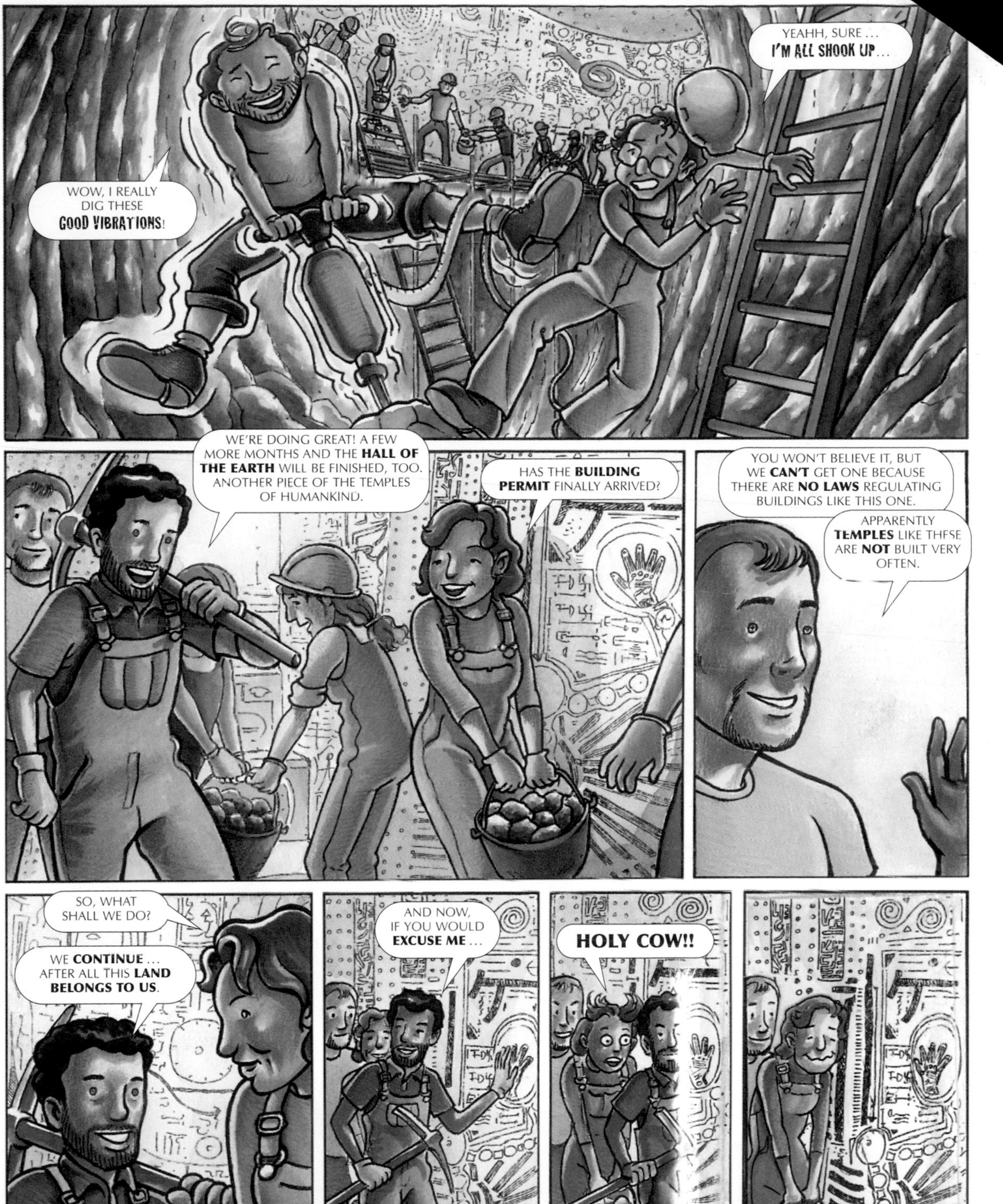
WOW, I REALLY DIG THESE GOOD VIBRATIONS!
YEAHH, SURE ... I'M ALL SHOOK UP ...
WE'RE DOING GREAT! A FEW MORE MONTHS AND THE HALL OF THE EARTH WILL BE FINISHED, TOO. ANOTHER PIECE OF THE TEMPLES OF HUMANKIND.
HAS THE BUILDING PERMIT FINALLY ARRIVED?
YOU WON'T BELIEVE IT, BUT WE CAN'T GET ONE BECAUSE THERE ARE NO LAWS REGULATING BUILDINGS LIKE THIS ONE.
APPARENTLY TEMPLES LIKE THESE ARE NOT BUILT VERY OFTEN.
SO, WHAT SHALL WE DO?
WE CONTINUE ... AFTER ALL THIS LAND BELONGS TO US.
AND NOW, IF YOU WOULD EXCUSE ME ...
HOLY COW!!
AWESOME!

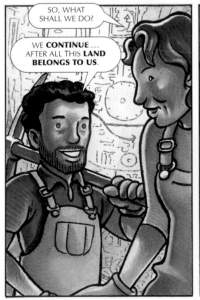

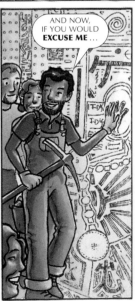

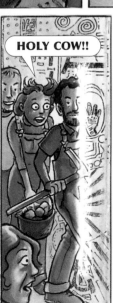

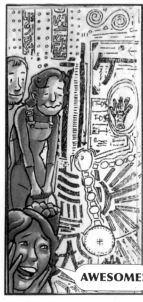

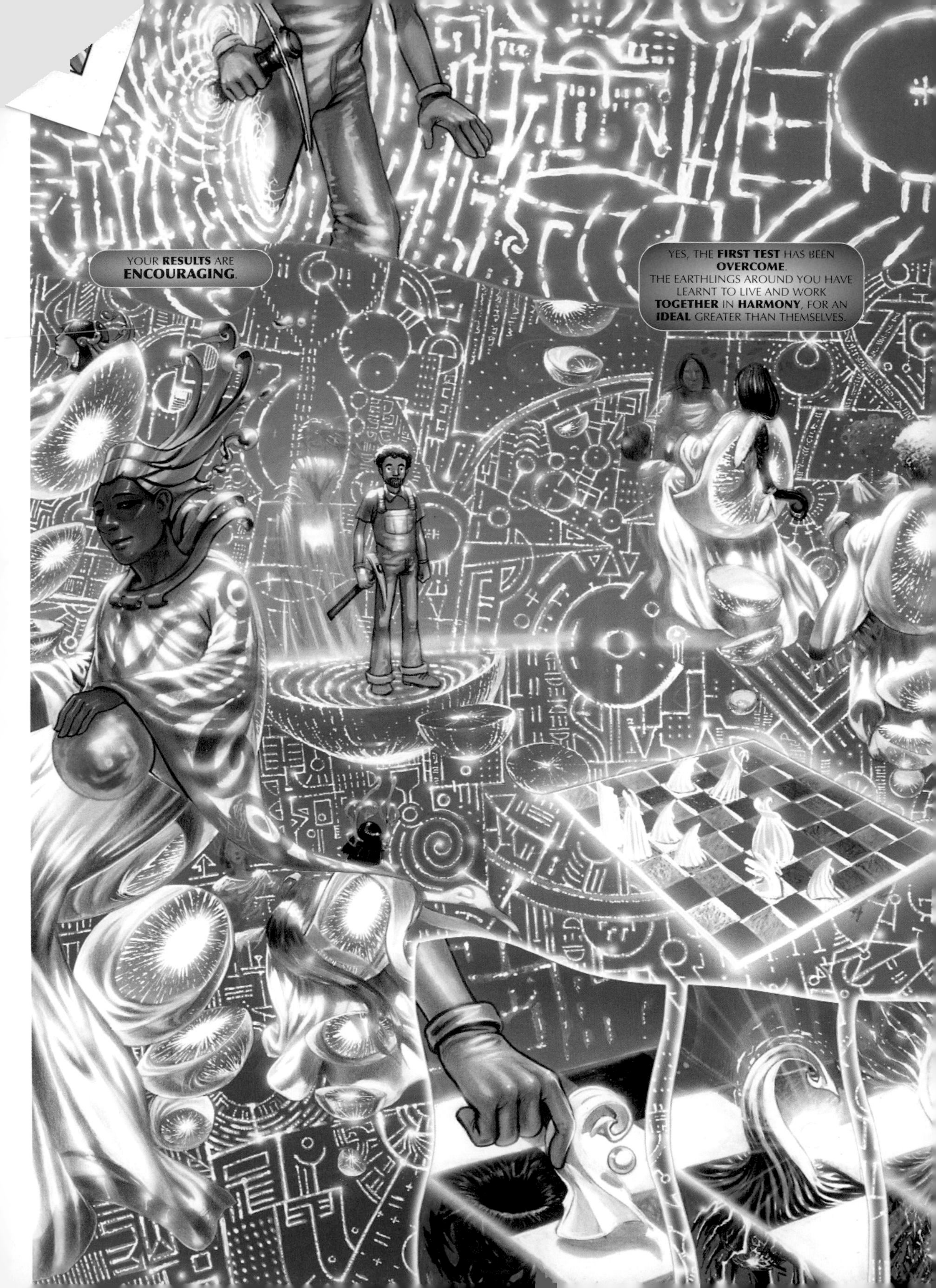
YOUR **RESULTS** ARE **ENCOURAGING**.
YES, THE **FIRST TEST** HAS BEEN **OVERCOME**. THE EARTHLINGS AROUND YOU HAVE LEARNT TO LIVE AND WORK **TOGETHER** IN **HARMONY**, FOR AN **IDEAL** GREATER THAN THEMSELVES.

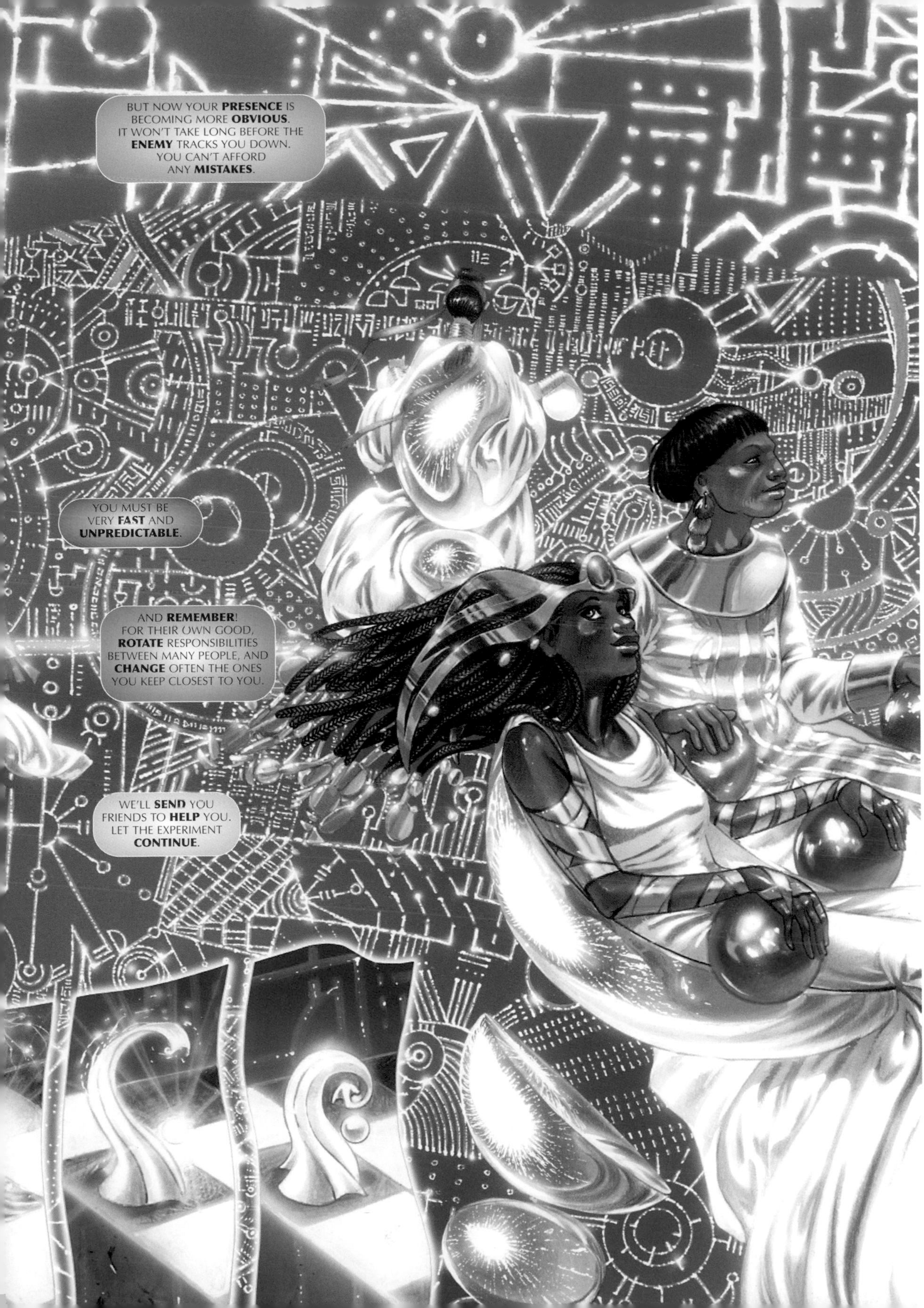
BUT NOW YOUR **PRESENCE** IS BECOMING MORE **OBVIOUS**. IT WON'T TAKE LONG BEFORE THE **ENEMY** TRACKS YOU DOWN. YOU CAN'T AFFORD ANY **MISTAKES**.
YOU MUST BE VERY **FAST** AND **UNPREDICTABLE**.
AND **REMEMBER**! FOR THEIR OWN GOOD, **ROTATE** RESPONSIBILITIES BETWEEN MANY PEOPLE, AND **CHANGE** OFTEN THE ONES YOU KEEP CLOSEST TO YOU.
WE'LL **SEND** YOU FRIENDS TO **HELP** YOU. LET THE EXPERIMENT **CONTINUE**.

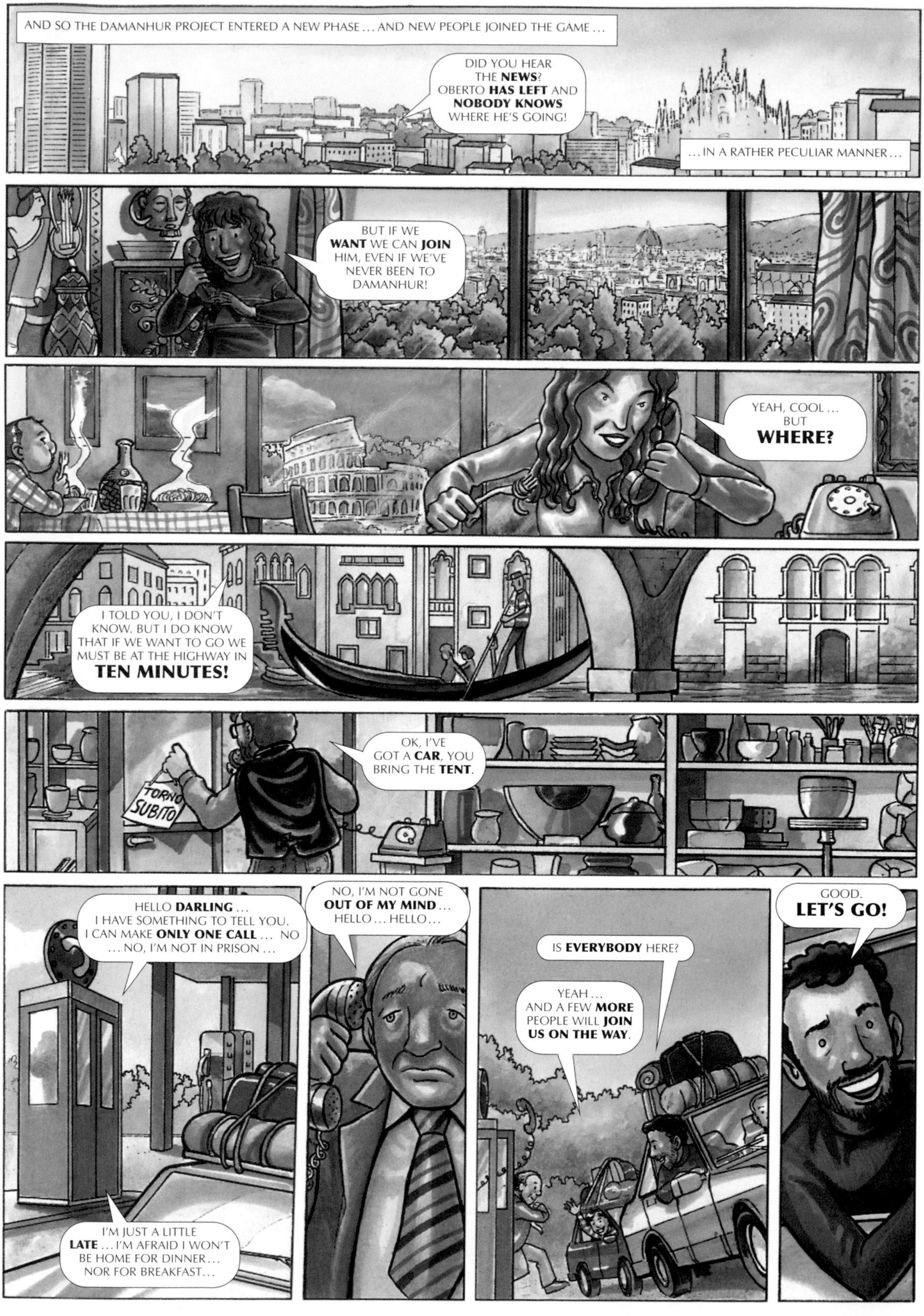
AND SO THE DAMANHUR PROJECT ENTERED A NEW PHASE . . . AND NEW PEOPLE JOINED THE GAME . . .
DID YOU HEAR THE **NEWS**? OBERTO **HAS LEFT** AND **NOBODY KNOWS** WHERE HE'S GOING!
. . . IN A RATHER PECULIAR MANNER . . .
BUT IF WE **WANT** WE CAN **JOIN** HIM, EVEN IF WE'VE NEVER BEEN TO DAMANHUR!
YEAH, COOL . . . BUT **WHERE?**
I TOLD YOU, I DON'T KNOW. BUT I DO KNOW THAT IF WE WANT TO GO WE MUST BE AT THE HIGHWAY IN **TEN MINUTES!**
TORNO SUBITO
OK, I'VE GOT A **CAR**, YOU BRING THE **TENT**.
HELLO **DARLING** . . . I HAVE SOMETHING TO TELL YOU. I CAN MAKE **ONLY ONE CALL** . . . NO . . . NO, I'M NOT IN PRISON . . .
I'M JUST A LITTLE **LATE** . . . I'M AFRAID I WON'T BE HOME FOR DINNER . . . NOR FOR BREAKFAST . . .
NO, I'M NOT GONE **OUT OF MY MIND** . . . HELLO . . . HELLO . . .
IS **EVERYBODY** HERE?
YEAH . . . AND A FEW **MORE** PEOPLE WILL **JOIN US ON THE WAY**.
GOOD. **LET'S GO!**

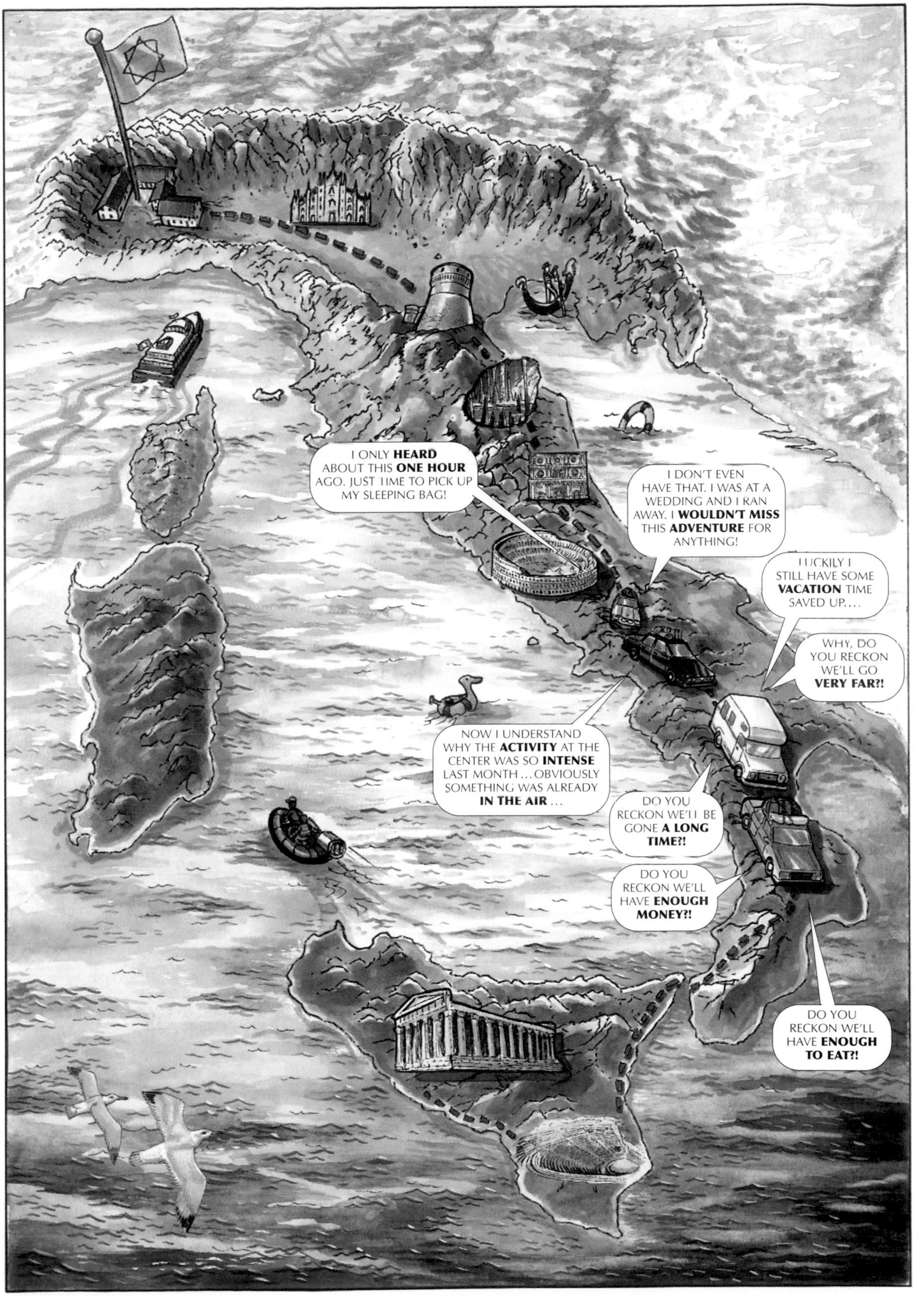
I ONLY **HEARD** ABOUT THIS **ONE HOUR** AGO. JUST TIME TO PICK UP MY SLEEPING BAG!
I DON'T EVEN HAVE THAT. I WAS AT A WEDDING AND I RAN AWAY. I **WOULDN'T MISS** THIS **ADVENTURE** FOR ANYTHING!
LUCKILY I STILL HAVE SOME **VACATION** TIME SAVED UP....
WHY, DO YOU RECKON WE'LL GO **VERY FAR?!**
NOW I UNDERSTAND WHY THE **ACTIVITY** AT THE CENTER WAS SO **INTENSE** LAST MONTH ... OBVIOUSLY SOMETHING WAS ALREADY **IN THE AIR** ...
DO YOU RECKON WE'LL BE GONE **A LONG TIME?!**
DO YOU RECKON WE'LL HAVE **ENOUGH MONEY?!**
DO YOU RECKON WE'LL HAVE **ENOUGH TO EAT?!**

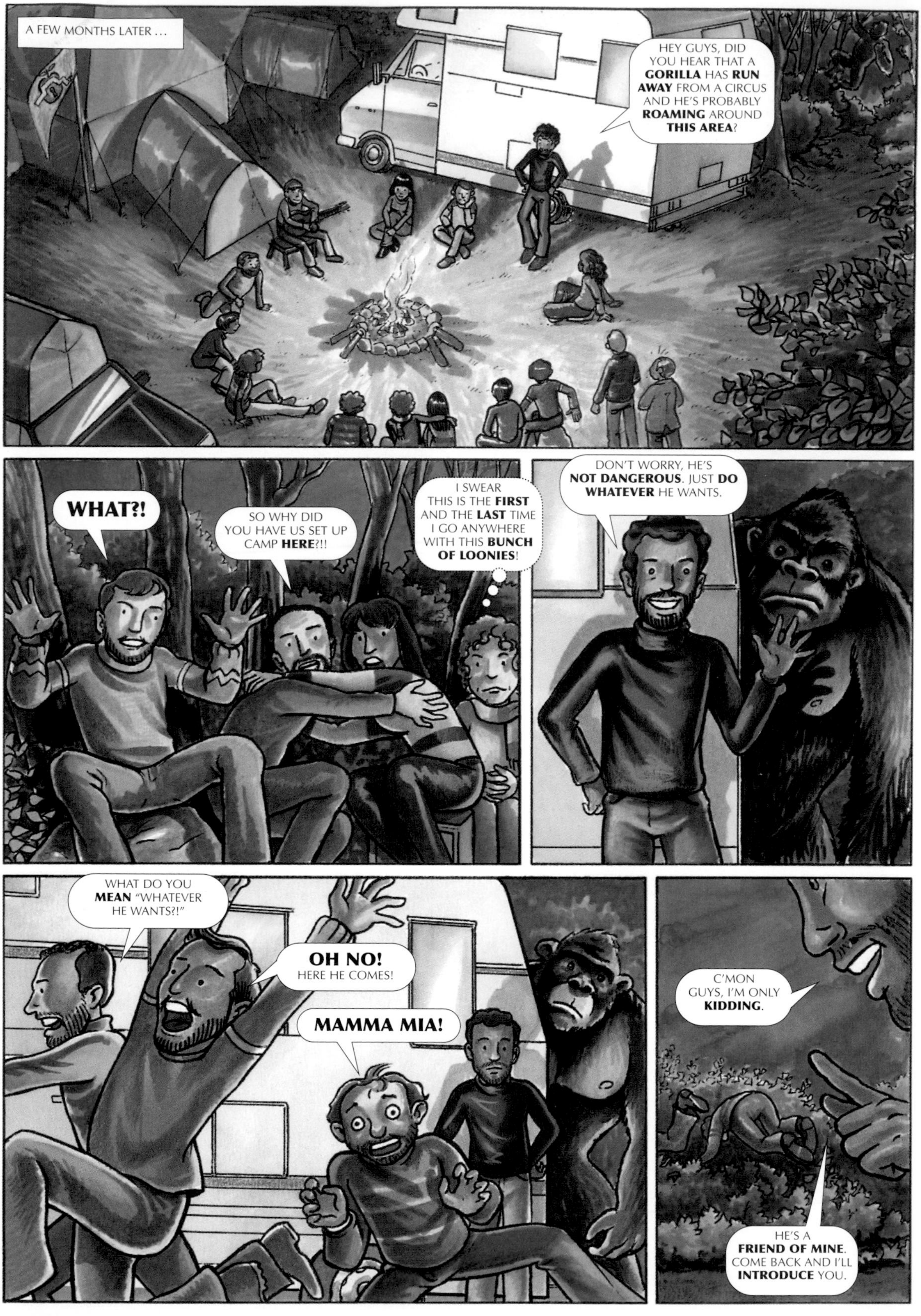
A FEW MONTHS LATER …
HEY GUYS, DID YOU HEAR THAT A **GORILLA** HAS **RUN AWAY** FROM A CIRCUS AND HE'S PROBABLY **ROAMING** AROUND **THIS AREA**?
WHAT?!
SO WHY DID YOU HAVE US SET UP CAMP **HERE**?!!
I SWEAR THIS IS THE **FIRST** AND THE **LAST** TIME I GO ANYWHERE WITH THIS **BUNCH OF LOONIES**!
DON'T WORRY, HE'S **NOT DANGEROUS**. JUST **DO WHATEVER** HE WANTS.
WHAT DO YOU **MEAN** "WHATEVER HE WANTS?!"
OH NO! HERE HE COMES!
MAMMA MIA!
C'MON GUYS, I'M ONLY **KIDDING**.
HE'S A **FRIEND OF MINE**. COME BACK AND I'LL **INTRODUCE** YOU.

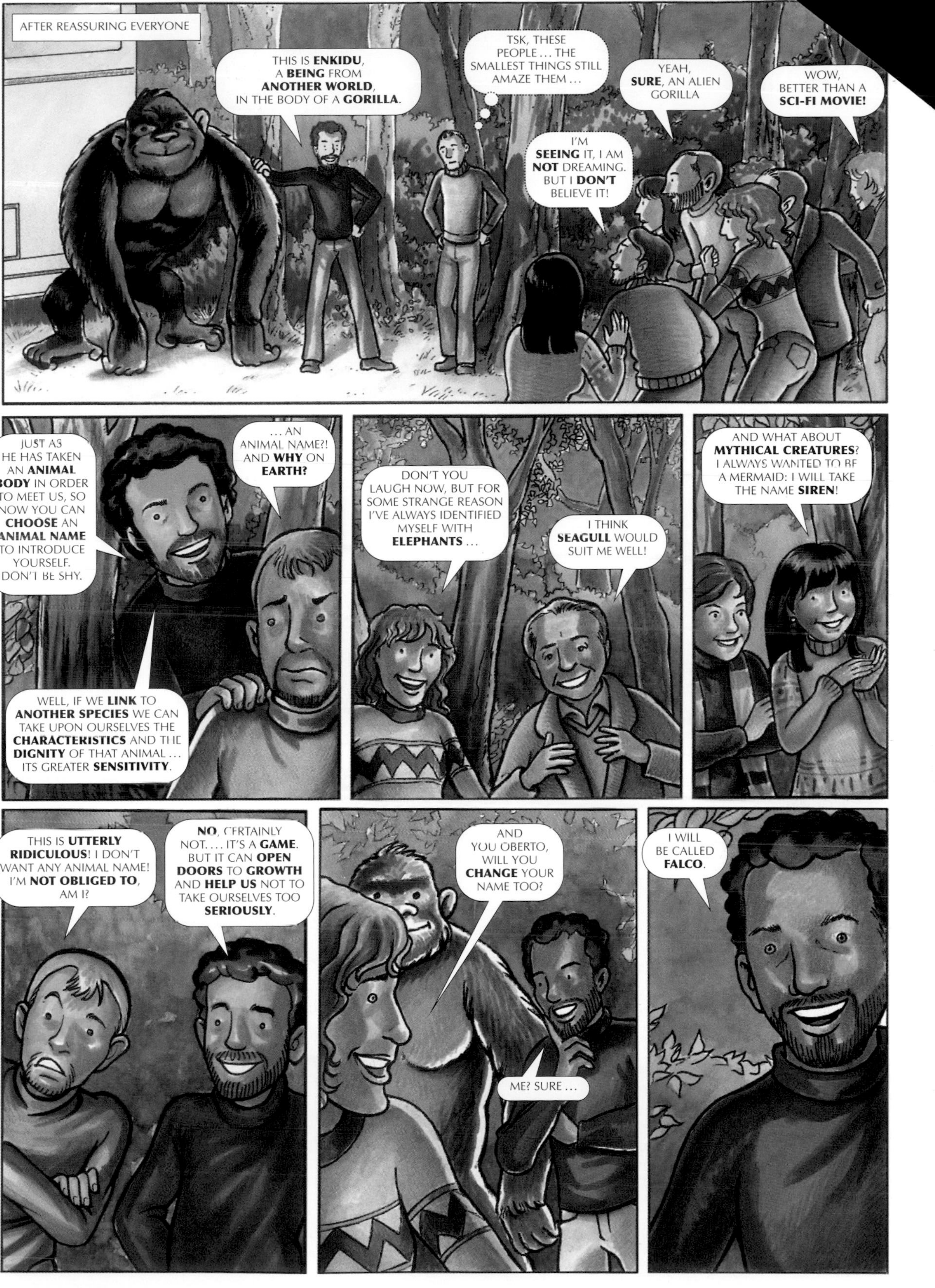
AFTER REASSURING EVERYONE
THIS IS ENKIDU, A BEING FROM ANOTHER WORLD, IN THE BODY OF A GORILLA.
TSK, THESE PEOPLE … THE SMALLEST THINGS STILL AMAZE THEM …
I'M SEEING IT, I AM NOT DREAMING. BUT I DON'T BELIEVE IT!
YEAH, SURE, AN ALIEN GORILLA
WOW, BETTER THAN A SCI-FI MOVIE!
JUST AS HE HAS TAKEN AN ANIMAL BODY IN ORDER TO MEET US, SO NOW YOU CAN CHOOSE AN ANIMAL NAME TO INTRODUCE YOURSELF. DON'T BE SHY.
… AN ANIMAL NAME?! AND WHY ON EARTH?
WELL, IF WE LINK TO ANOTHER SPECIES WE CAN TAKE UPON OURSELVES THE CHARACTERISTICS AND THE DIGNITY OF THAT ANIMAL … ITS GREATER SENSITIVITY.
DON'T YOU LAUGH NOW, BUT FOR SOME STRANGE REASON I'VE ALWAYS IDENTIFIED MYSELF WITH ELEPHANTS …
I THINK SEAGULL WOULD SUIT ME WELL!
AND WHAT ABOUT MYTHICAL CREATURES? I ALWAYS WANTED TO BE A MERMAID: I WILL TAKE THE NAME SIREN!
THIS IS UTTERLY RIDICULOUS! I DON'T WANT ANY ANIMAL NAME! I'M NOT OBLIGED TO, AM I?
NO, CERTAINLY NOT. … IT'S A GAME. BUT IT CAN OPEN DOORS TO GROWTH AND HELP US NOT TO TAKE OURSELVES TOO SERIOUSLY.
AND YOU OBERTO, WILL YOU CHANGE YOUR NAME TOO?
ME? SURE …
I WILL BE CALLED FALCO.

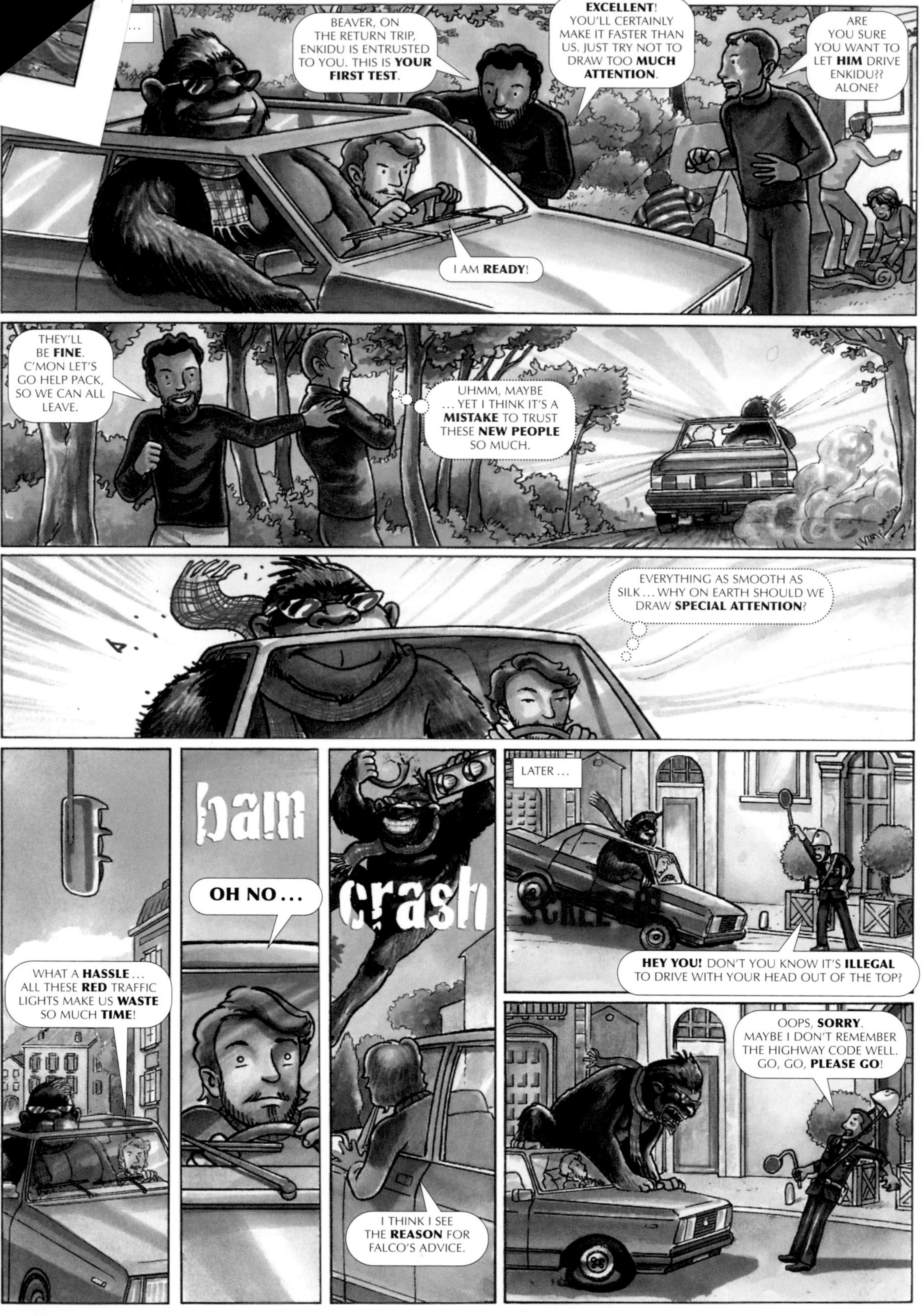
…
BEAVER, ON THE RETURN TRIP, ENKIDU IS ENTRUSTED TO YOU. THIS IS **YOUR FIRST TEST**.
EXCELLENT! YOU'LL CERTAINLY MAKE IT FASTER THAN US. JUST TRY NOT TO DRAW TOO **MUCH ATTENTION**.
ARE YOU SURE YOU WANT TO LET **HIM** DRIVE ENKIDU?? ALONE?
I AM **READY**!
THEY'LL BE **FINE**. C'MON LET'S GO HELP PACK, SO WE CAN ALL LEAVE.
UHMM, MAYBE … YET I THINK IT'S A **MISTAKE** TO TRUST THESE **NEW PEOPLE** SO MUCH.
EVERYTHING AS SMOOTH AS SILK … WHY ON EARTH SHOULD WE DRAW **SPECIAL ATTENTION**?
WHAT A **HASSLE** … ALL THESE **RED** TRAFFIC LIGHTS MAKE US **WASTE** SO MUCH **TIME**!
bam
OH NO …
crash
I THINK I SEE THE **REASON** FOR FALCO'S ADVICE.
LATER …
HEY YOU! DON'T YOU KNOW IT'S **ILLEGAL** TO DRIVE WITH YOUR HEAD OUT OF THE TOP?
OOPS, **SORRY**. MAYBE I DON'T REMEMBER THE HIGHWAY CODE WELL. GO, GO, **PLEASE GO**!

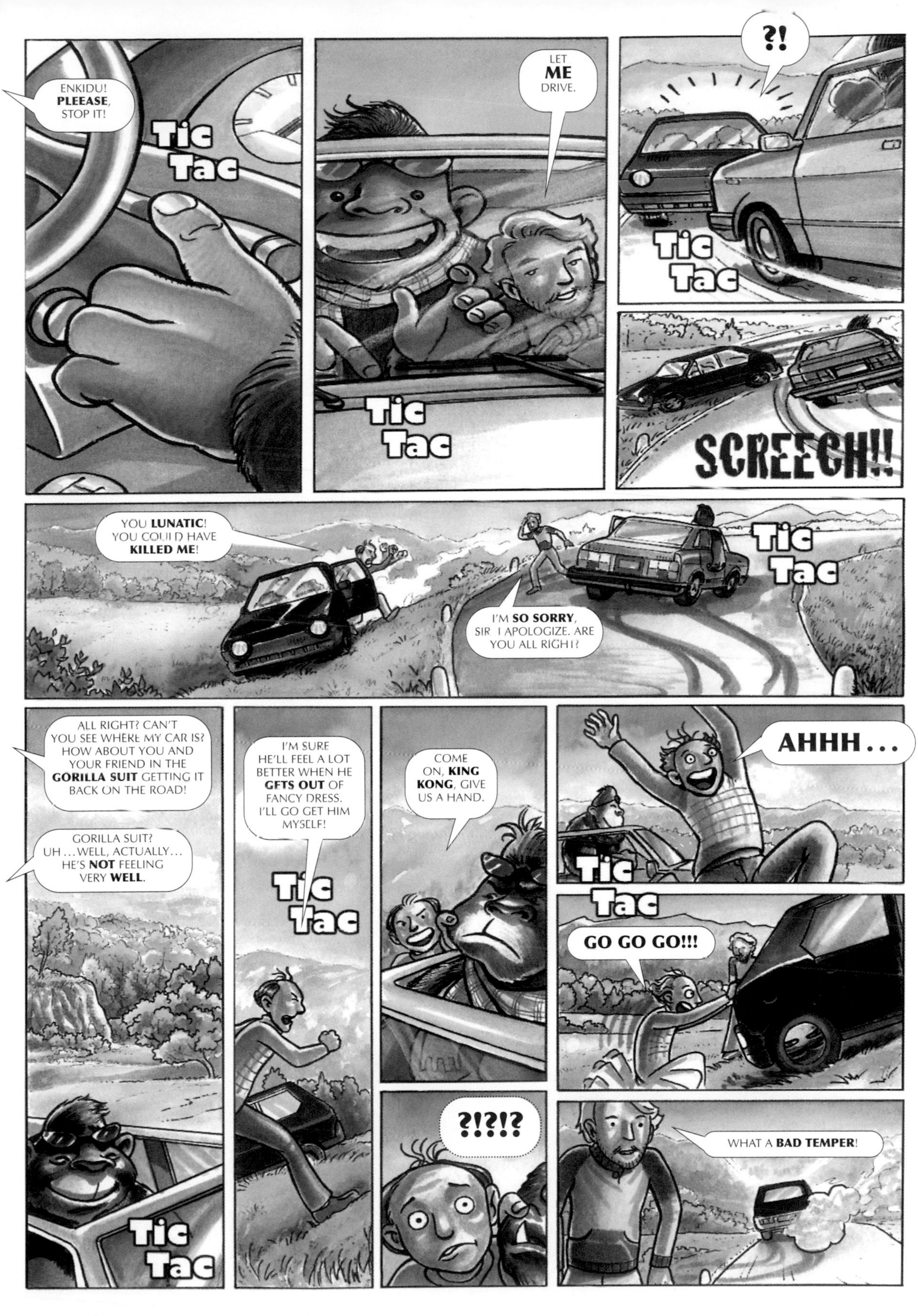

ENKIDU! **PLEEASE**, STOP IT!
Tic Tac
LET **ME** DRIVE.
Tic Tac
?!
Tic Tac
SCREECH!!
YOU **LUNATIC**! YOU COULD HAVE **KILLED ME**!
Tic Tac
I'M **SO SORRY**, SIR. I APOLOGIZE. ARE YOU ALL RIGHT?
ALL RIGHT? CAN'T YOU SEE WHERE MY CAR IS? HOW ABOUT YOU AND YOUR FRIEND IN THE **GORILLA SUIT** GETTING IT BACK ON THE ROAD!
GORILLA SUIT? UH ...WELL, ACTUALLY... HE'S **NOT** FEELING VERY **WELL**.
Tic Tac
I'M SURE HE'LL FEEL A LOT BETTER WHEN HE **GETS OUT** OF FANCY DRESS. I'LL GO GET HIM MYSELF!
Tic Tac
COME ON, **KING KONG**, GIVE US A HAND.
AHHH . . .
Tic Tac
GO GO GO!!!
?!?!?
WHAT A **BAD TEMPER**!

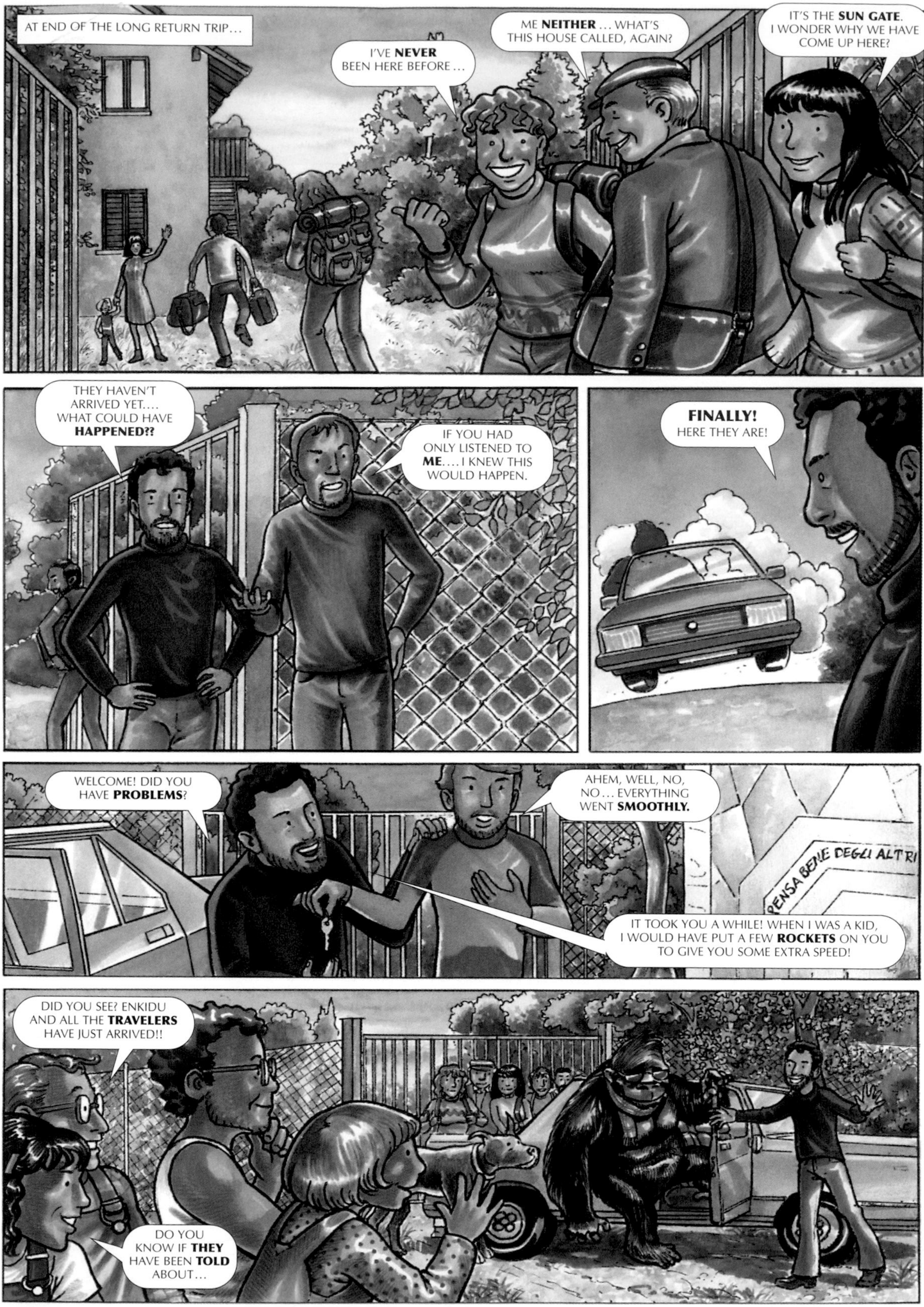
AT END OF THE LONG RETURN TRIP…
I'VE **NEVER** BEEN HERE BEFORE…
ME **NEITHER**… WHAT'S THIS HOUSE CALLED, AGAIN?
IT'S THE **SUN GATE**. I WONDER WHY WE HAVE COME UP HERE?
THEY HAVEN'T ARRIVED YET…. WHAT COULD HAVE **HAPPENED??**
IF YOU HAD ONLY LISTENED TO **ME**…. I KNEW THIS WOULD HAPPEN.
FINALLY! HERE THEY ARE!
WELCOME! DID YOU HAVE **PROBLEMS**?
AHEM, WELL, NO, NO… EVERYTHING WENT **SMOOTHLY.**
PENSA BENE DEGLI ALTRI
IT TOOK YOU A WHILE! WHEN I WAS A KID, I WOULD HAVE PUT A FEW **ROCKETS** ON YOU TO GIVE YOU SOME EXTRA SPEED!
DID YOU SEE? ENKIDU AND ALL THE **TRAVELERS** HAVE JUST ARRIVED!!
DO YOU KNOW IF **THEY** HAVE BEEN **TOLD** ABOUT…

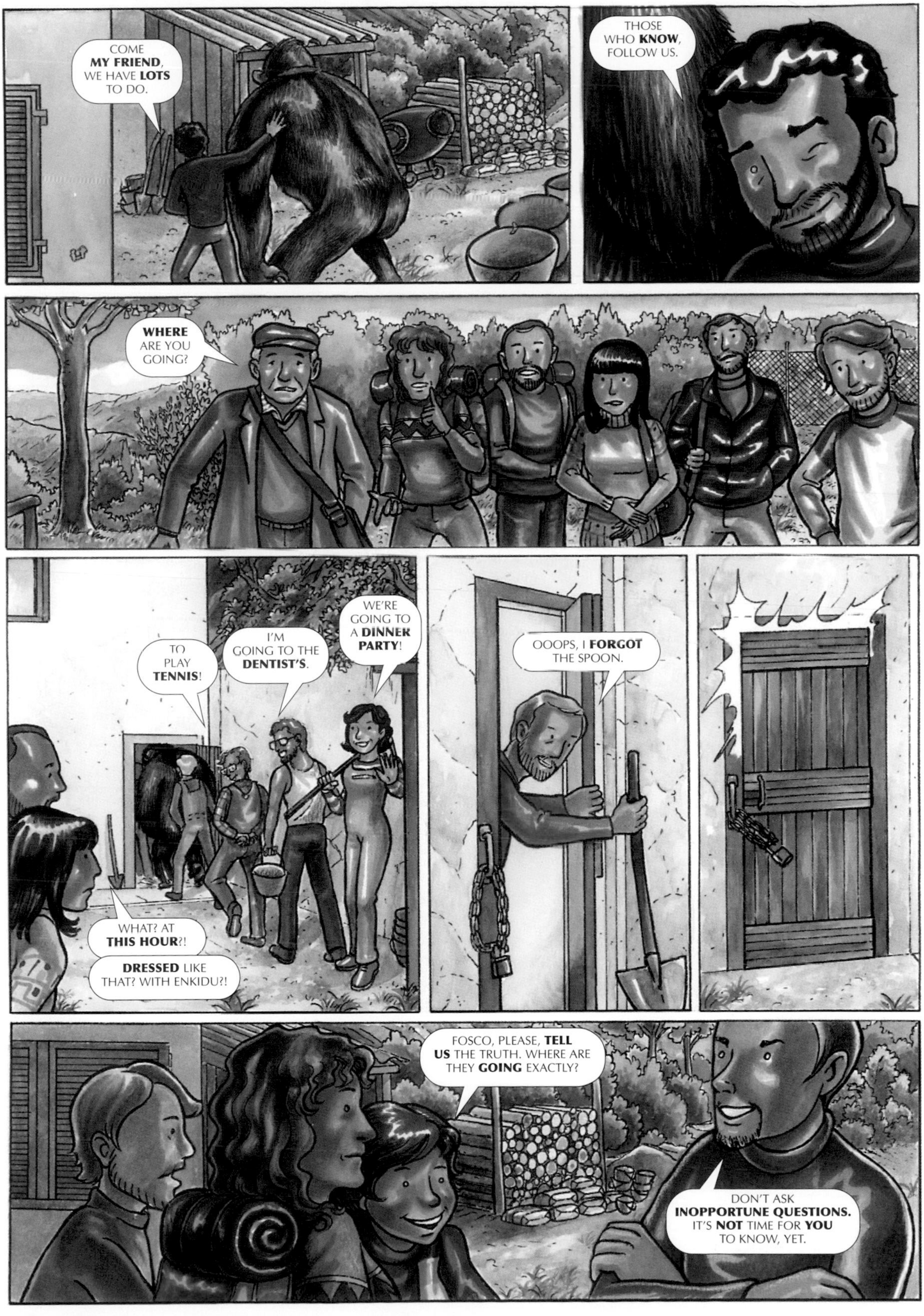
COME MY FRIEND, WE HAVE LOTS TO DO.
THOSE WHO KNOW, FOLLOW US.
WHERE ARE YOU GOING?
TO PLAY TENNIS!
I'M GOING TO THE DENTIST'S.
WE'RE GOING TO A DINNER PARTY!
WHAT? AT THIS HOUR?!
DRESSED LIKE THAT? WITH ENKIDU?!
OOOPS, I FORGOT THE SPOON.
FOSCO, PLEASE, TELL US THE TRUTH. WHERE ARE THEY GOING EXACTLY?
DON'T ASK INOPPORTUNE QUESTIONS. IT'S NOT TIME FOR YOU TO KNOW, YET.

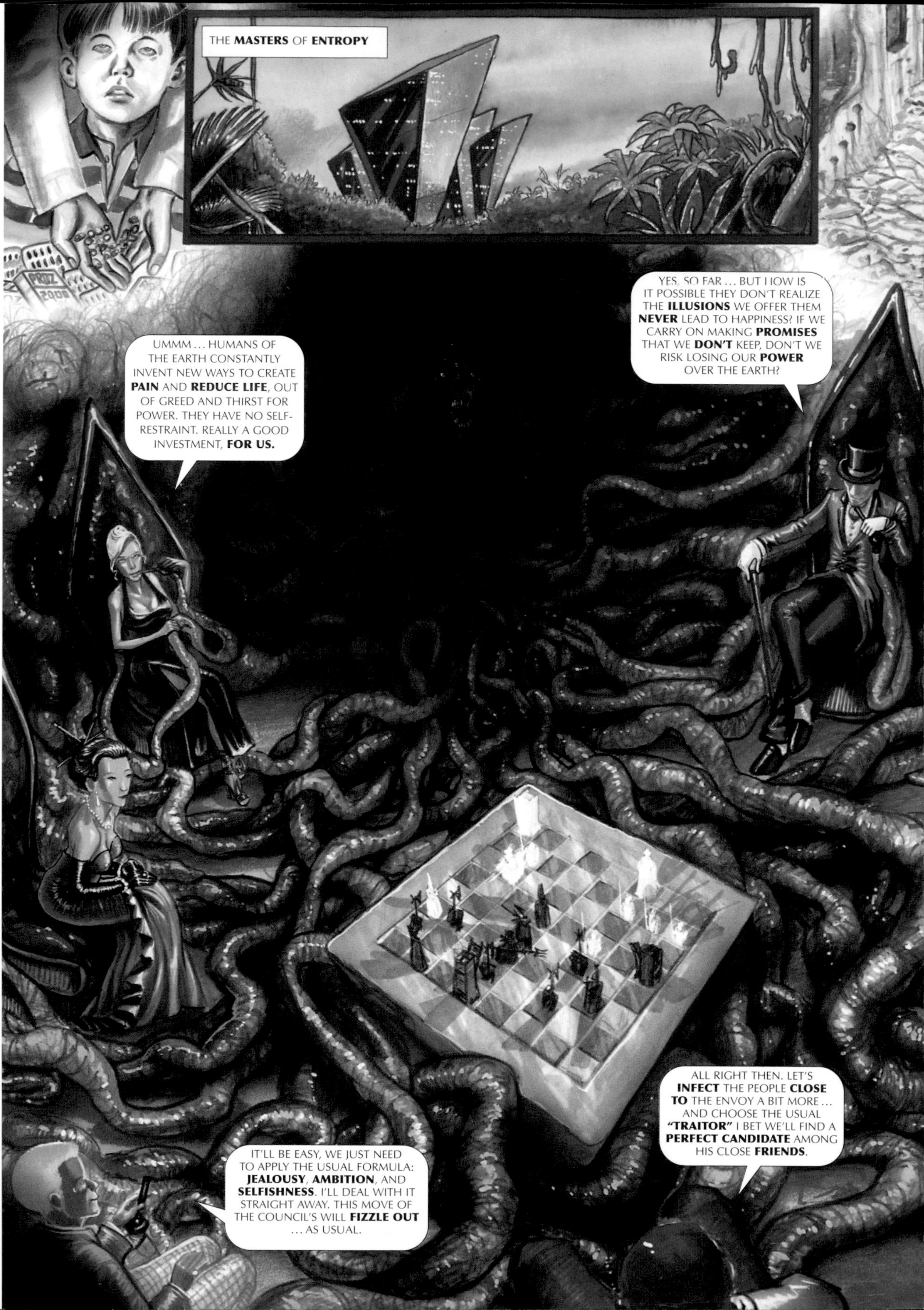
THE MASTERS OF ENTROPY
UMMM . . . HUMANS OF THE EARTH CONSTANTLY INVENT NEW WAYS TO CREATE PAIN AND REDUCE LIFE, OUT OF GREED AND THIRST FOR POWER. THEY HAVE NO SELF-RESTRAINT. REALLY A GOOD INVESTMENT, FOR US.
YES, SO FAR . . . BUT HOW IS IT POSSIBLE THEY DON'T REALIZE THE ILLUSIONS WE OFFER THEM NEVER LEAD TO HAPPINESS? IF WE CARRY ON MAKING PROMISES THAT WE DON'T KEEP, DON'T WE RISK LOSING OUR POWER OVER THE EARTH?
ALL RIGHT THEN. LET'S INFECT THE PEOPLE CLOSE TO THE ENVOY A BIT MORE . . . AND CHOOSE THE USUAL "TRAITOR" I BET WE'LL FIND A PERFECT CANDIDATE AMONG HIS CLOSE FRIENDS.
IT'LL BE EASY, WE JUST NEED TO APPLY THE USUAL FORMULA: JEALOUSY, AMBITION, AND SELFISHNESS. I'LL DEAL WITH IT STRAIGHT AWAY. THIS MOVE OF THE COUNCIL'S WILL FIZZLE OUT . . . AS USUAL.

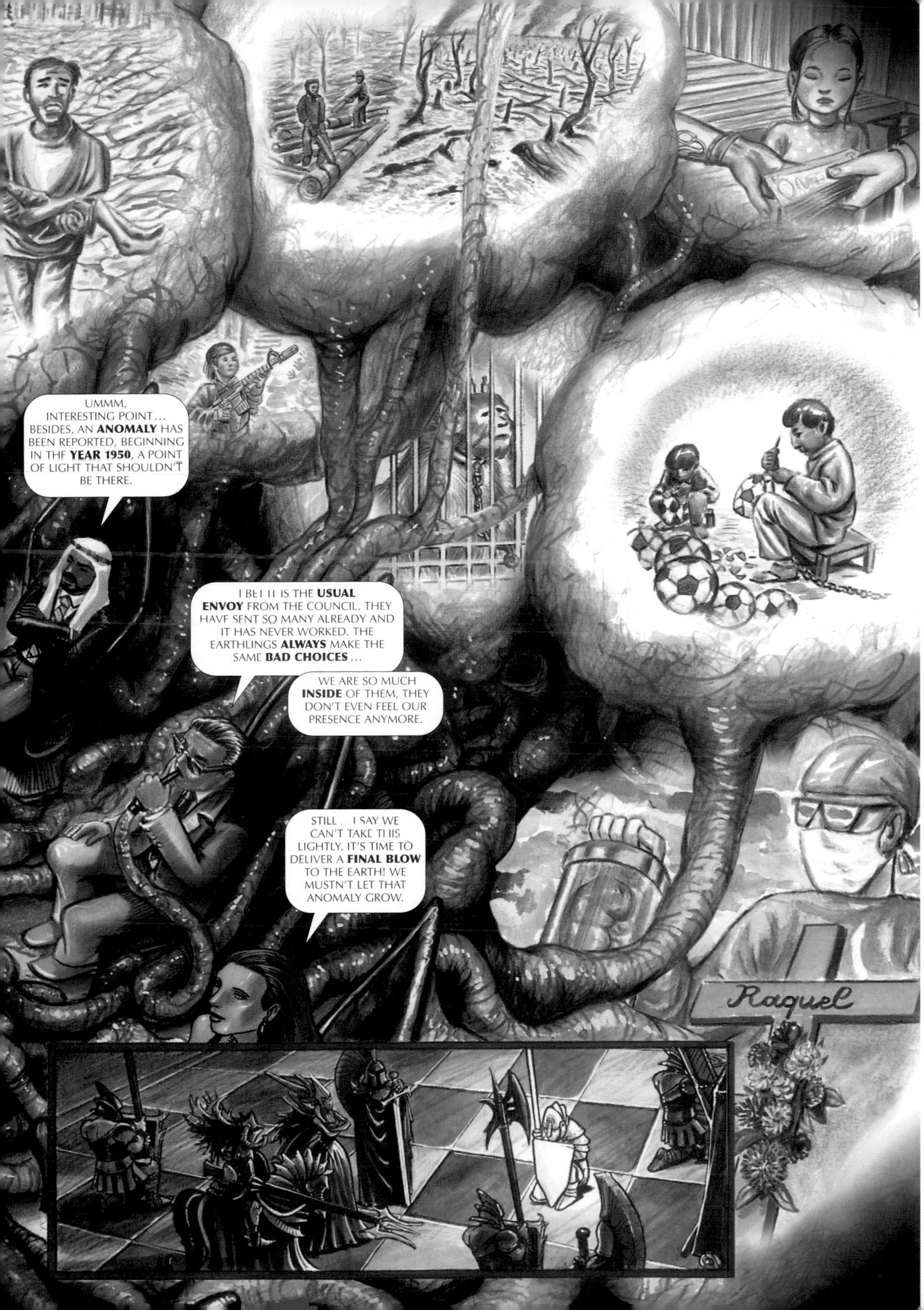
UMMM, INTERESTING POINT… BESIDES, AN **ANOMALY** HAS BEEN REPORTED, BEGINNING IN THE **YEAR 1950**, A POINT OF LIGHT THAT SHOULDN'T BE THERE.
I BET IT IS THE **USUAL ENVOY** FROM THE COUNCIL. THEY HAVE SENT SO MANY ALREADY AND IT HAS NEVER WORKED. THE EARTHLINGS **ALWAYS** MAKE THE SAME **BAD CHOICES**…
WE ARE SO MUCH **INSIDE** OF THEM, THEY DON'T EVEN FEEL OUR PRESENCE ANYMORE.
STILL . . . I SAY WE CAN'T TAKE THIS LIGHTLY. IT'S TIME TO DELIVER A **FINAL BLOW** TO THE EARTH! WE MUSTN'T LET THAT ANOMALY GROW.
Raquel

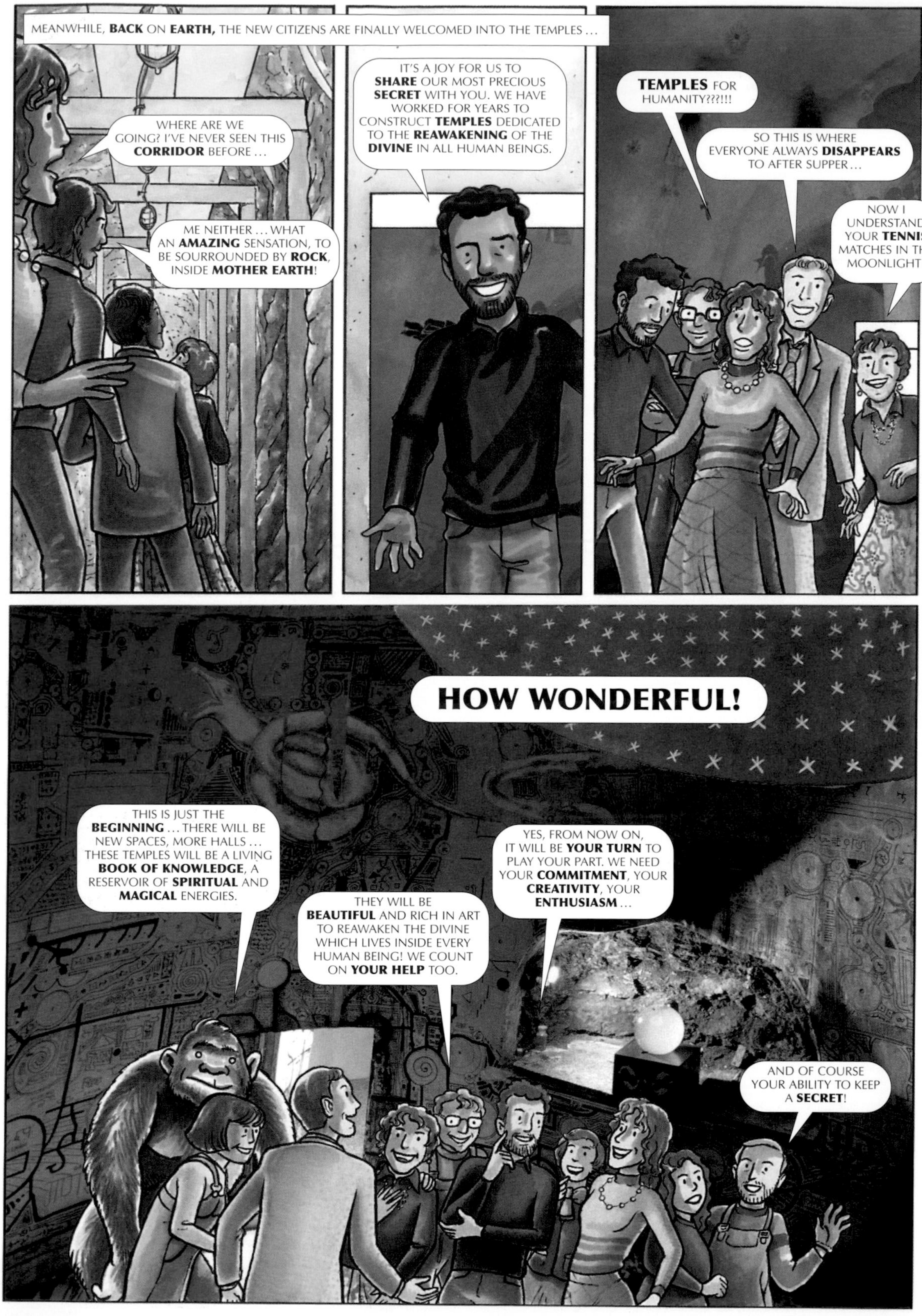
MEANWHILE, BACK ON EARTH, THE NEW CITIZENS ARE FINALLY WELCOMED INTO THE TEMPLES …
WHERE ARE WE GOING? I'VE NEVER SEEN THIS CORRIDOR BEFORE …
ME NEITHER … WHAT AN AMAZING SENSATION, TO BE SOURROUNDED BY ROCK, INSIDE MOTHER EARTH!
IT'S A JOY FOR US TO SHARE OUR MOST PRECIOUS SECRET WITH YOU. WE HAVE WORKED FOR YEARS TO CONSTRUCT TEMPLES DEDICATED TO THE REAWAKENING OF THE DIVINE IN ALL HUMAN BEINGS.
TEMPLES FOR HUMANITY???!!!
SO THIS IS WHERE EVERYONE ALWAYS DISAPPEARS TO AFTER SUPPER …
NOW I UNDERSTAND YOUR TENNIS MATCHES IN THE MOONLIGHT!
HOW WONDERFUL!
THIS IS JUST THE BEGINNING … THERE WILL BE NEW SPACES, MORE HALLS … THESE TEMPLES WILL BE A LIVING BOOK OF KNOWLEDGE, A RESERVOIR OF SPIRITUAL AND MAGICAL ENERGIES.
THEY WILL BE BEAUTIFUL AND RICH IN ART TO REAWAKEN THE DIVINE WHICH LIVES INSIDE EVERY HUMAN BEING! WE COUNT ON YOUR HELP TOO.
YES, FROM NOW ON, IT WILL BE YOUR TURN TO PLAY YOUR PART. WE NEED YOUR COMMITMENT, YOUR CREATIVITY, YOUR ENTHUSIASM …
AND OF COURSE YOUR ABILITY TO KEEP A SECRET!

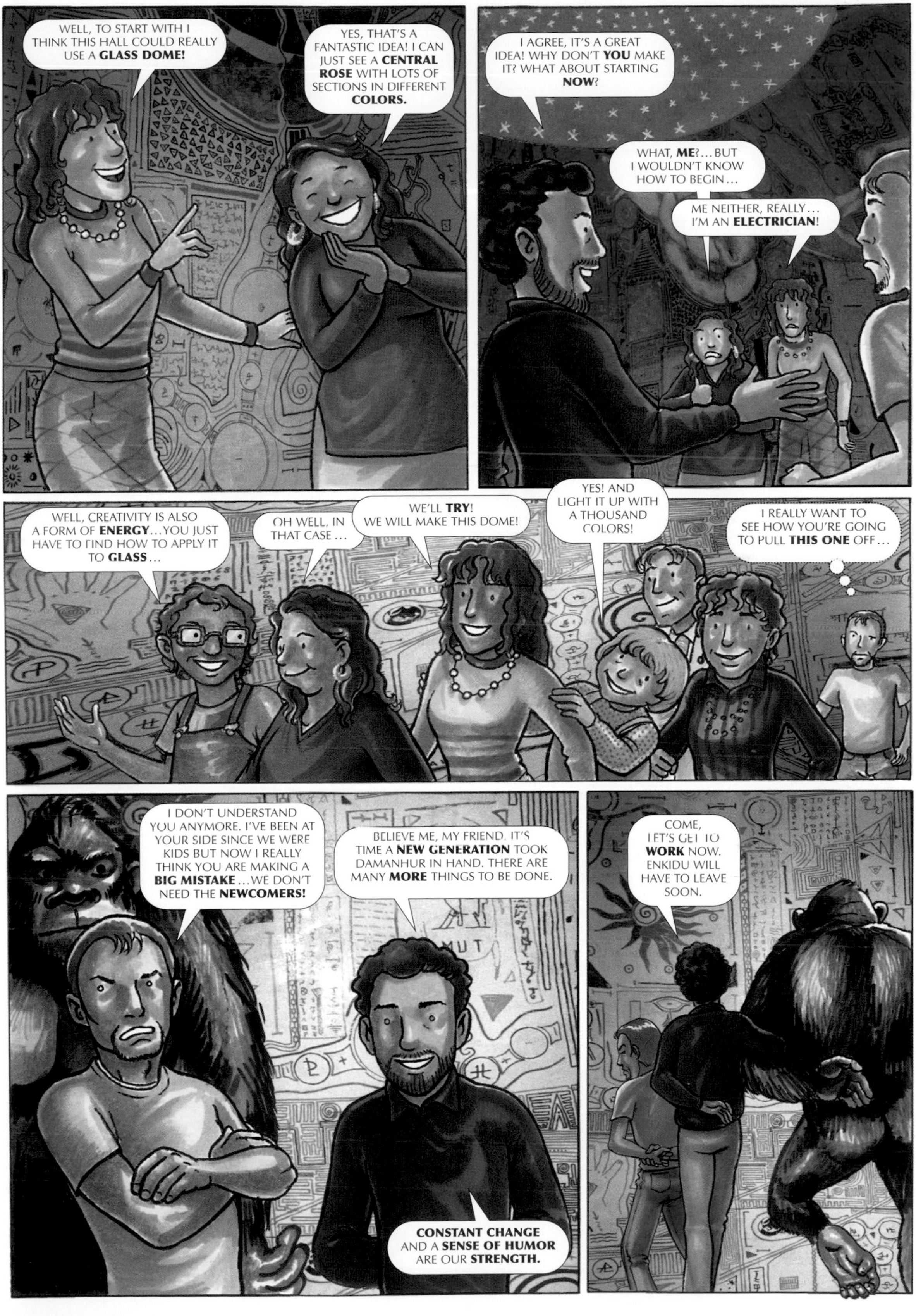
WELL, TO START WITH I THINK THIS HALL COULD REALLY USE A **GLASS DOME!**
YES, THAT'S A FANTASTIC IDEA! I CAN JUST SEE A **CENTRAL ROSE** WITH LOTS OF SECTIONS IN DIFFERENT **COLORS.**
I AGREE, IT'S A GREAT IDEA! WHY DON'T **YOU** MAKE IT? WHAT ABOUT STARTING **NOW**?
WHAT, **ME**?... BUT I WOULDN'T KNOW HOW TO BEGIN...
ME NEITHER, REALLY... I'M AN **ELECTRICIAN**!
WELL, CREATIVITY IS ALSO A FORM OF **ENERGY**... YOU JUST HAVE TO FIND HOW TO APPLY IT TO **GLASS**...
OH WELL, IN THAT CASE...
WE'LL **TRY**! WE WILL MAKE THIS DOME!
YES! AND LIGHT IT UP WITH A THOUSAND COLORS!
I REALLY WANT TO SEE HOW YOU'RE GOING TO PULL **THIS ONE** OFF...
I DON'T UNDERSTAND YOU ANYMORE. I'VE BEEN AT YOUR SIDE SINCE WE WERE KIDS BUT NOW I REALLY THINK YOU ARE MAKING A **BIG MISTAKE**... WE DON'T NEED THE **NEWCOMERS!**
BELIEVE ME, MY FRIEND. IT'S TIME A **NEW GENERATION** TOOK DAMANHUR IN HAND. THERE ARE MANY **MORE** THINGS TO BE DONE.
CONSTANT CHANGE AND A **SENSE OF HUMOR** ARE OUR **STRENGTH.**
COME, LET'S GET TO **WORK** NOW. ENKIDU WILL HAVE TO LEAVE SOON.

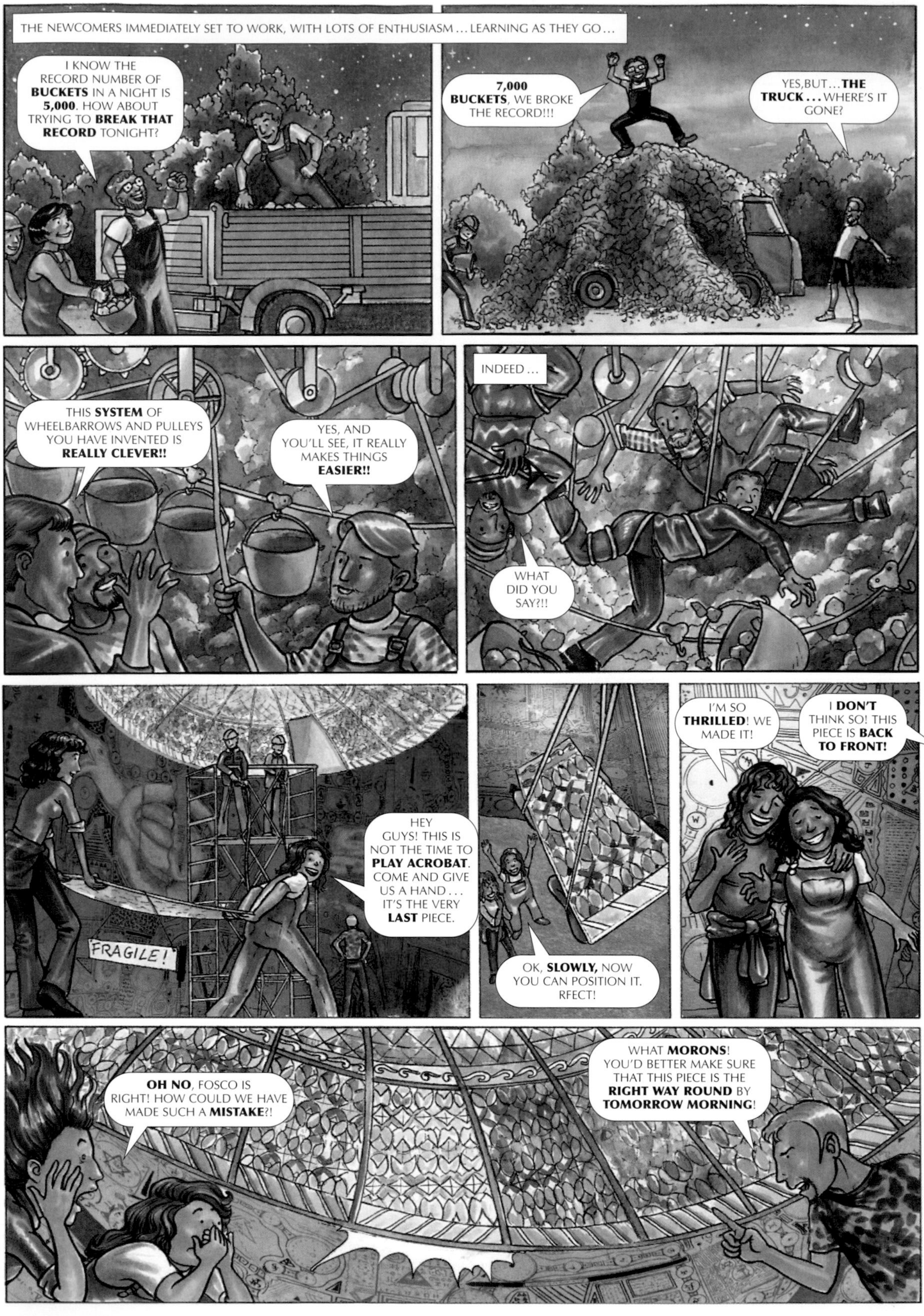
THE NEWCOMERS IMMEDIATELY SET TO WORK, WITH LOTS OF ENTHUSIASM … LEARNING AS THEY GO …
I KNOW THE RECORD NUMBER OF BUCKETS IN A NIGHT IS 5,000. HOW ABOUT TRYING TO BREAK THAT RECORD TONIGHT?
7,000 BUCKETS, WE BROKE THE RECORD!!!
YES,BUT… THE TRUCK … WHERE'S IT GONE?
THIS SYSTEM OF WHEELBARROWS AND PULLEYS YOU HAVE INVENTED IS REALLY CLEVER!!
YES, AND YOU'LL SEE, IT REALLY MAKES THINGS EASIER!!
INDEED …
WHAT DID YOU SAY?!!
HEY GUYS! THIS IS NOT THE TIME TO PLAY ACROBAT. COME AND GIVE US A HAND . . . IT'S THE VERY LAST PIECE.
FRAGILE!
OK, SLOWLY, NOW YOU CAN POSITION IT. RFECT!
I'M SO THRILLED! WE MADE IT!
I DON'T THINK SO! THIS PIECE IS BACK TO FRONT!
OH NO, FOSCO IS RIGHT! HOW COULD WE HAVE MADE SUCH A MISTAKE?!
WHAT MORONS! YOU'D BETTER MAKE SURE THAT THIS PIECE IS THE RIGHT WAY ROUND BY TOMORROW MORNING!

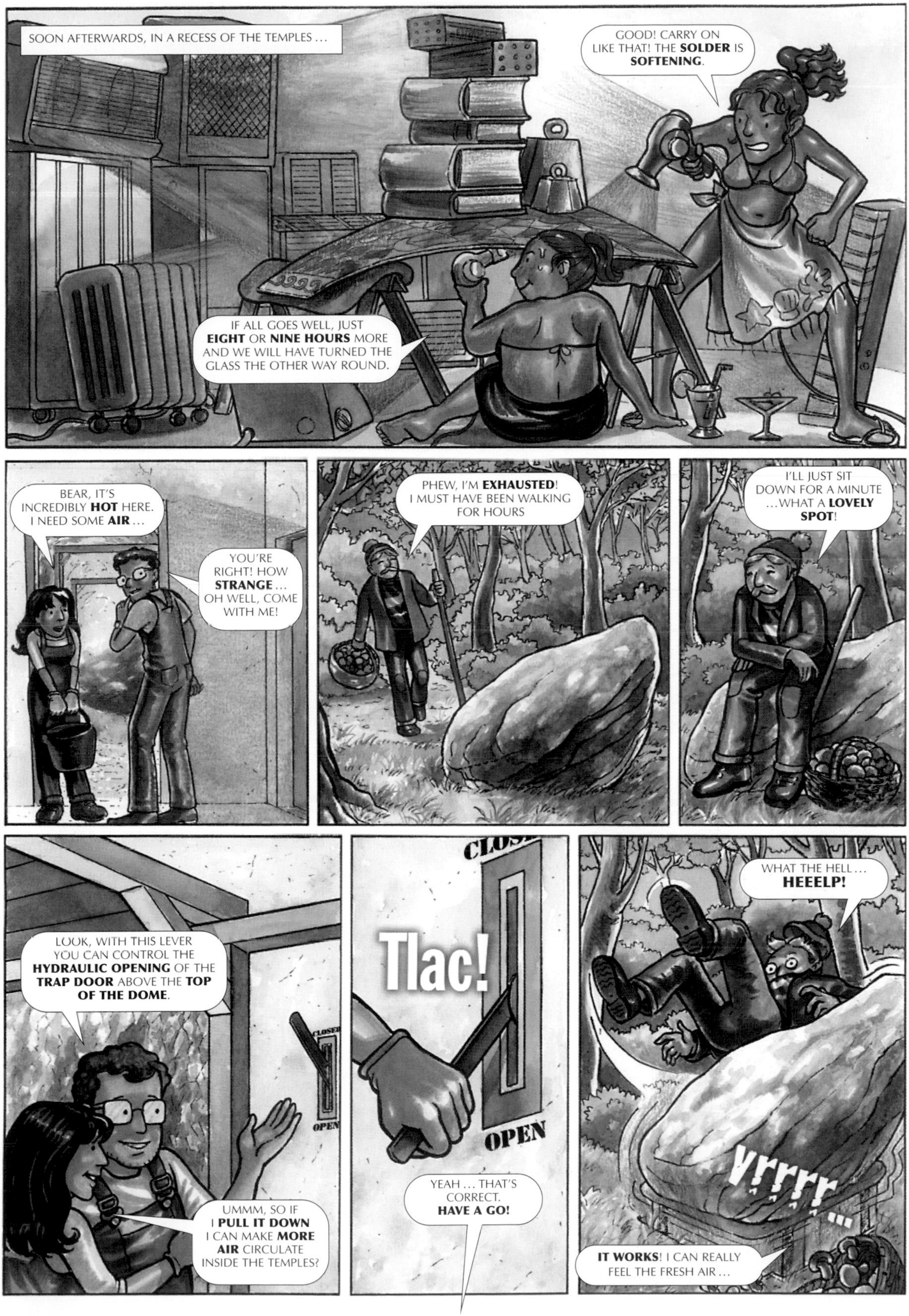
SOON AFTERWARDS, IN A RECESS OF THE TEMPLES ...
GOOD! CARRY ON LIKE THAT! THE **SOLDER** IS **SOFTENING**.
IF ALL GOES WELL, JUST **EIGHT** OR **NINE HOURS** MORE AND WE WILL HAVE TURNED THE GLASS THE OTHER WAY ROUND.
BEAR, IT'S INCREDIBLY **HOT** HERE. I NEED SOME **AIR** ...
YOU'RE RIGHT! HOW **STRANGE** ... OH WELL, COME WITH ME!
PHEW, I'M **EXHAUSTED**! I MUST HAVE BEEN WALKING FOR HOURS
I'LL JUST SIT DOWN FOR A MINUTE ...WHAT A **LOVELY SPOT**!
LOOK, WITH THIS LEVER YOU CAN CONTROL THE **HYDRAULIC OPENING** OF THE **TRAP DOOR** ABOVE THE **TOP OF THE DOME**.
CLOSED
OPEN
UMMM, SO IF I **PULL IT DOWN** I CAN MAKE **MORE AIR** CIRCULATE INSIDE THE TEMPLES?
CLOS
Tlac!
OPEN
YEAH ... THAT'S CORRECT. **HAVE A GO!**
WHAT THE HELL ... **HEEELP!**
vrrrr...
IT WORKS! I CAN REALLY FEEL THE FRESH AIR ...

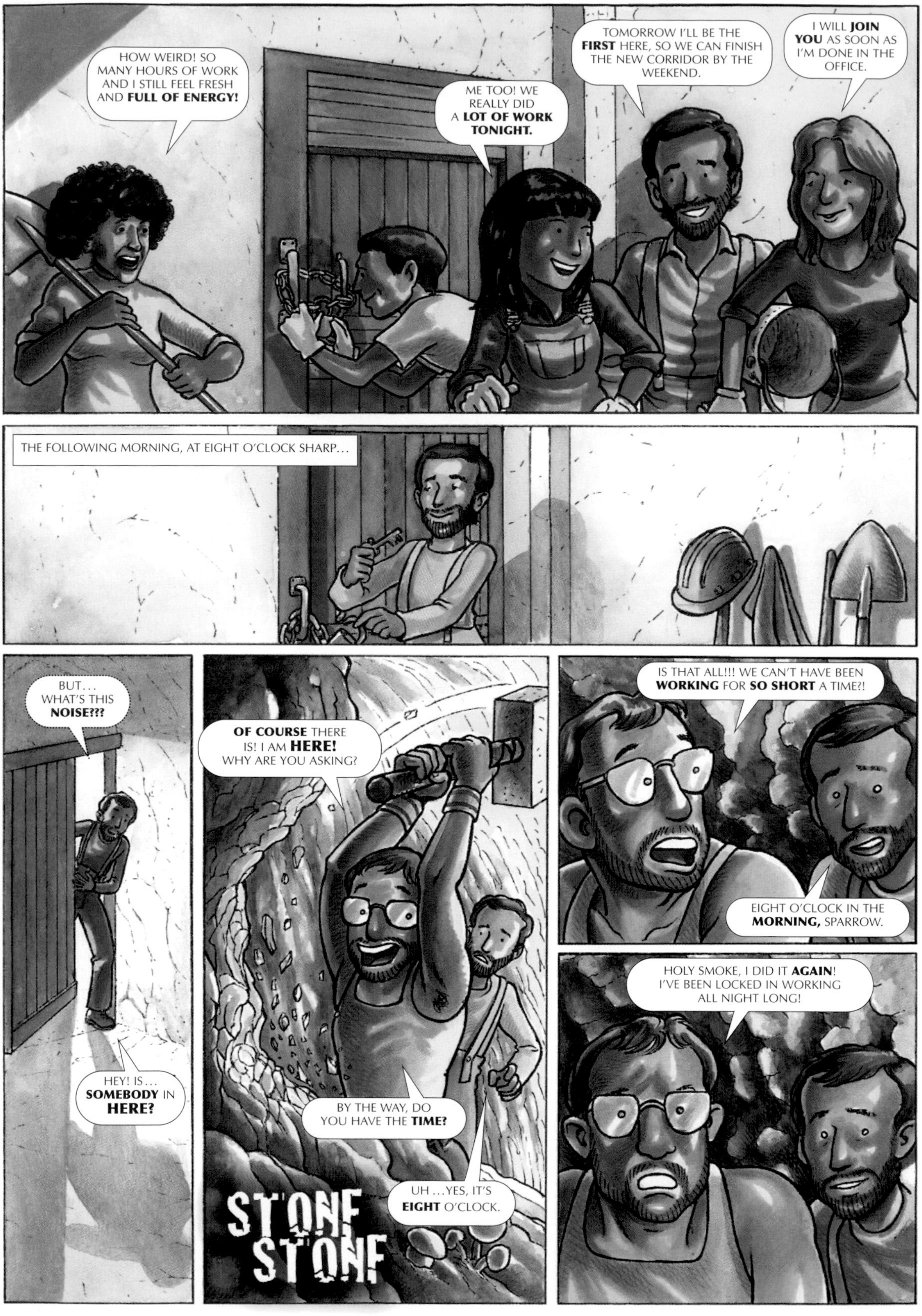
HOW WEIRD! SO MANY HOURS OF WORK AND I STILL FEEL FRESH AND FULL OF ENERGY!
ME TOO! WE REALLY DID A LOT OF WORK TONIGHT.
TOMORROW I'LL BE THE FIRST HERE, SO WE CAN FINISH THE NEW CORRIDOR BY THE WEEKEND.
I WILL JOIN YOU AS SOON AS I'M DONE IN THE OFFICE.
THE FOLLOWING MORNING, AT EIGHT O'CLOCK SHARP...
BUT... WHAT'S THIS NOISE???
HEY! IS... SOMEBODY IN HERE?
OF COURSE THERE IS! I AM HERE! WHY ARE YOU ASKING?
BY THE WAY, DO YOU HAVE THE TIME?
UH ...YES, IT'S EIGHT O'CLOCK.
STONE STONE
IS THAT ALL!!! WE CAN'T HAVE BEEN WORKING FOR SO SHORT A TIME?!
EIGHT O'CLOCK IN THE MORNING, SPARROW.
HOLY SMOKE, I DID IT AGAIN! I'VE BEEN LOCKED IN WORKING ALL NIGHT LONG!

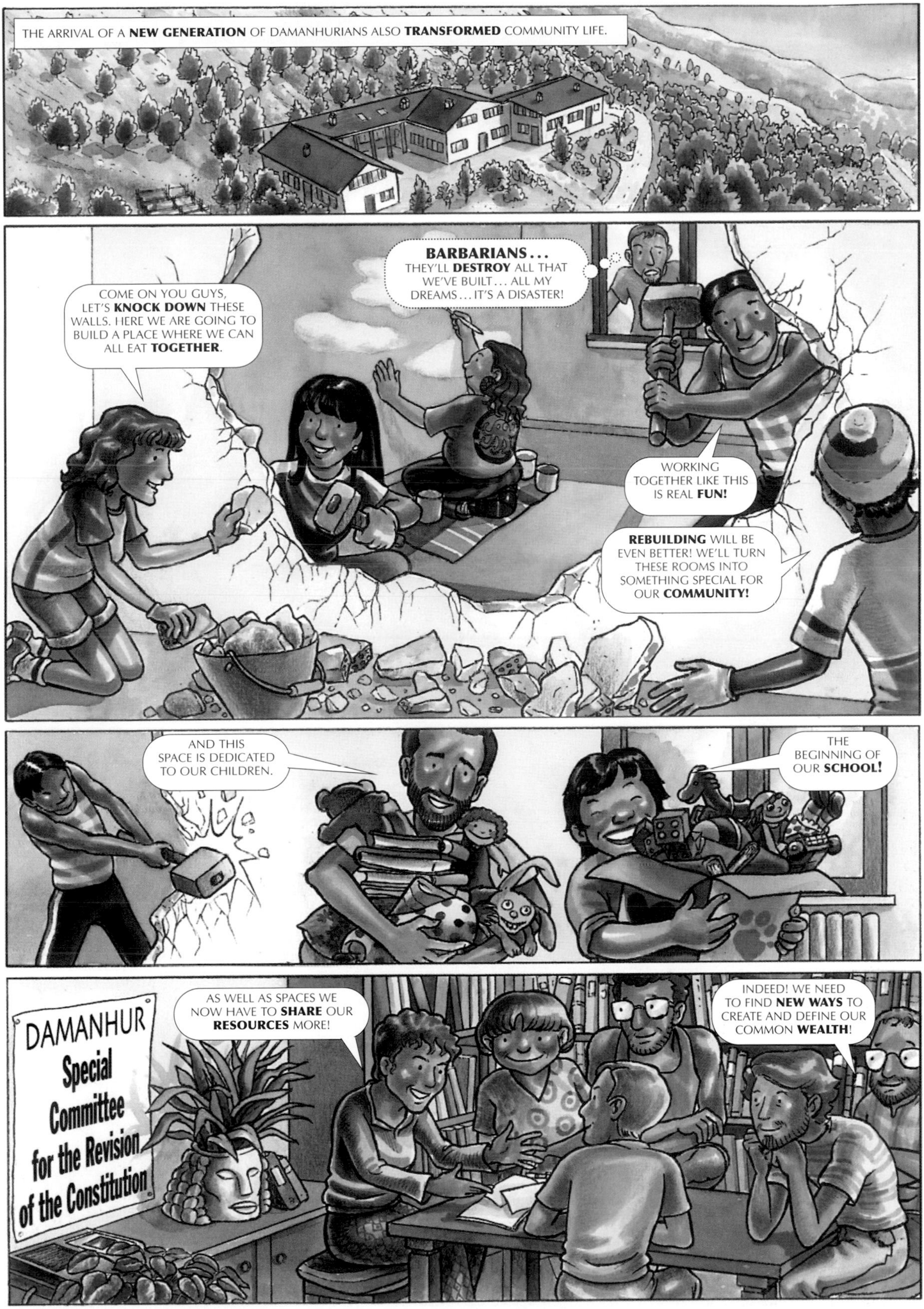
THE ARRIVAL OF A NEW GENERATION OF DAMANHURIANS ALSO TRANSFORMED COMMUNITY LIFE.
COME ON YOU GUYS, LET'S KNOCK DOWN THESE WALLS. HERE WE ARE GOING TO BUILD A PLACE WHERE WE CAN ALL EAT TOGETHER.
BARBARIANS... THEY'LL DESTROY ALL THAT WE'VE BUILT... ALL MY DREAMS... IT'S A DISASTER!
WORKING TOGETHER LIKE THIS IS REAL FUN!
REBUILDING WILL BE EVEN BETTER! WE'LL TURN THESE ROOMS INTO SOMETHING SPECIAL FOR OUR COMMUNITY!
AND THIS SPACE IS DEDICATED TO OUR CHILDREN.
THE BEGINNING OF OUR SCHOOL!
DAMANHUR Special Committee for the Revision of the Constitution
AS WELL AS SPACES WE NOW HAVE TO SHARE OUR RESOURCES MORE!
INDEED! WE NEED TO FIND NEW WAYS TO CREATE AND DEFINE OUR COMMON WEALTH!

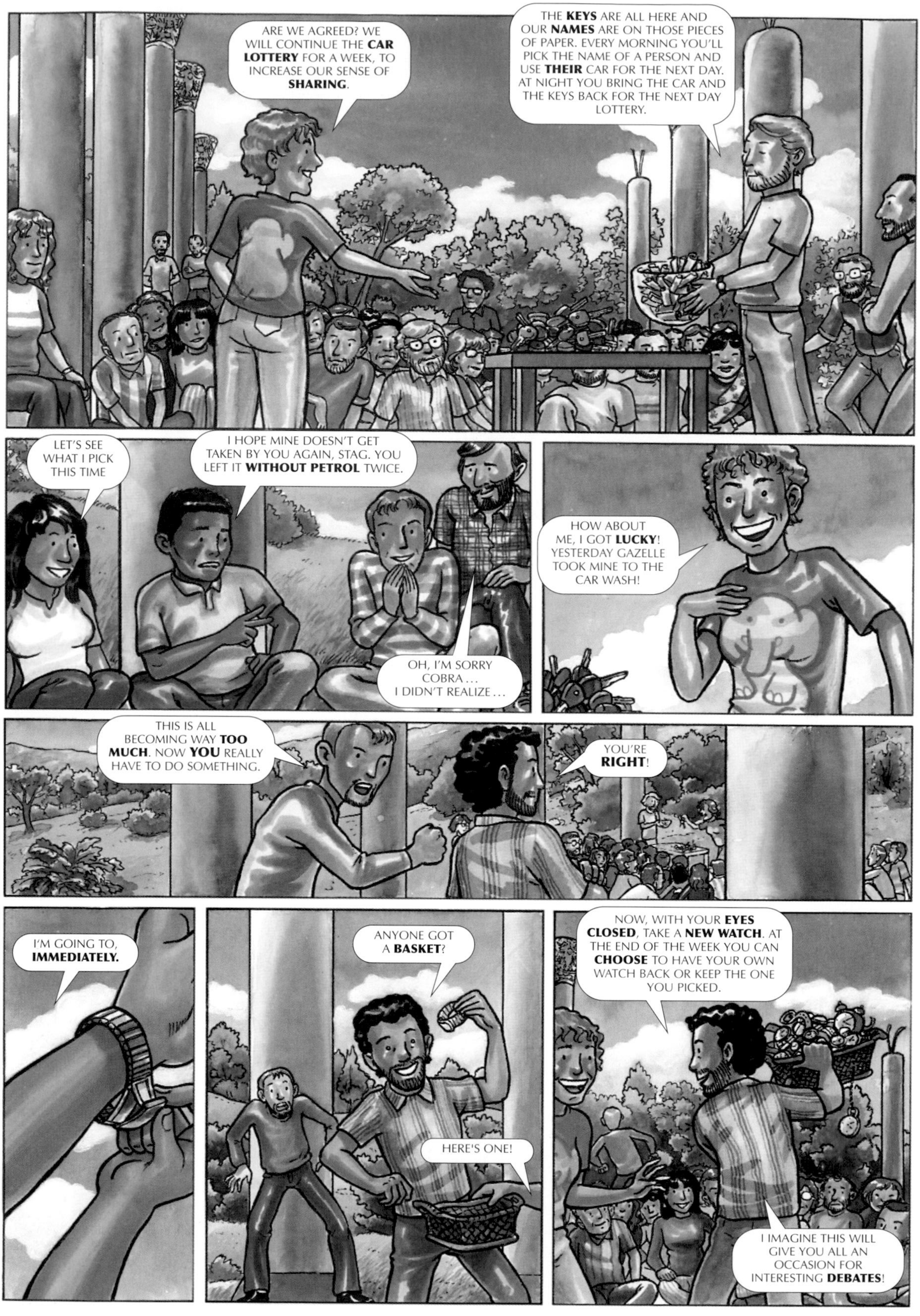
ARE WE AGREED? WE WILL CONTINUE THE **CAR LOTTERY** FOR A WEEK, TO INCREASE OUR SENSE OF **SHARING**.
THE **KEYS** ARE ALL HERE AND OUR **NAMES** ARE ON THOSE PIECES OF PAPER. EVERY MORNING YOU'LL PICK THE NAME OF A PERSON AND USE **THEIR** CAR FOR THE NEXT DAY. AT NIGHT YOU BRING THE CAR AND THE KEYS BACK FOR THE NEXT DAY LOTTERY.
LET'S SEE WHAT I PICK THIS TIME
I HOPE MINE DOESN'T GET TAKEN BY YOU AGAIN, STAG. YOU LEFT IT **WITHOUT PETROL** TWICE.
OH, I'M SORRY COBRA… I DIDN'T REALIZE…
HOW ABOUT ME, I GOT **LUCKY**! YESTERDAY GAZELLE TOOK MINE TO THE CAR WASH!
THIS IS ALL BECOMING WAY **TOO MUCH**. NOW **YOU** REALLY HAVE TO DO SOMETHING.
YOU'RE **RIGHT**!
I'M GOING TO, **IMMEDIATELY.**
ANYONE GOT A **BASKET**?
HERE'S ONE!
NOW, WITH YOUR **EYES CLOSED**, TAKE A **NEW WATCH**. AT THE END OF THE WEEK YOU CAN **CHOOSE** TO HAVE YOUR OWN WATCH BACK OR KEEP THE ONE YOU PICKED.
I IMAGINE THIS WILL GIVE YOU ALL AN OCCASION FOR INTERESTING **DEBATES**!

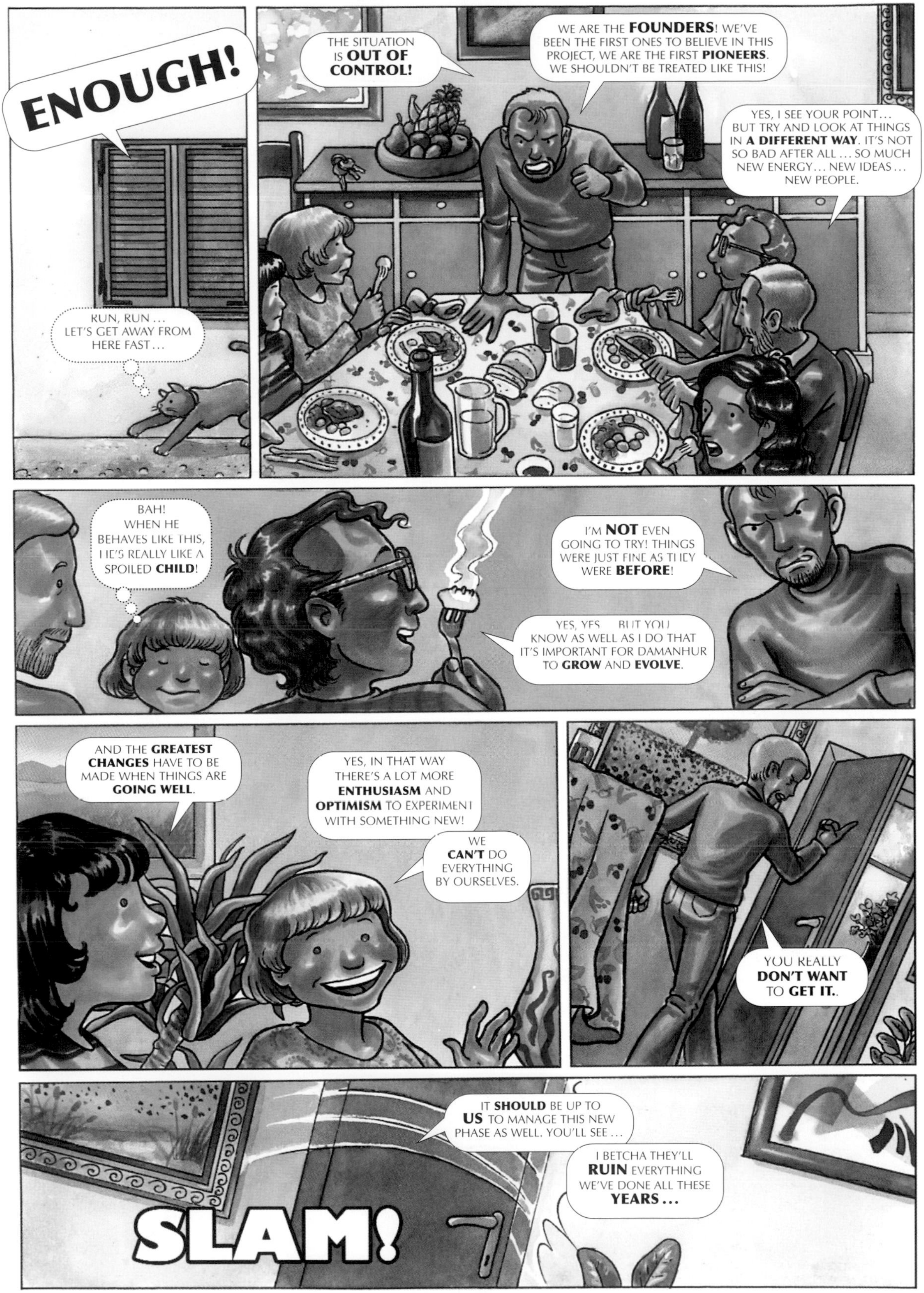
ENOUGH!
RUN, RUN … LET'S GET AWAY FROM HERE FAST …
THE SITUATION IS OUT OF CONTROL!
WE ARE THE FOUNDERS! WE'VE BEEN THE FIRST ONES TO BELIEVE IN THIS PROJECT, WE ARE THE FIRST PIONEERS. WE SHOULDN'T BE TREATED LIKE THIS!
YES, I SEE YOUR POINT… BUT TRY AND LOOK AT THINGS IN A DIFFERENT WAY. IT'S NOT SO BAD AFTER ALL … SO MUCH NEW ENERGY… NEW IDEAS… NEW PEOPLE.
BAH! WHEN HE BEHAVES LIKE THIS, HE'S REALLY LIKE A SPOILED CHILD!
I'M NOT EVEN GOING TO TRY! THINGS WERE JUST FINE AS THEY WERE BEFORE!
YES, YES … BUT YOU KNOW AS WELL AS I DO THAT IT'S IMPORTANT FOR DAMANHUR TO GROW AND EVOLVE.
AND THE GREATEST CHANGES HAVE TO BE MADE WHEN THINGS ARE GOING WELL.
YES, IN THAT WAY THERE'S A LOT MORE ENTHUSIASM AND OPTIMISM TO EXPERIMENT WITH SOMETHING NEW!
WE CAN'T DO EVERYTHING BY OURSELVES.
YOU REALLY DON'T WANT TO GET IT..
IT SHOULD BE UP TO US TO MANAGE THIS NEW PHASE AS WELL. YOU'LL SEE …
I BETCHA THEY'LL RUIN EVERYTHING WE'VE DONE ALL THESE YEARS …
SLAM!

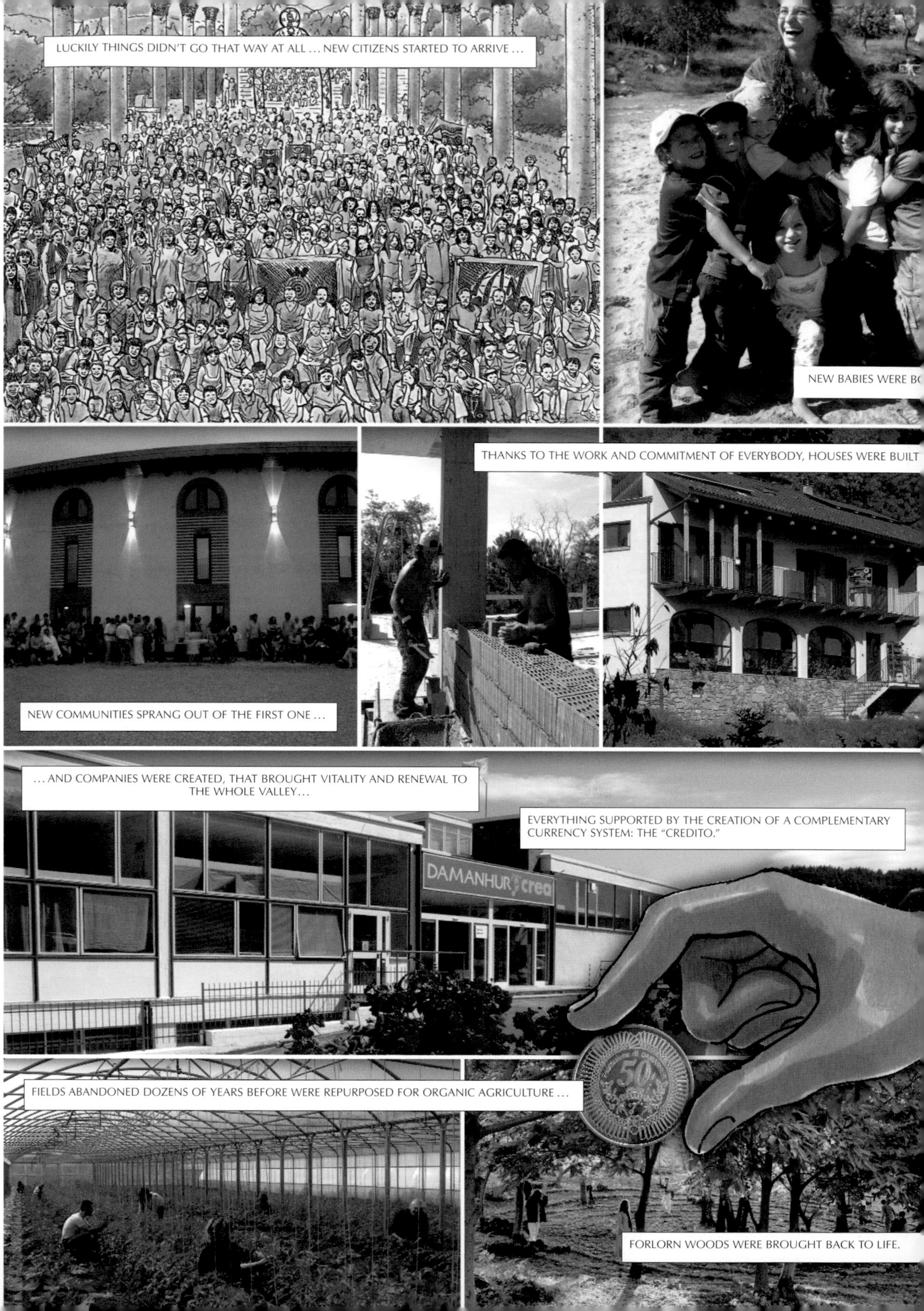
LUCKILY THINGS DIDN'T GO THAT WAY AT ALL … NEW CITIZENS STARTED TO ARRIVE …
NEW BABIES WERE BO
NEW COMMUNITIES SPRANG OUT OF THE FIRST ONE …
THANKS TO THE WORK AND COMMITMENT OF EVERYBODY, HOUSES WERE BUILT
… AND COMPANIES WERE CREATED, THAT BROUGHT VITALITY AND RENEWAL TO THE WHOLE VALLEY…
DAMANHUR crea
EVERYTHING SUPPORTED BY THE CREATION OF A COMPLEMENTARY CURRENCY SYSTEM: THE "CREDITO."
FIELDS ABANDONED DOZENS OF YEARS BEFORE WERE REPURPOSED FOR ORGANIC AGRICULTURE …
FORLORN WOODS WERE BROUGHT BACK TO LIFE.

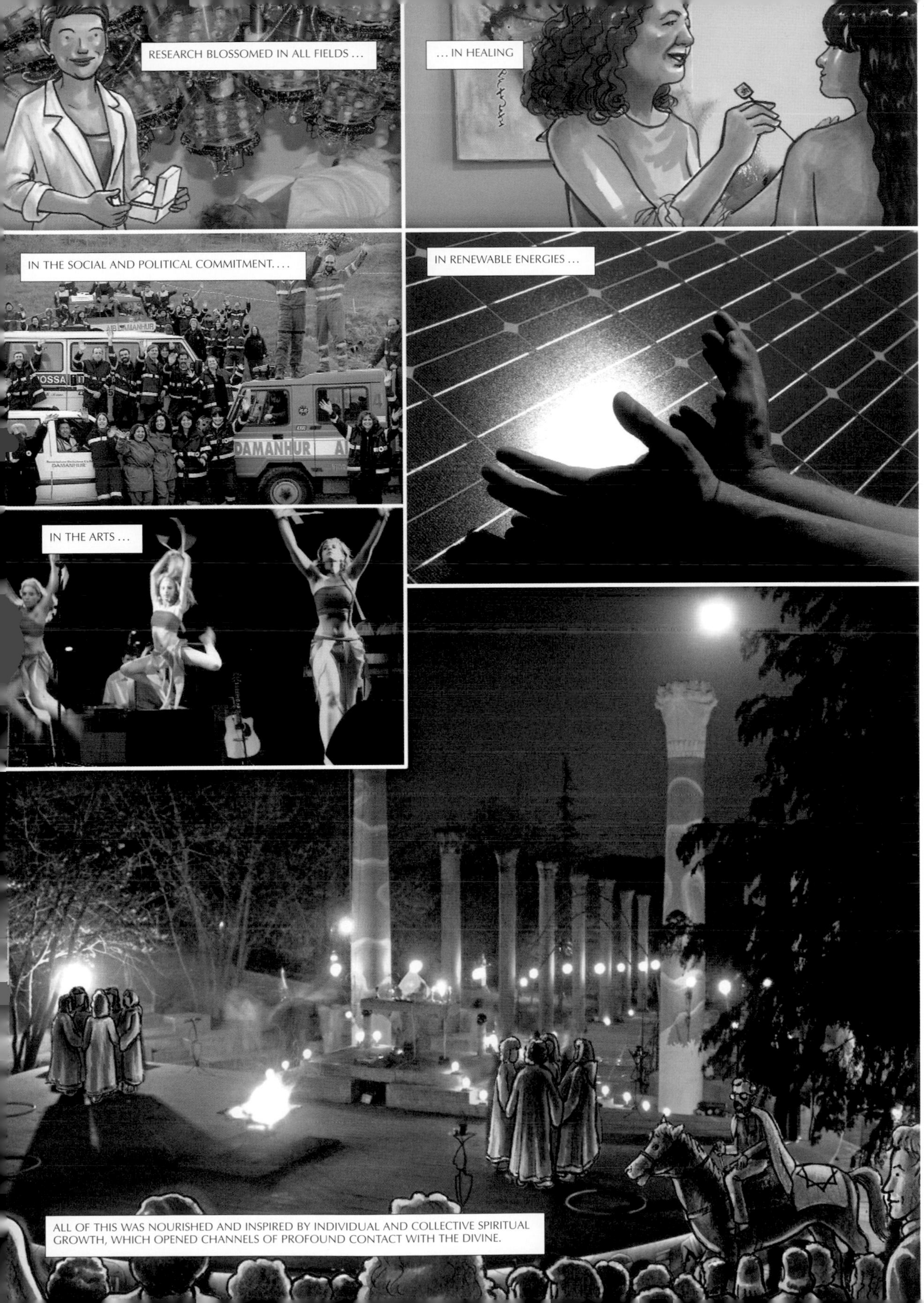
RESEARCH BLOSSOMED IN ALL FIELDS ...
... IN HEALING
IN THE SOCIAL AND POLITICAL COMMITMENT. . . .
DAMANHUR
IN RENEWABLE ENERGIES ...
IN THE ARTS ...
ALL OF THIS WAS NOURISHED AND INSPIRED BY INDIVIDUAL AND COLLECTIVE SPIRITUAL GROWTH, WHICH OPENED CHANNELS OF PROFOUND CONTACT WITH THE DIVINE.

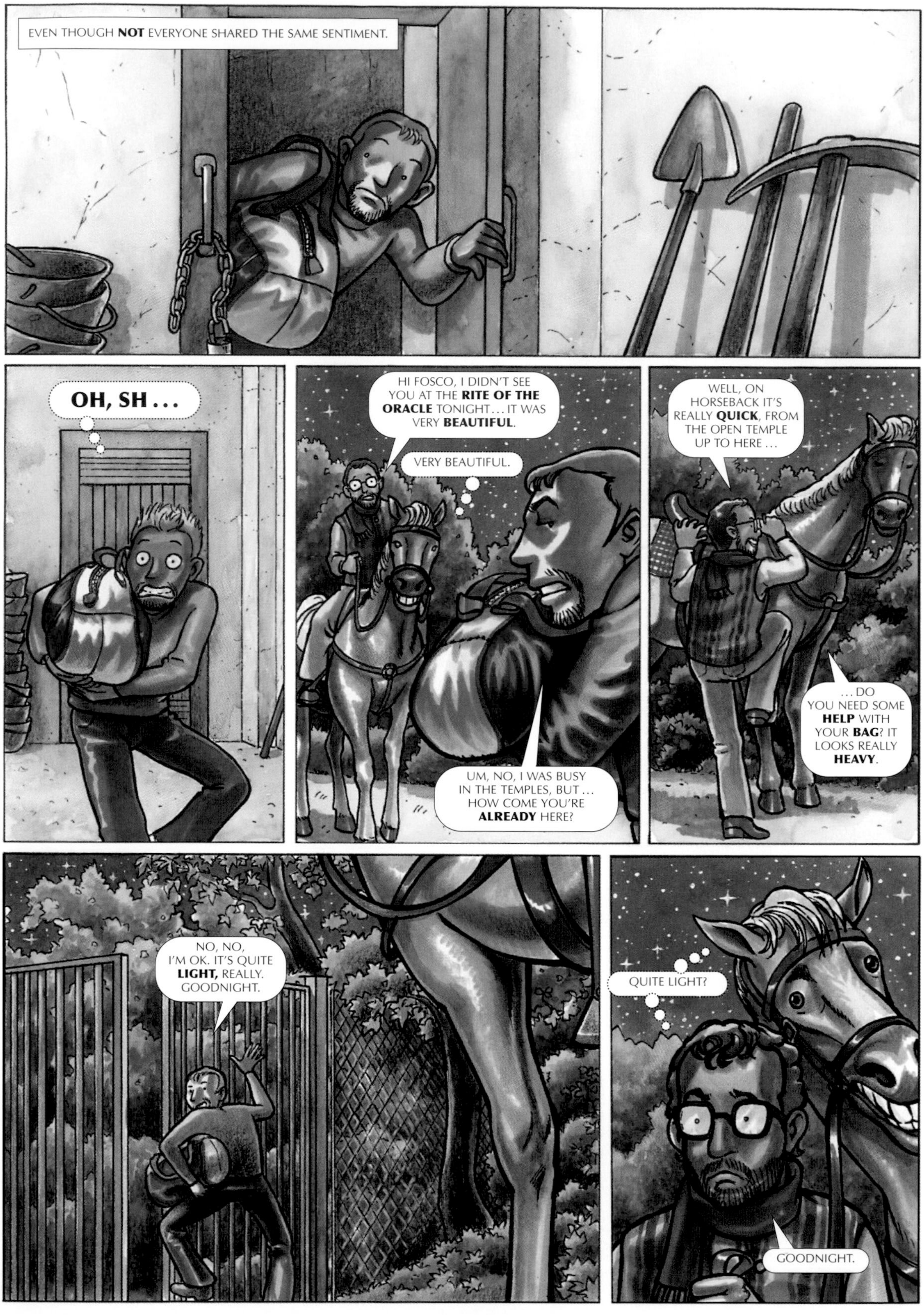
EVEN THOUGH NOT EVERYONE SHARED THE SAME SENTIMENT.
OH, SH . . .
HI FOSCO, I DIDN'T SEE YOU AT THE RITE OF THE ORACLE TONIGHT . . . IT WAS VERY BEAUTIFUL.
VERY BEAUTIFUL.
UM, NO, I WAS BUSY IN THE TEMPLES, BUT . . . HOW COME YOU'RE ALREADY HERE?
WELL, ON HORSEBACK IT'S REALLY QUICK, FROM THE OPEN TEMPLE UP TO HERE . . .
. . . DO YOU NEED SOME HELP WITH YOUR BAG? IT LOOKS REALLY HEAVY.
NO, NO, I'M OK. IT'S QUITE LIGHT, REALLY. GOODNIGHT.
QUITE LIGHT?
GOODNIGHT.

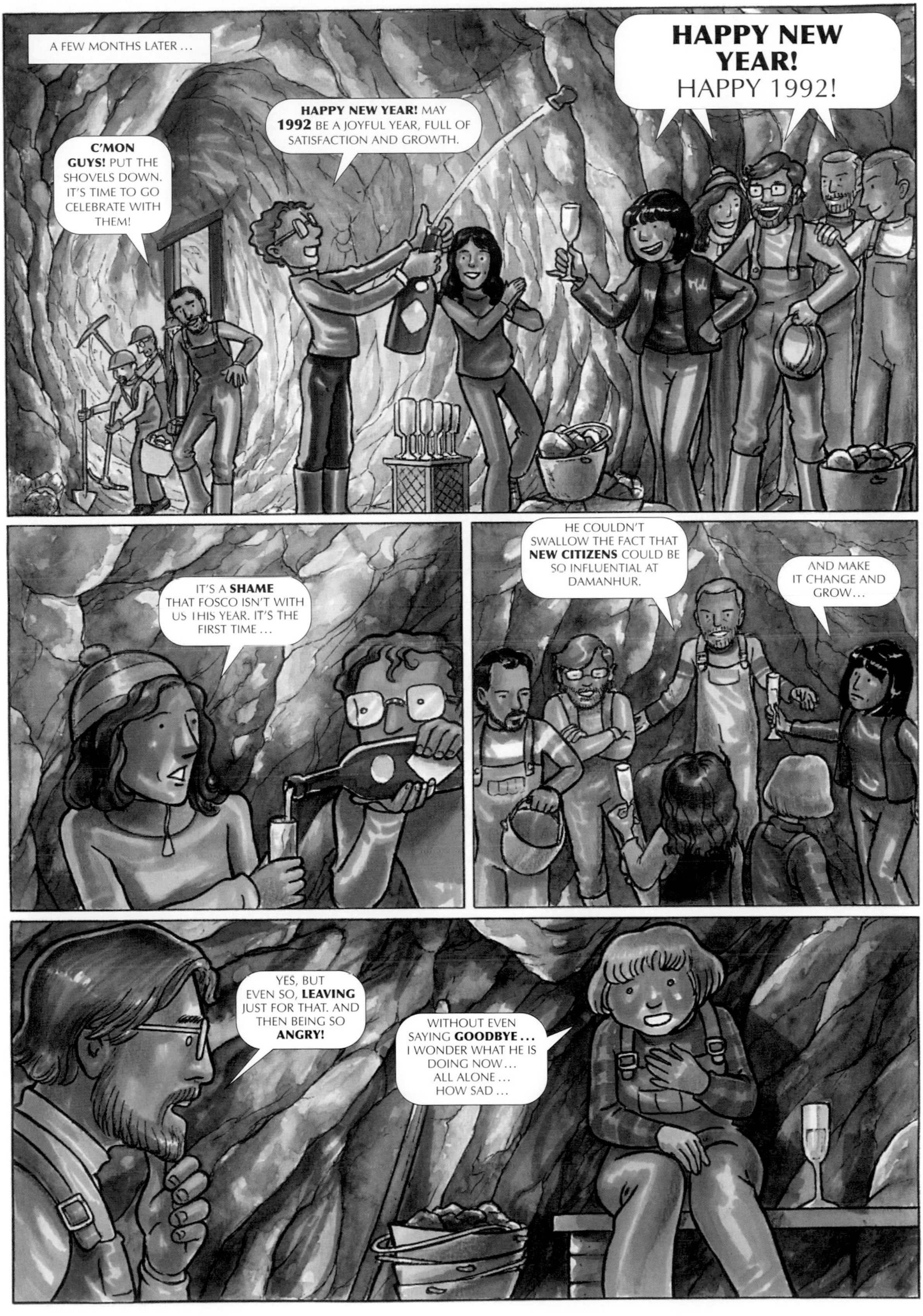
A FEW MONTHS LATER …
C'MON GUYS! PUT THE SHOVELS DOWN. IT'S TIME TO GO CELEBRATE WITH THEM!
HAPPY NEW YEAR! MAY 1992 BE A JOYFUL YEAR, FULL OF SATISFACTION AND GROWTH.
HAPPY NEW YEAR! HAPPY 1992!
IT'S A SHAME THAT FOSCO ISN'T WITH US THIS YEAR. IT'S THE FIRST TIME …
HE COULDN'T SWALLOW THE FACT THAT NEW CITIZENS COULD BE SO INFLUENTIAL AT DAMANHUR.
AND MAKE IT CHANGE AND GROW…
YES, BUT EVEN SO, LEAVING JUST FOR THAT. AND THEN BEING SO ANGRY!
WITHOUT EVEN SAYING GOODBYE … I WONDER WHAT HE IS DOING NOW… ALL ALONE … HOW SAD …

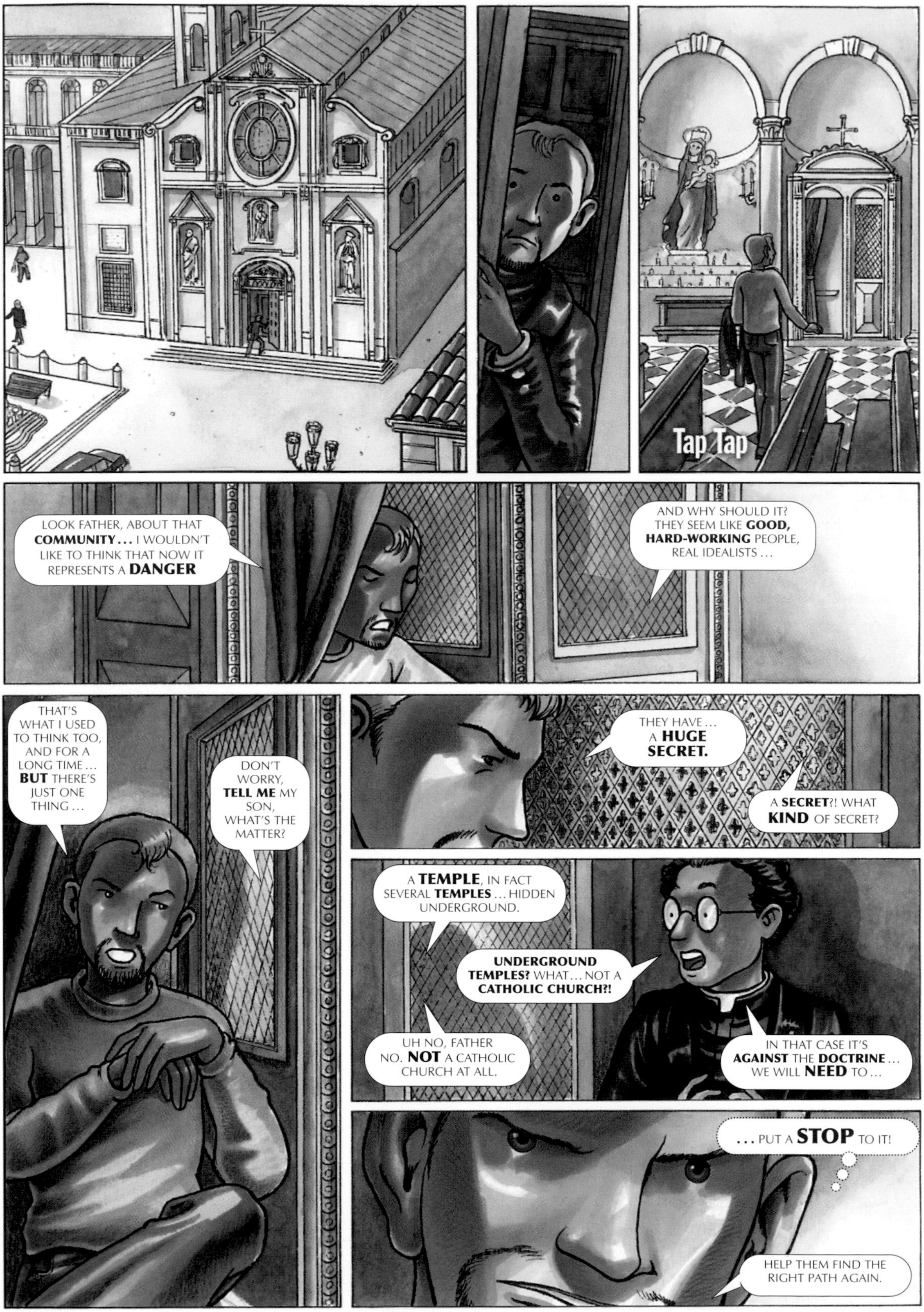
Tap Tap
LOOK FATHER, ABOUT THAT **COMMUNITY...** I WOULDN'T LIKE TO THINK THAT NOW IT REPRESENTS A **DANGER**
AND WHY SHOULD IT? THEY SEEM LIKE **GOOD, HARD-WORKING** PEOPLE, REAL IDEALISTS ...
THAT'S WHAT I USED TO THINK TOO, AND FOR A LONG TIME ... **BUT** THERE'S JUST ONE THING ...
DON'T WORRY, **TELL ME** MY SON, WHAT'S THE MATTER?
THEY HAVE ... A **HUGE SECRET.**
A **SECRET**?! WHAT **KIND** OF SECRET?
A **TEMPLE**, IN FACT SEVERAL **TEMPLES** ... HIDDEN UNDERGROUND.
UNDERGROUND TEMPLES? WHAT... NOT A **CATHOLIC CHURCH?!**
UH NO, FATHER NO. **NOT** A CATHOLIC CHURCH AT ALL.
IN THAT CASE IT'S **AGAINST** THE **DOCTRINE** ... WE WILL **NEED** TO ...
... PUT A **STOP** TO IT!
HELP THEM FIND THE RIGHT PATH AGAIN.

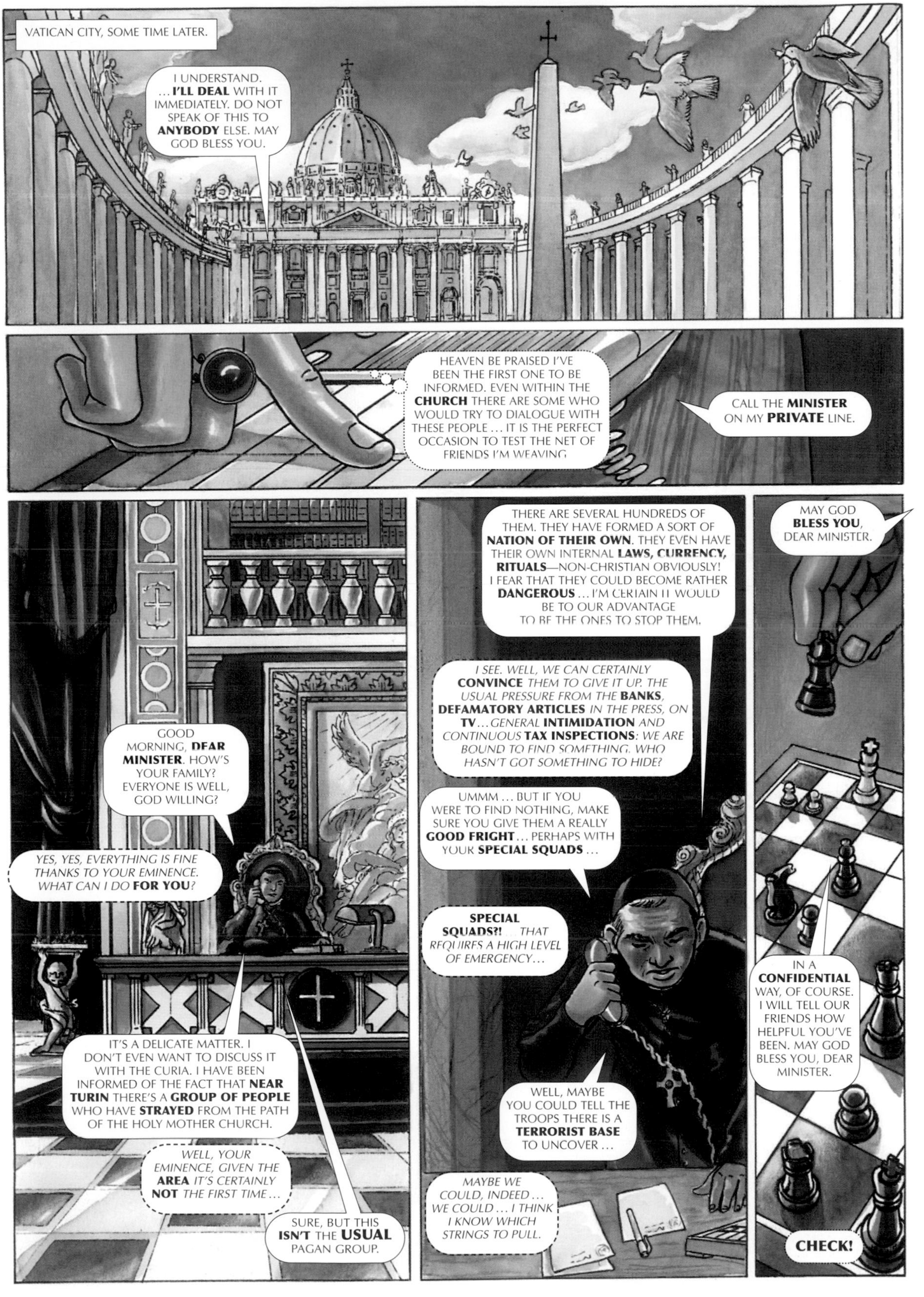
VATICAN CITY, SOME TIME LATER.
I UNDERSTAND. …I'LL DEAL WITH IT IMMEDIATELY. DO NOT SPEAK OF THIS TO ANYBODY ELSE. MAY GOD BLESS YOU.
HEAVEN BE PRAISED I'VE BEEN THE FIRST ONE TO BE INFORMED. EVEN WITHIN THE CHURCH THERE ARE SOME WHO WOULD TRY TO DIALOGUE WITH THESE PEOPLE … IT IS THE PERFECT OCCASION TO TEST THE NET OF FRIENDS I'M WEAVING.
CALL THE MINISTER ON MY PRIVATE LINE.
GOOD MORNING, DEAR MINISTER. HOW'S YOUR FAMILY? EVERYONE IS WELL, GOD WILLING?
YES, YES, EVERYTHING IS FINE THANKS TO YOUR EMINENCE. WHAT CAN I DO FOR YOU?
IT'S A DELICATE MATTER. I DON'T EVEN WANT TO DISCUSS IT WITH THE CURIA. I HAVE BEEN INFORMED OF THE FACT THAT NEAR TURIN THERE'S A GROUP OF PEOPLE WHO HAVE STRAYED FROM THE PATH OF THE HOLY MOTHER CHURCH.
WELL, YOUR EMINENCE, GIVEN THE AREA IT'S CERTAINLY NOT THE FIRST TIME …
SURE, BUT THIS ISN'T THE USUAL PAGAN GROUP.
THERE ARE SEVERAL HUNDREDS OF THEM. THEY HAVE FORMED A SORT OF NATION OF THEIR OWN. THEY EVEN HAVE THEIR OWN INTERNAL LAWS, CURRENCY, RITUALS—NON-CHRISTIAN OBVIOUSLY! I FEAR THAT THEY COULD BECOME RATHER DANGEROUS … I'M CERTAIN IT WOULD BE TO OUR ADVANTAGE TO BE THE ONES TO STOP THEM.
I SEE. WELL, WE CAN CERTAINLY CONVINCE THEM TO GIVE IT UP. THE USUAL PRESSURE FROM THE BANKS, DEFAMATORY ARTICLES IN THE PRESS, ON TV…GENERAL INTIMIDATION AND CONTINUOUS TAX INSPECTIONS: WE ARE BOUND TO FIND SOMETHING. WHO HASN'T GOT SOMETHING TO HIDE?
UMMM … BUT IF YOU WERE TO FIND NOTHING, MAKE SURE YOU GIVE THEM A REALLY GOOD FRIGHT… PERHAPS WITH YOUR SPECIAL SQUADS …
SPECIAL SQUADS?! … THAT REQUIRES A HIGH LEVEL OF EMERGENCY…
WELL, MAYBE YOU COULD TELL THE TROOPS THERE IS A TERRORIST BASE TO UNCOVER …
MAYBE WE COULD, INDEED … WE COULD … I THINK I KNOW WHICH STRINGS TO PULL.
MAY GOD BLESS YOU, DEAR MINISTER.
IN A CONFIDENTIAL WAY, OF COURSE. I WILL TELL OUR FRIENDS HOW HELPFUL YOU'VE BEEN. MAY GOD BLESS YOU, DEAR MINISTER.
CHECK!

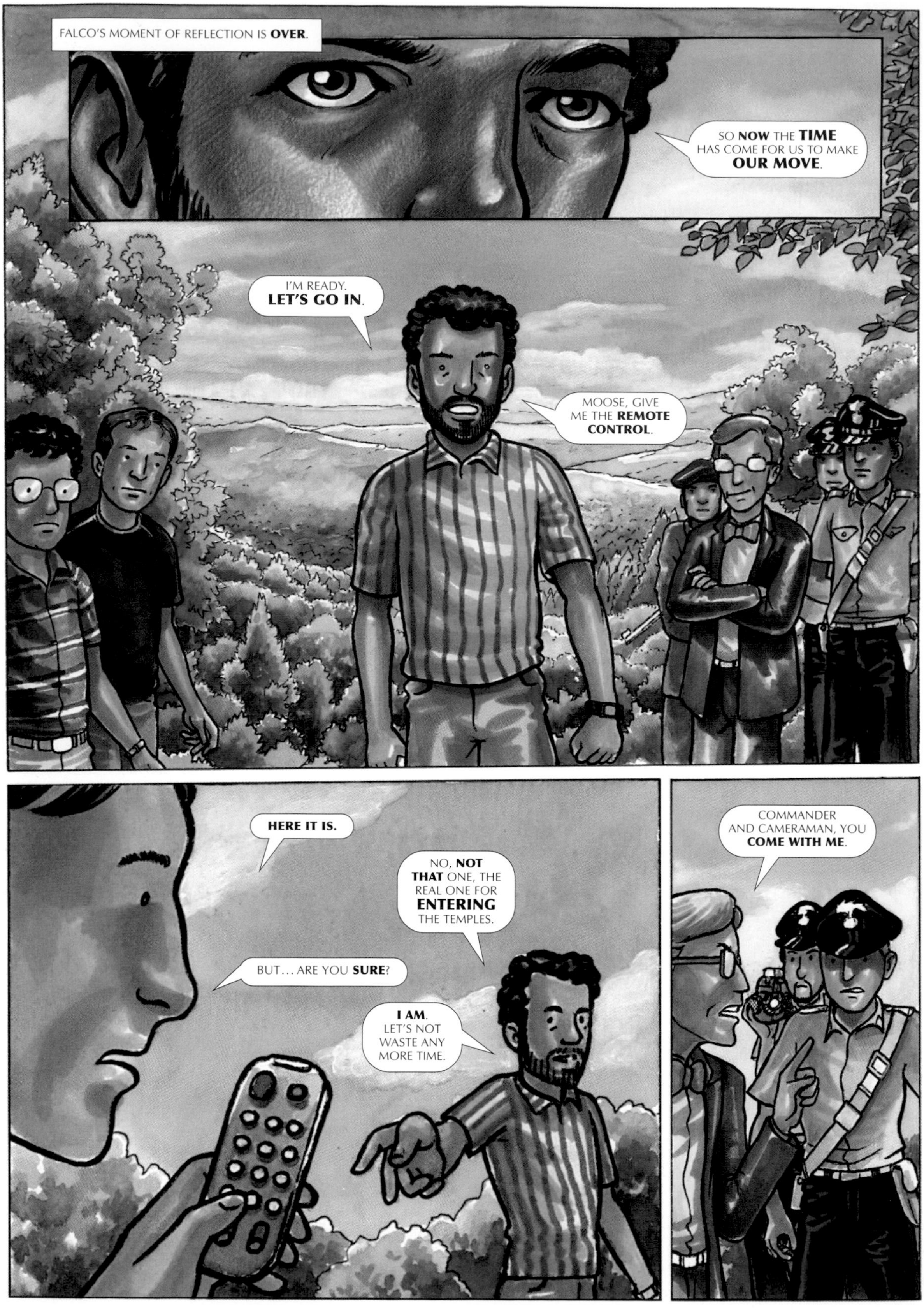
FALCO'S MOMENT OF REFLECTION IS **OVER**.
SO **NOW** THE **TIME** HAS COME FOR US TO MAKE **OUR MOVE**.
I'M READY. **LET'S GO IN**.
MOOSE, GIVE ME THE **REMOTE CONTROL**.
HERE IT IS.
NO, **NOT THAT** ONE, THE REAL ONE FOR **ENTERING** THE TEMPLES.
BUT… ARE YOU **SURE**?
I AM. LET'S NOT WASTE ANY MORE TIME.
COMMANDER AND CAMERAMAN, YOU **COME WITH ME**.

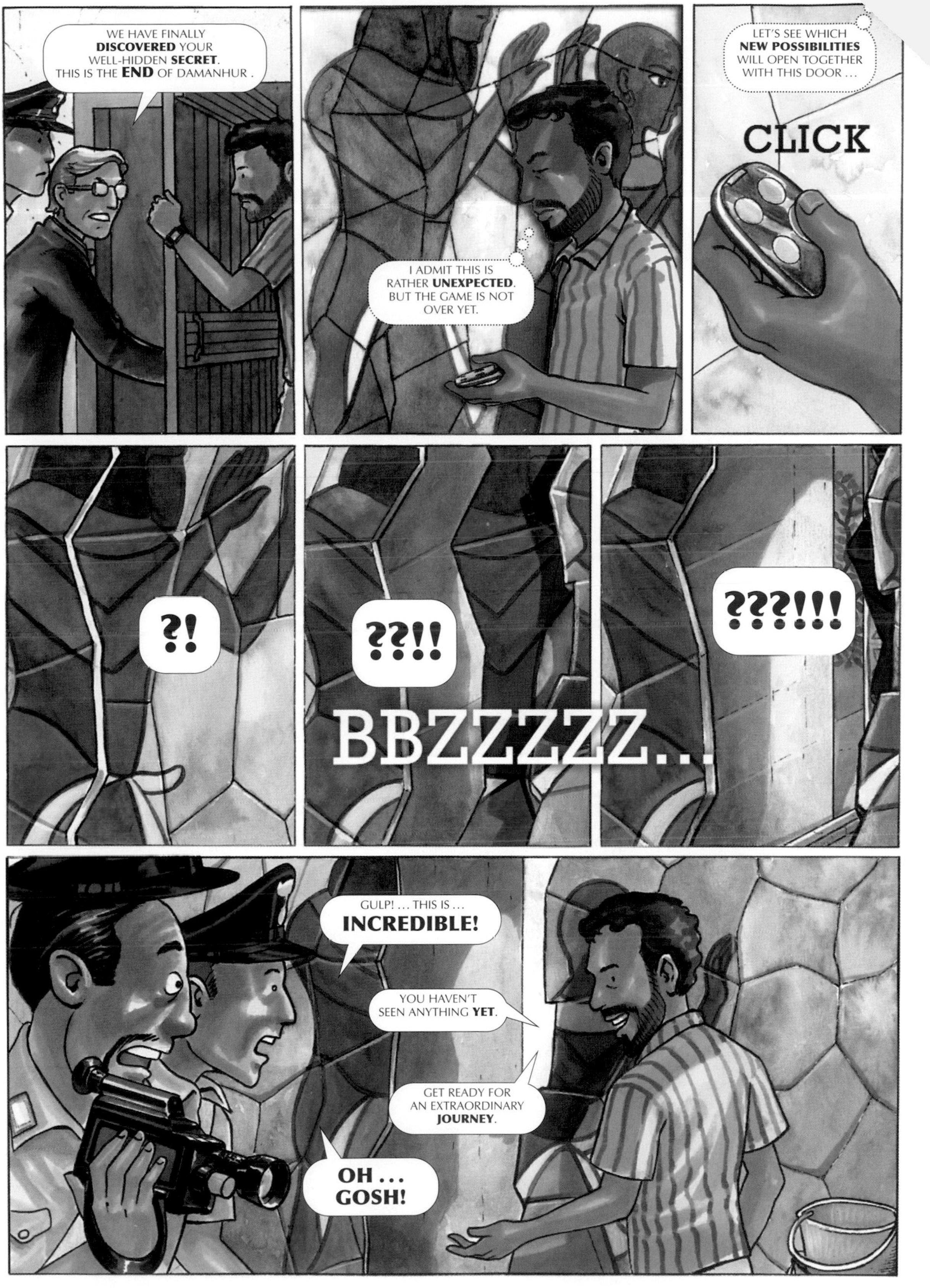
WE HAVE FINALLY DISCOVERED YOUR WELL-HIDDEN SECRET. THIS IS THE END OF DAMANHUR .
I ADMIT THIS IS RATHER UNEXPECTED. BUT THE GAME IS NOT OVER YET.
LET'S SEE WHICH NEW POSSIBILITIES WILL OPEN TOGETHER WITH THIS DOOR ...
CLICK
?!
??!!
???!!!
BBZZZZZ...
GULP! ... THIS IS ... INCREDIBLE!
YOU HAVEN'T SEEN ANYTHING YET.
GET READY FOR AN EXTRAORDINARY JOURNEY.
OH ... GOSH!

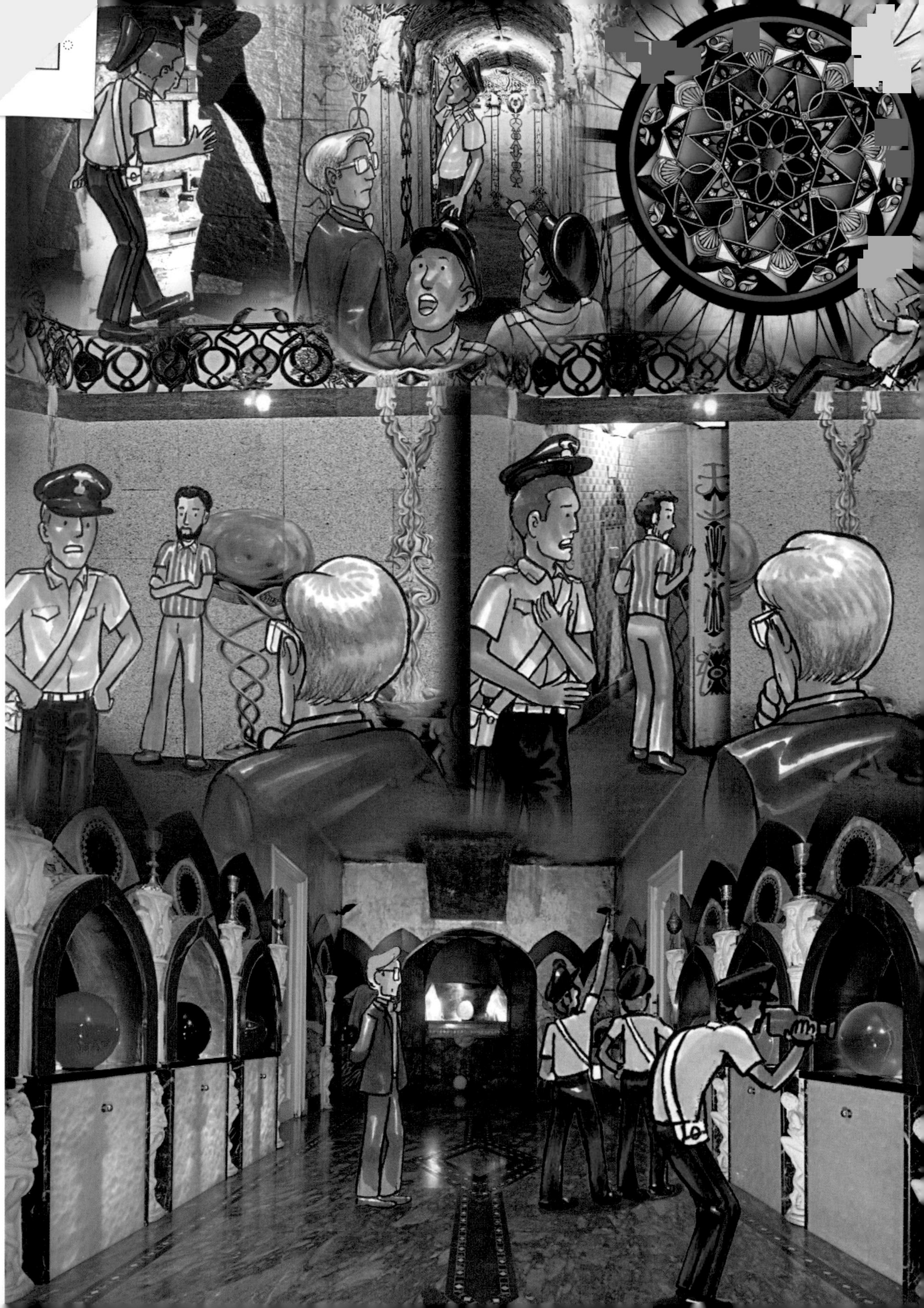

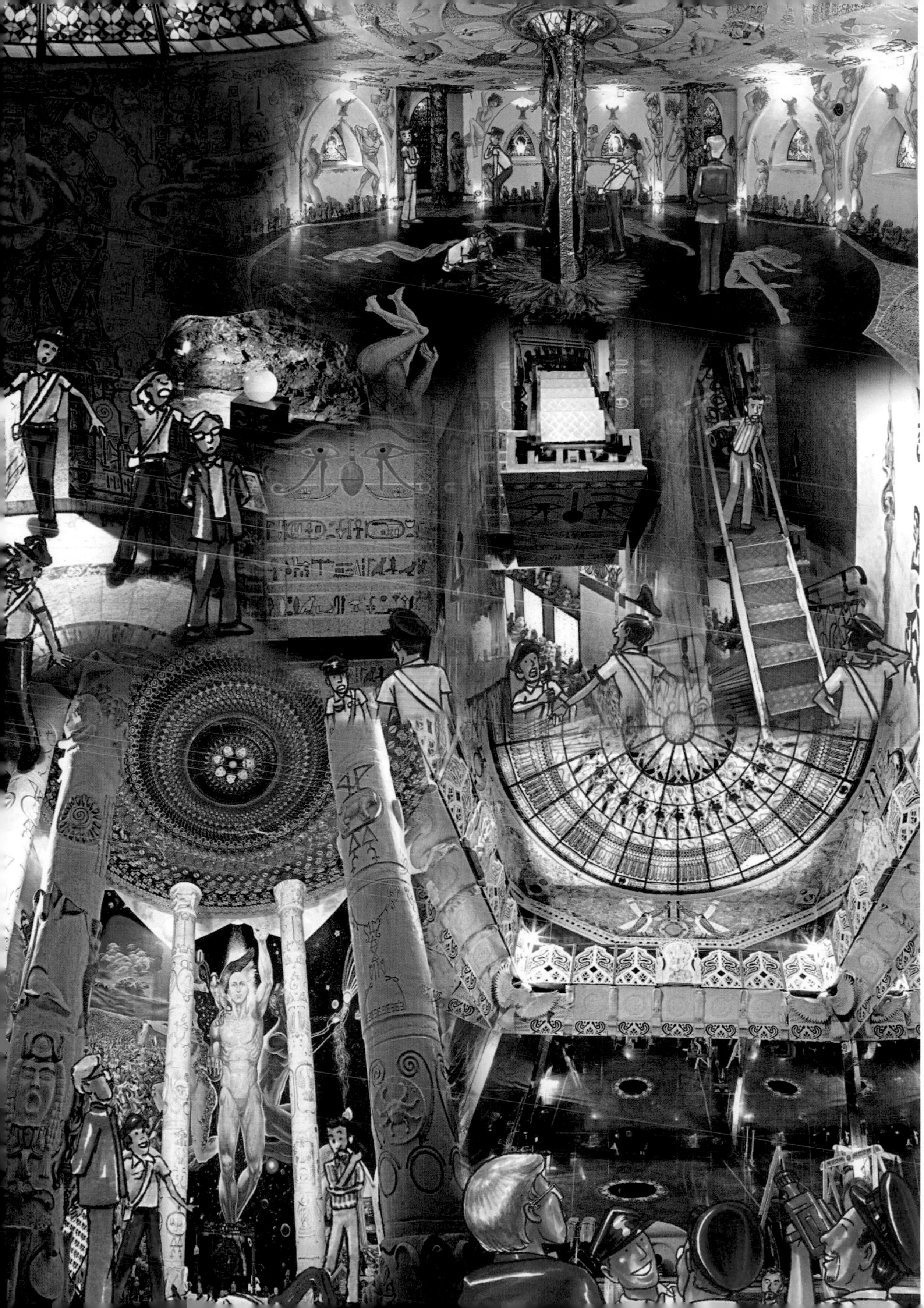

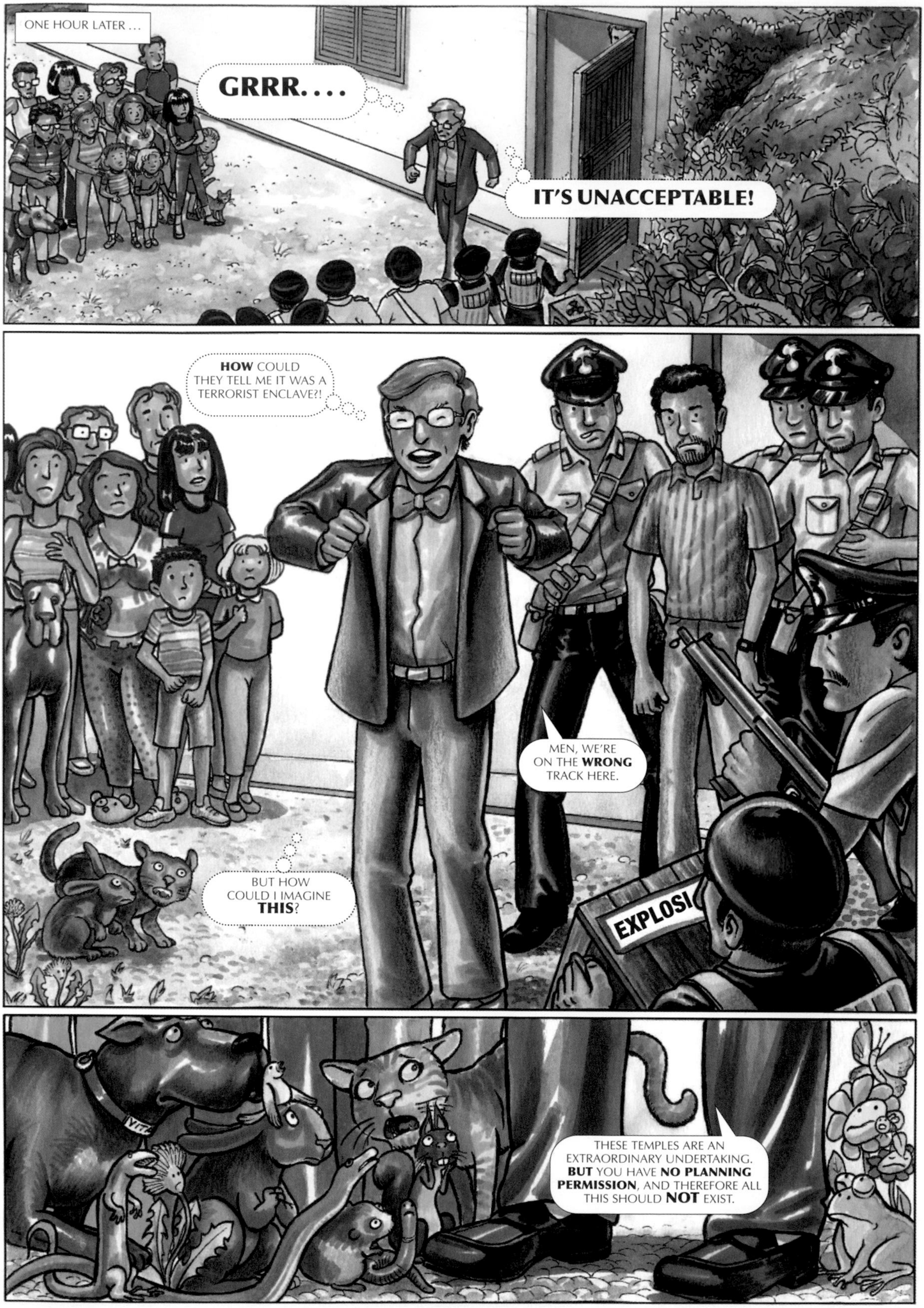
ONE HOUR LATER ...
GRRR....
IT'S UNACCEPTABLE!
HOW COULD THEY TELL ME IT WAS A TERRORIST ENCLAVE?!
MEN, WE'RE ON THE WRONG TRACK HERE.
BUT HOW COULD I IMAGINE THIS?
EXPLOSI
THESE TEMPLES ARE AN EXTRAORDINARY UNDERTAKING. BUT YOU HAVE NO PLANNING PERMISSION, AND THEREFORE ALL THIS SHOULD NOT EXIST.

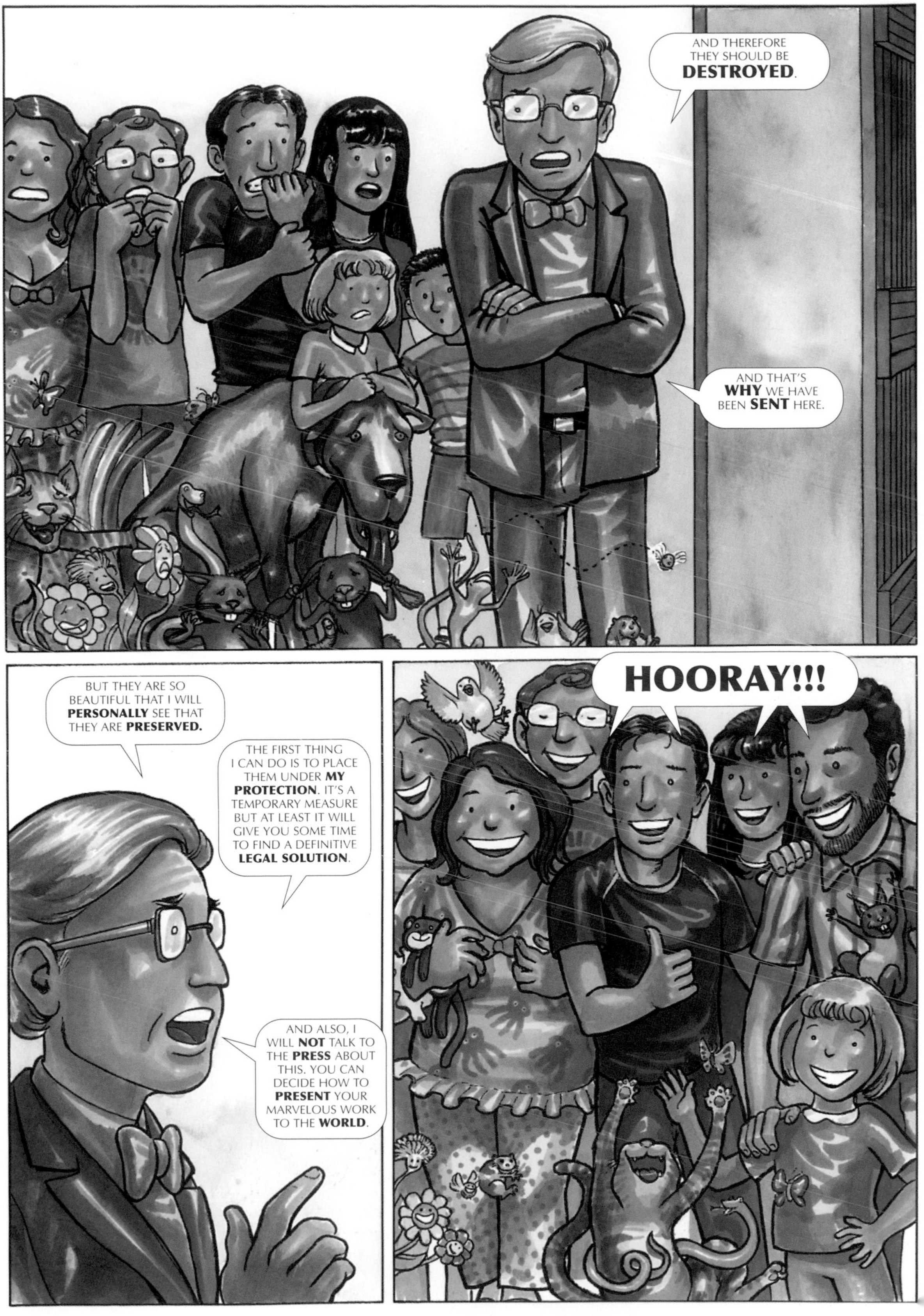
AND THEREFORE THEY SHOULD BE DESTROYED.
AND THAT'S WHY WE HAVE BEEN SENT HERE.
BUT THEY ARE SO BEAUTIFUL THAT I WILL PERSONALLY SEE THAT THEY ARE PRESERVED.
THE FIRST THING I CAN DO IS TO PLACE THEM UNDER MY PROTECTION. IT'S A TEMPORARY MEASURE BUT AT LEAST IT WILL GIVE YOU SOME TIME TO FIND A DEFINITIVE LEGAL SOLUTION.
AND ALSO, I WILL NOT TALK TO THE PRESS ABOUT THIS. YOU CAN DECIDE HOW TO PRESENT YOUR MARVELOUS WORK TO THE WORLD.
HOORAY!!!

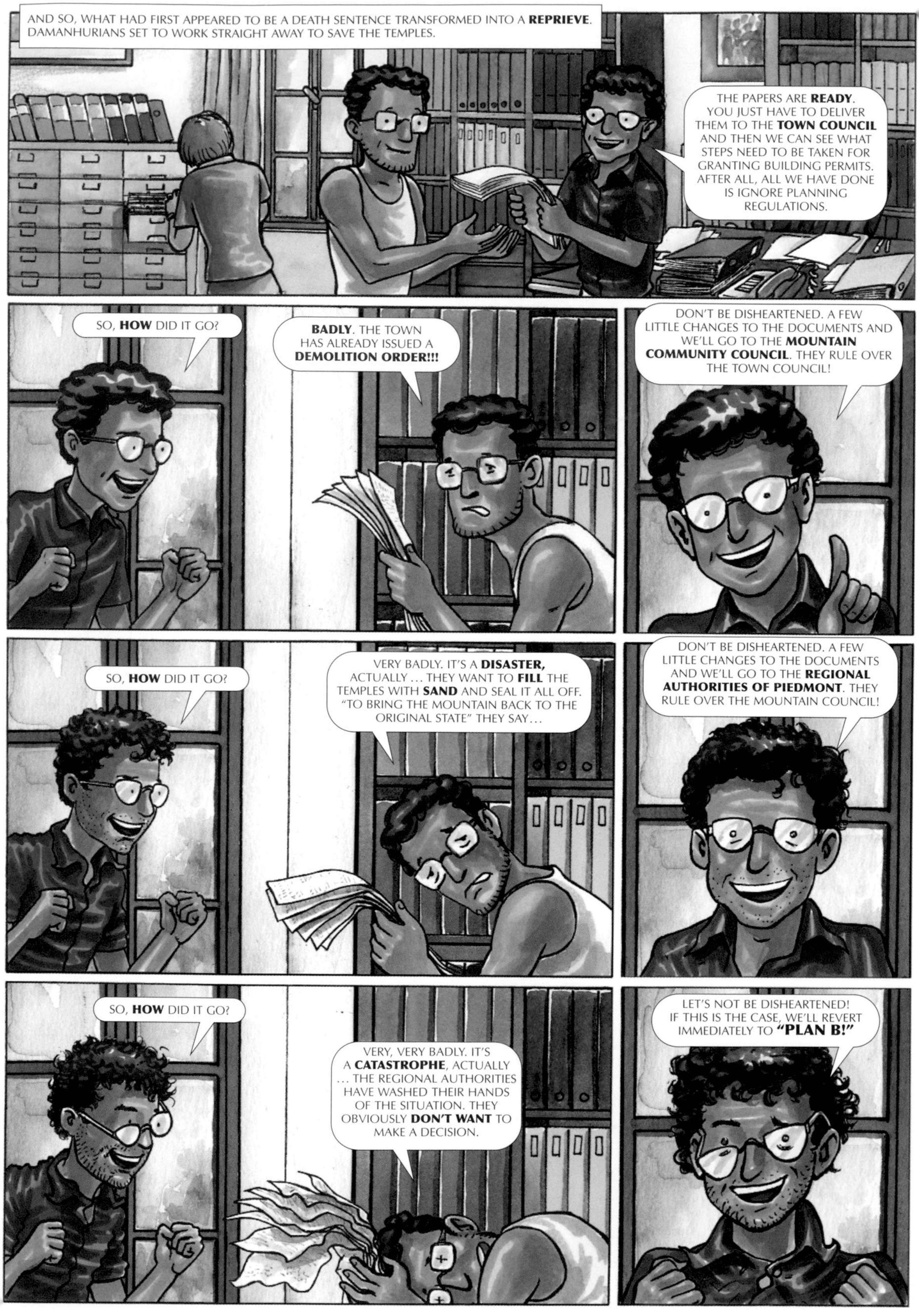
AND SO, WHAT HAD FIRST APPEARED TO BE A DEATH SENTENCE TRANSFORMED INTO A **REPRIEVE**. DAMANHURIANS SET TO WORK STRAIGHT AWAY TO SAVE THE TEMPLES.
THE PAPERS ARE **READY**. YOU JUST HAVE TO DELIVER THEM TO THE **TOWN COUNCIL** AND THEN WE CAN SEE WHAT STEPS NEED TO BE TAKEN FOR GRANTING BUILDING PERMITS. AFTER ALL, ALL WE HAVE DONE IS IGNORE PLANNING REGULATIONS.
SO, **HOW** DID IT GO?
BADLY. THE TOWN HAS ALREADY ISSUED A **DEMOLITION ORDER!!!**
DON'T BE DISHEARTENED. A FEW LITTLE CHANGES TO THE DOCUMENTS AND WE'LL GO TO THE **MOUNTAIN COMMUNITY COUNCIL**. THEY RULE OVER THE TOWN COUNCIL!
SO, **HOW** DID IT GO?
VERY BADLY. IT'S A **DISASTER,** ACTUALLY ... THEY WANT TO **FILL** THE TEMPLES WITH **SAND** AND SEAL IT ALL OFF. "TO BRING THE MOUNTAIN BACK TO THE ORIGINAL STATE" THEY SAY...
DON'T BE DISHEARTENED. A FEW LITTLE CHANGES TO THE DOCUMENTS AND WE'LL GO TO THE **REGIONAL AUTHORITIES OF PIEDMONT**. THEY RULE OVER THE MOUNTAIN COUNCIL!
SO, **HOW** DID IT GO?
VERY, VERY BADLY. IT'S A **CATASTROPHE**, ACTUALLY ... THE REGIONAL AUTHORITIES HAVE WASHED THEIR HANDS OF THE SITUATION. THEY OBVIOUSLY **DON'T WANT** TO MAKE A DECISION.
LET'S NOT BE DISHEARTENED! IF THIS IS THE CASE, WE'LL REVERT IMMEDIATELY TO **"PLAN B!"**

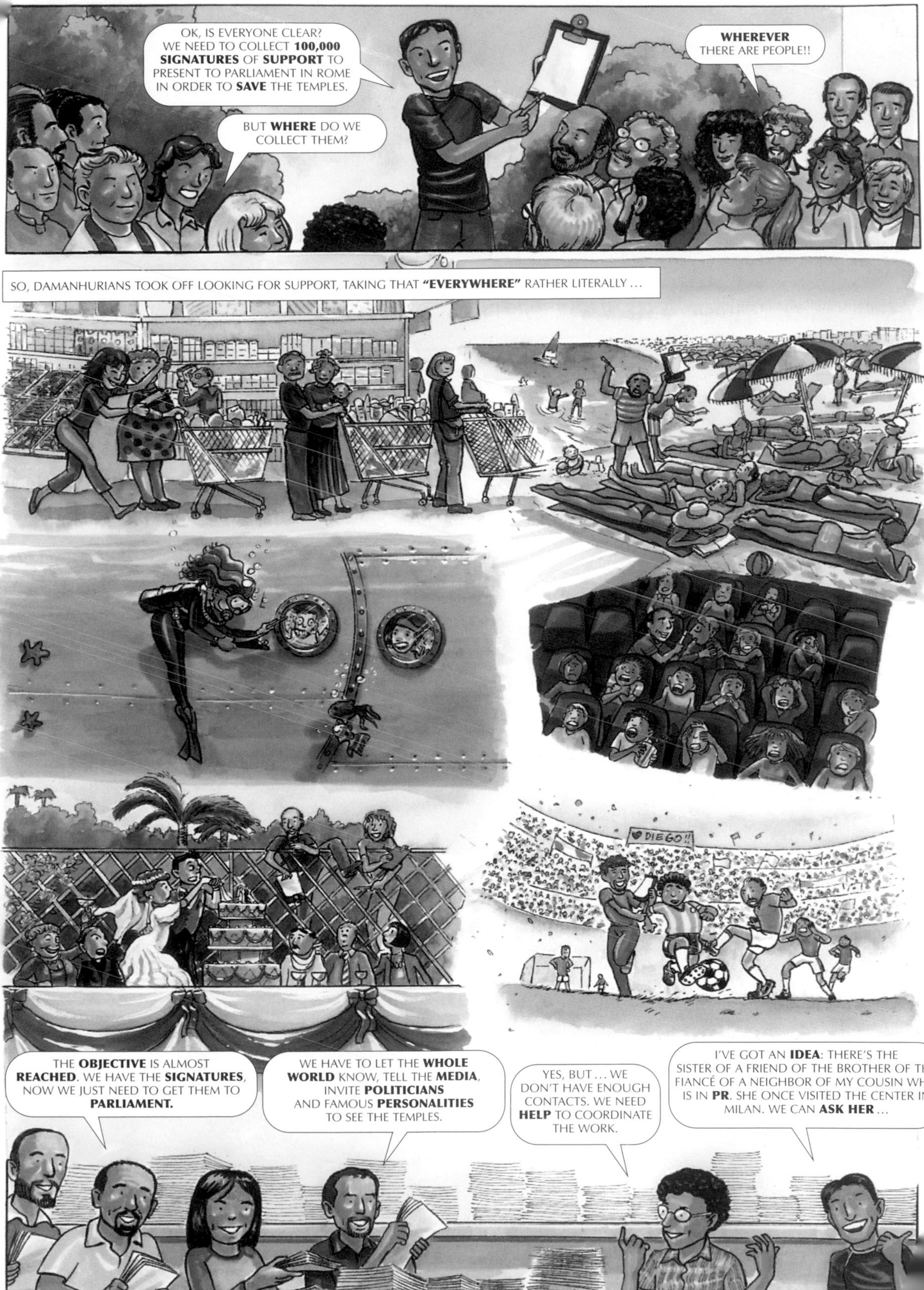
OK, IS EVERYONE CLEAR? WE NEED TO COLLECT **100,000 SIGNATURES** OF **SUPPORT** TO PRESENT TO PARLIAMENT IN ROME IN ORDER TO **SAVE** THE TEMPLES.
BUT **WHERE** DO WE COLLECT THEM?
WHEREVER THERE ARE PEOPLE!!
SO, DAMANHURIANS TOOK OFF LOOKING FOR SUPPORT, TAKING THAT **"EVERYWHERE"** RATHER LITERALLY ...
DIEGO!!
THE **OBJECTIVE** IS ALMOST **REACHED**. WE HAVE THE **SIGNATURES**, NOW WE JUST NEED TO GET THEM TO **PARLIAMENT.**
WE HAVE TO LET THE **WHOLE WORLD** KNOW, TELL THE **MEDIA**, INVITE **POLITICIANS** AND FAMOUS **PERSONALITIES** TO SEE THE TEMPLES.
YES, BUT ... WE DON'T HAVE ENOUGH CONTACTS. WE NEED **HELP** TO COORDINATE THE WORK.
I'VE GOT AN **IDEA**: THERE'S THE SISTER OF A FRIEND OF THE BROTHER OF THE FIANCÉ OF A NEIGHBOR OF MY COUSIN WHO IS IN **PR**. SHE ONCE VISITED THE CENTER IN MILAN. WE CAN **ASK HER** ...

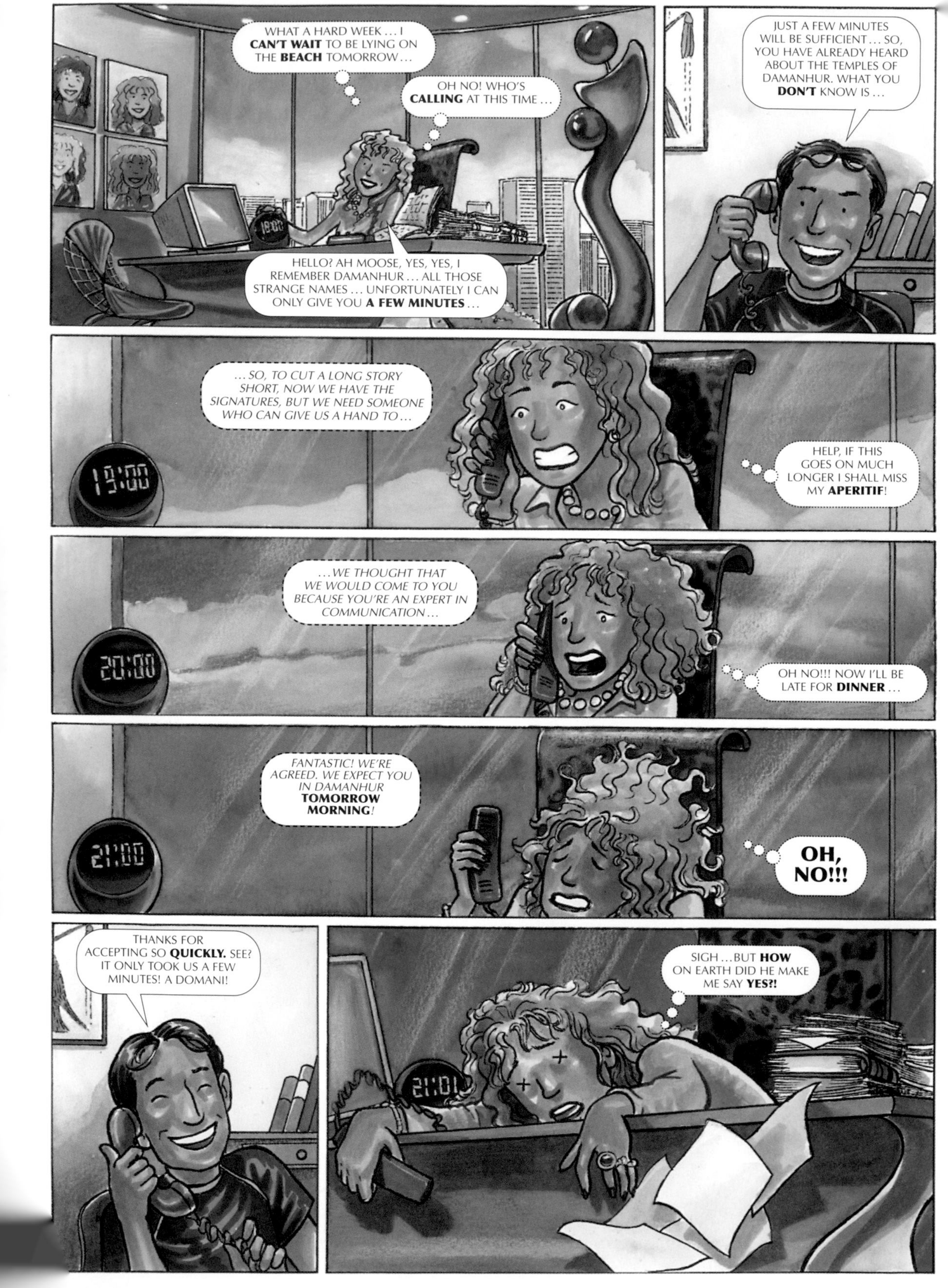
WHAT A HARD WEEK ... I CAN'T WAIT TO BE LYING ON THE BEACH TOMORROW ...
OH NO! WHO'S CALLING AT THIS TIME ...
HELLO? AH MOOSE, YES, YES, I REMEMBER DAMANHUR ... ALL THOSE STRANGE NAMES ... UNFORTUNATELY I CAN ONLY GIVE YOU A FEW MINUTES ...
JUST A FEW MINUTES WILL BE SUFFICIENT ... SO, YOU HAVE ALREADY HEARD ABOUT THE TEMPLES OF DAMANHUR. WHAT YOU DON'T KNOW IS ...
... SO, TO CUT A LONG STORY SHORT, NOW WE HAVE THE SIGNATURES, BUT WE NEED SOMEONE WHO CAN GIVE US A HAND TO ...
19:00
HELP, IF THIS GOES ON MUCH LONGER I SHALL MISS MY APERITIF!
... WE THOUGHT THAT WE WOULD COME TO YOU BECAUSE YOU'RE AN EXPERT IN COMMUNICATION ...
20:00
OH NO!!! NOW I'LL BE LATE FOR DINNER ...
FANTASTIC! WE'RE AGREED. WE EXPECT YOU IN DAMANHUR TOMORROW MORNING!
21:00
OH, NO!!!
THANKS FOR ACCEPTING SO QUICKLY. SEE? IT ONLY TOOK US A FEW MINUTES! A DOMANI!
SIGH ... BUT HOW ON EARTH DID HE MAKE ME SAY YES?!
21:01

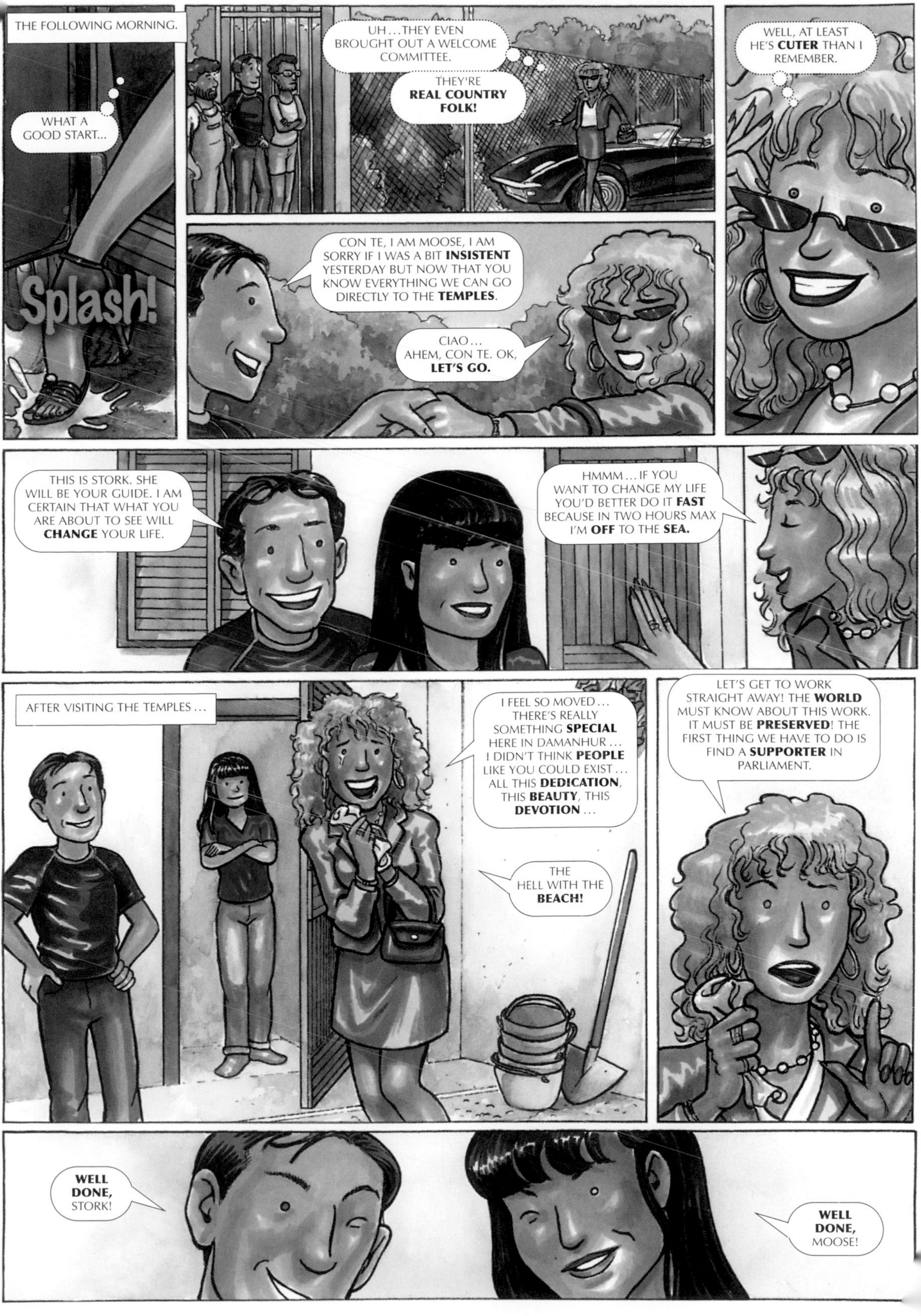
THE FOLLOWING MORNING.
WHAT A GOOD START...
Splash!
UH . . . THEY EVEN BROUGHT OUT A WELCOME COMMITTEE.
THEY'RE **REAL COUNTRY FOLK!**
CON TE, I AM MOOSE, I AM SORRY IF I WAS A BIT **INSISTENT** YESTERDAY BUT NOW THAT YOU KNOW EVERYTHING WE CAN GO DIRECTLY TO THE **TEMPLES**.
CIAO . . . AHEM, CON TE. OK, **LET'S GO.**
WELL, AT LEAST HE'S **CUTER** THAN I REMEMBER.
THIS IS STORK. SHE WILL BE YOUR GUIDE. I AM CERTAIN THAT WHAT YOU ARE ABOUT TO SEE WILL **CHANGE** YOUR LIFE.
HMMM . . . IF YOU WANT TO CHANGE MY LIFE YOU'D BETTER DO IT **FAST** BECAUSE IN TWO HOURS MAX I'M **OFF** TO THE **SEA.**
AFTER VISITING THE TEMPLES . . .
I FEEL SO MOVED . . . THERE'S REALLY SOMETHING **SPECIAL** HERE IN DAMANHUR . . . I DIDN'T THINK **PEOPLE** LIKE YOU COULD EXIST . . . ALL THIS **DEDICATION**, THIS **BEAUTY**, THIS **DEVOTION** . . .
THE HELL WITH THE **BEACH!**
LET'S GET TO WORK STRAIGHT AWAY! THE **WORLD** MUST KNOW ABOUT THIS WORK. IT MUST BE **PRESERVED**! THE FIRST THING WE HAVE TO DO IS FIND A **SUPPORTER** IN PARLIAMENT.
WELL DONE, STORK!
WELL DONE, MOOSE!

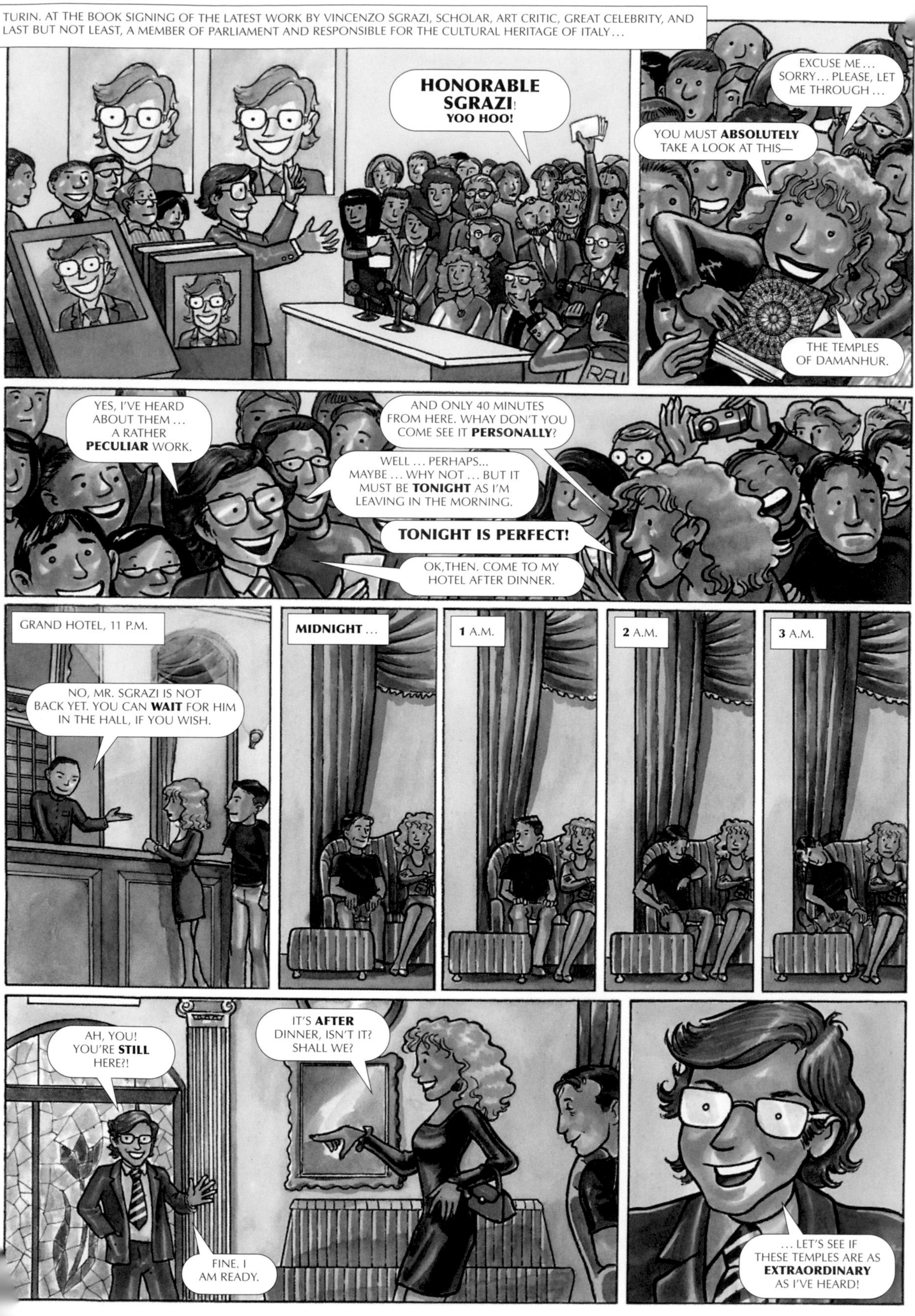
TURIN. AT THE BOOK SIGNING OF THE LATEST WORK BY VINCENZO SGRAZI, SCHOLAR, ART CRITIC, GREAT CELEBRITY, AND LAST BUT NOT LEAST, A MEMBER OF PARLIAMENT AND RESPONSIBLE FOR THE CULTURAL HERITAGE OF ITALY…
HONORABLE SGRAZI! YOO HOO!
RAI
EXCUSE ME… SORRY… PLEASE, LET ME THROUGH…
YOU MUST ABSOLUTELY TAKE A LOOK AT THIS—
THE TEMPLES OF DAMANHUR.
YES, I'VE HEARD ABOUT THEM… A RATHER PECULIAR WORK.
AND ONLY 40 MINUTES FROM HERE. WHAY DON'T YOU COME SEE IT PERSONALLY?
WELL… PERHAPS... MAYBE… WHY NOT… BUT IT MUST BE TONIGHT AS I'M LEAVING IN THE MORNING.
TONIGHT IS PERFECT!
OK,THEN. COME TO MY HOTEL AFTER DINNER.
GRAND HOTEL, 11 P.M.
NO, MR. SGRAZI IS NOT BACK YET. YOU CAN WAIT FOR HIM IN THE HALL, IF YOU WISH.
MIDNIGHT…
1 A.M.
2 A.M.
3 A.M.
AH, YOU! YOU'RE STILL HERE?!
FINE. I AM READY.
IT'S AFTER DINNER, ISN'T IT? SHALL WE?
… LET'S SEE IF THESE TEMPLES ARE AS EXTRAORDINARY AS I'VE HEARD!

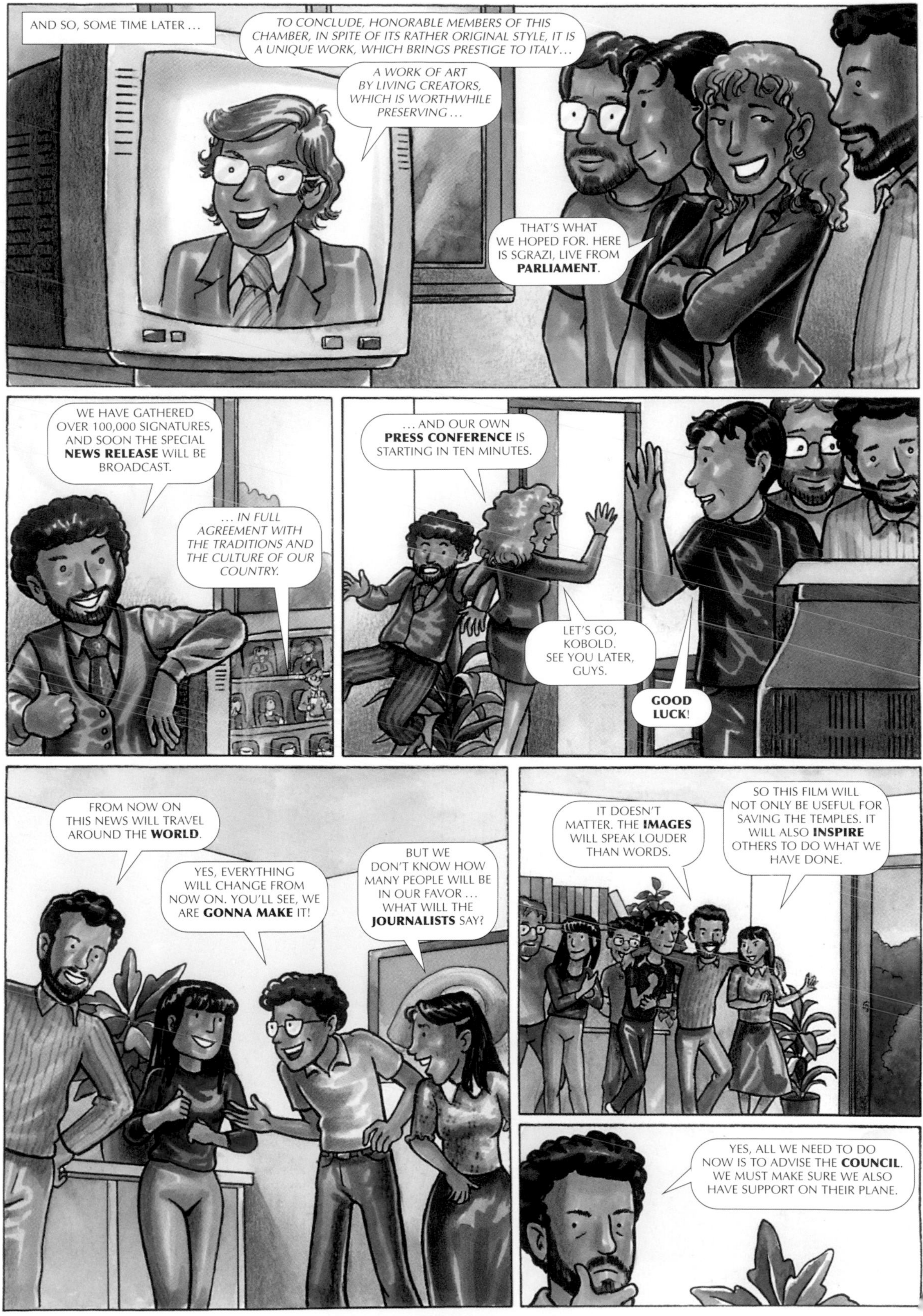
AND SO, SOME TIME LATER …
TO CONCLUDE, HONORABLE MEMBERS OF THIS CHAMBER, IN SPITE OF ITS RATHER ORIGINAL STYLE, IT IS A UNIQUE WORK, WHICH BRINGS PRESTIGE TO ITALY …
A WORK OF ART BY LIVING CREATORS, WHICH IS WORTHWHILE PRESERVING …
THAT'S WHAT WE HOPED FOR. HERE IS SGRAZI, LIVE FROM **PARLIAMENT**.
WE HAVE GATHERED OVER 100,000 SIGNATURES, AND SOON THE SPECIAL **NEWS RELEASE** WILL BE BROADCAST.
… IN FULL AGREEMENT WITH THE TRADITIONS AND THE CULTURE OF OUR COUNTRY.
… AND OUR OWN **PRESS CONFERENCE** IS STARTING IN TEN MINUTES.
LET'S GO, KOBOLD. SEE YOU LATER, GUYS.
GOOD LUCK!
FROM NOW ON THIS NEWS WILL TRAVEL AROUND THE **WORLD**.
YES, EVERYTHING WILL CHANGE FROM NOW ON. YOU'LL SEE, WE ARE **GONNA MAKE** IT!
BUT WE DON'T KNOW HOW MANY PEOPLE WILL BE IN OUR FAVOR … WHAT WILL THE **JOURNALISTS** SAY?
IT DOESN'T MATTER. THE **IMAGES** WILL SPEAK LOUDER THAN WORDS.
SO THIS FILM WILL NOT ONLY BE USEFUL FOR SAVING THE TEMPLES. IT WILL ALSO **INSPIRE** OTHERS TO DO WHAT WE HAVE DONE.
YES, ALL WE NEED TO DO NOW IS TO ADVISE THE **COUNCIL**. WE MUST MAKE SURE WE ALSO HAVE SUPPORT ON THEIR PLANE.

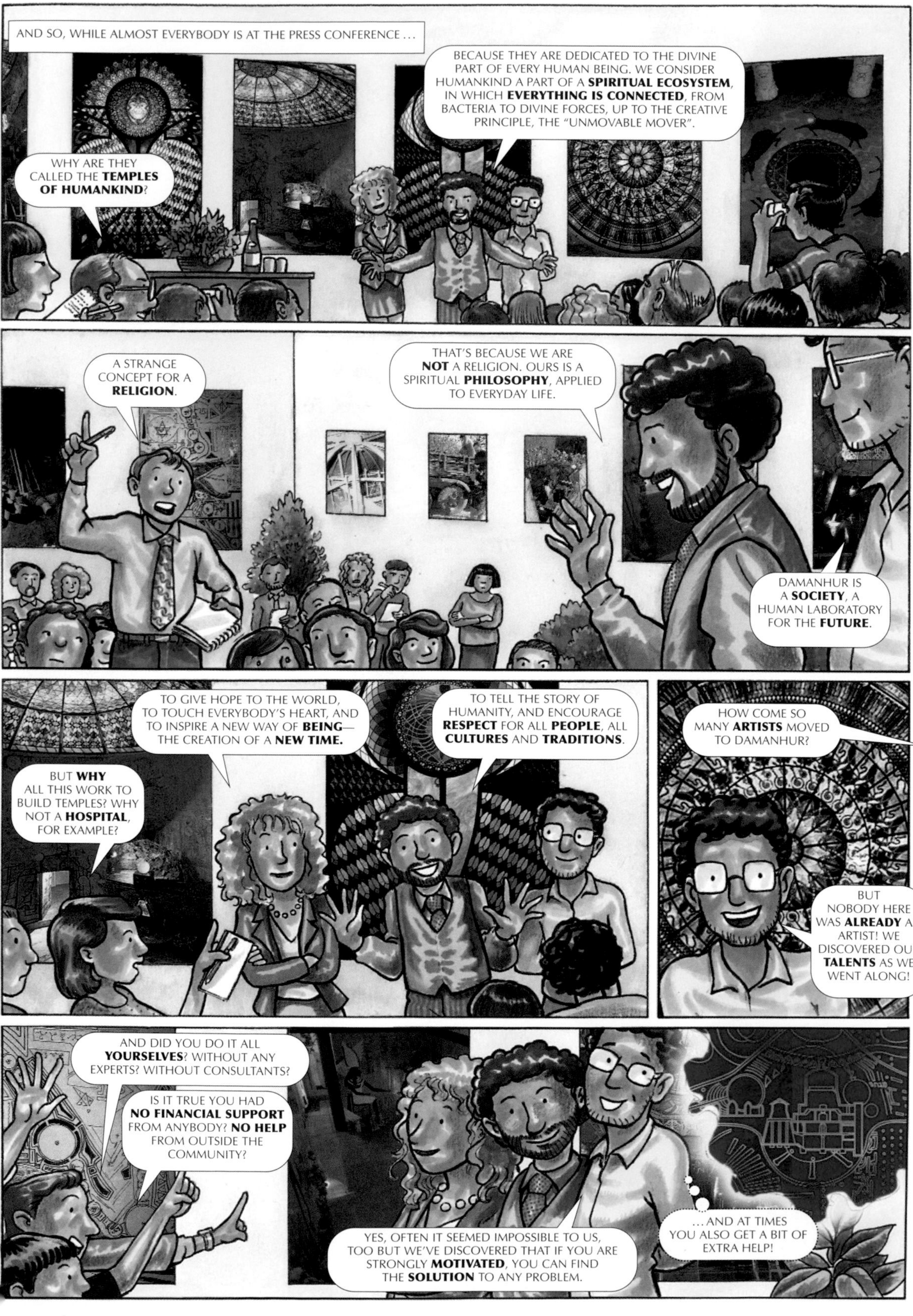
AND SO, WHILE ALMOST EVERYBODY IS AT THE PRESS CONFERENCE . . .
WHY ARE THEY CALLED THE **TEMPLES OF HUMANKIND**?
BECAUSE THEY ARE DEDICATED TO THE DIVINE PART OF EVERY HUMAN BEING. WE CONSIDER HUMANKIND A PART OF A **SPIRITUAL ECOSYSTEM**, IN WHICH **EVERYTHING IS CONNECTED**, FROM BACTERIA TO DIVINE FORCES, UP TO THE CREATIVE PRINCIPLE, THE "UNMOVABLE MOVER".
A STRANGE CONCEPT FOR A **RELIGION**.
THAT'S BECAUSE WE ARE **NOT** A RELIGION. OURS IS A SPIRITUAL **PHILOSOPHY**, APPLIED TO EVERYDAY LIFE.
DAMANHUR IS A **SOCIETY**, A HUMAN LABORATORY FOR THE **FUTURE**.
BUT **WHY** ALL THIS WORK TO BUILD TEMPLES? WHY NOT A **HOSPITAL**, FOR EXAMPLE?
TO GIVE HOPE TO THE WORLD, TO TOUCH EVERYBODY'S HEART, AND TO INSPIRE A NEW WAY OF **BEING**— THE CREATION OF A **NEW TIME.**
TO TELL THE STORY OF HUMANITY, AND ENCOURAGE **RESPECT** FOR ALL **PEOPLE**, ALL **CULTURES** AND **TRADITIONS**.
HOW COME SO MANY **ARTISTS** MOVED TO DAMANHUR?
BUT NOBODY HERE WAS **ALREADY** AN ARTIST! WE DISCOVERED OUR **TALENTS** AS WE WENT ALONG!
AND DID YOU DO IT ALL **YOURSELVES**? WITHOUT ANY EXPERTS? WITHOUT CONSULTANTS?
IS IT TRUE YOU HAD **NO FINANCIAL SUPPORT** FROM ANYBODY? **NO HELP** FROM OUTSIDE THE COMMUNITY?
YES, OFTEN IT SEEMED IMPOSSIBLE TO US, TOO BUT WE'VE DISCOVERED THAT IF YOU ARE STRONGLY **MOTIVATED**, YOU CAN FIND THE **SOLUTION** TO ANY PROBLEM.
. . . AND AT TIMES YOU ALSO GET A BIT OF EXTRA HELP!

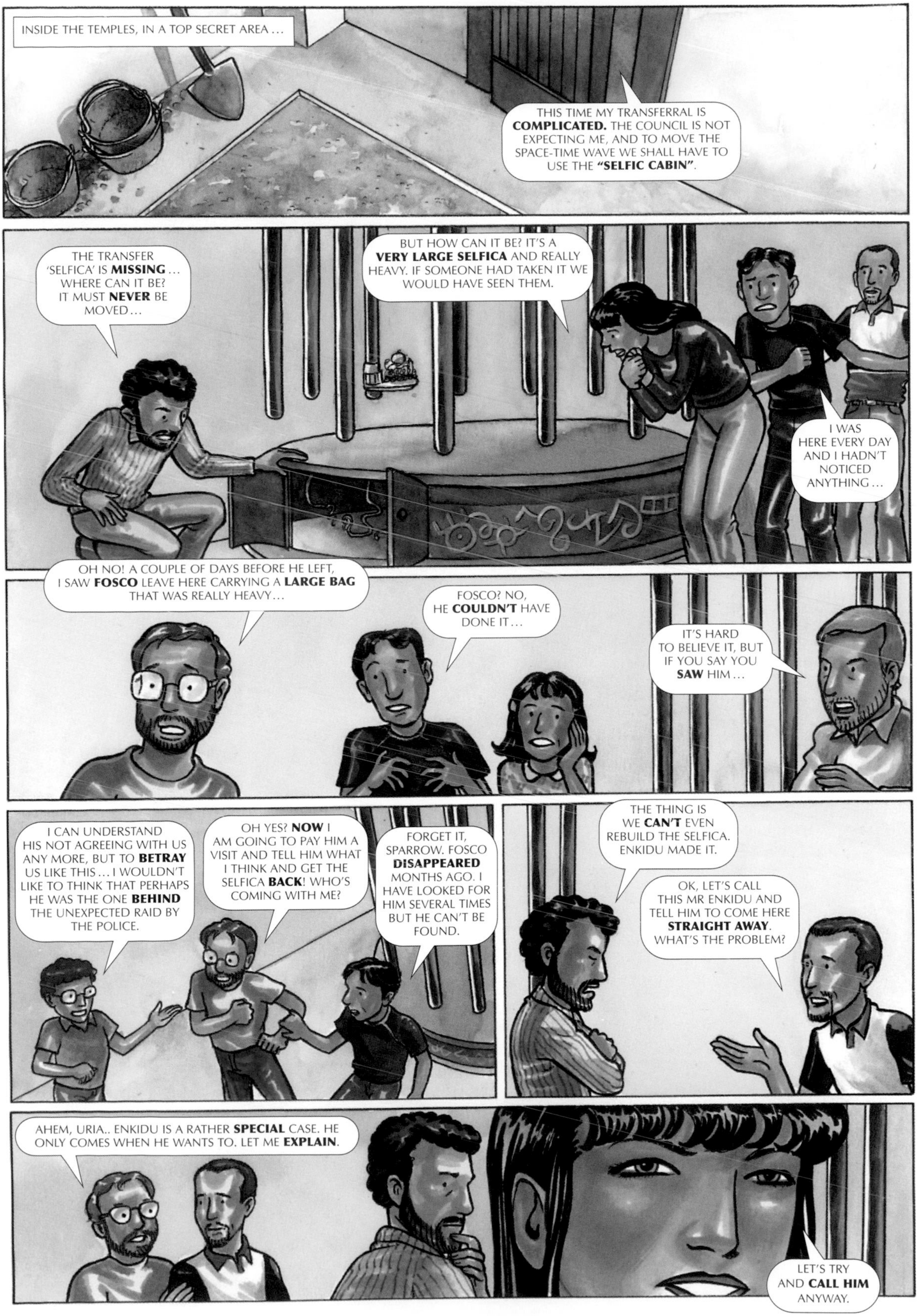
INSIDE THE TEMPLES, IN A TOP SECRET AREA …
THIS TIME MY TRANSFERRAL IS COMPLICATED. THE COUNCIL IS NOT EXPECTING ME, AND TO MOVE THE SPACE-TIME WAVE WE SHALL HAVE TO USE THE "SELFIC CABIN".
THE TRANSFER 'SELFICA' IS MISSING … WHERE CAN IT BE? IT MUST NEVER BE MOVED …
BUT HOW CAN IT BE? IT'S A VERY LARGE SELFICA AND REALLY HEAVY. IF SOMEONE HAD TAKEN IT WE WOULD HAVE SEEN THEM.
I WAS HERE EVERY DAY AND I HADN'T NOTICED ANYTHING …
OH NO! A COUPLE OF DAYS BEFORE HE LEFT, I SAW FOSCO LEAVE HERE CARRYING A LARGE BAG THAT WAS REALLY HEAVY…
FOSCO? NO, HE COULDN'T HAVE DONE IT …
IT'S HARD TO BELIEVE IT, BUT IF YOU SAY YOU SAW HIM …
I CAN UNDERSTAND HIS NOT AGREEING WITH US ANY MORE, BUT TO BETRAY US LIKE THIS … I WOULDN'T LIKE TO THINK THAT PERHAPS HE WAS THE ONE BEHIND THE UNEXPECTED RAID BY THE POLICE.
OH YES? NOW I AM GOING TO PAY HIM A VISIT AND TELL HIM WHAT I THINK AND GET THE SELFICA BACK! WHO'S COMING WITH ME?
FORGET IT, SPARROW. FOSCO DISAPPEARED MONTHS AGO. I HAVE LOOKED FOR HIM SEVERAL TIMES BUT HE CAN'T BE FOUND.
THE THING IS WE CAN'T EVEN REBUILD THE SELFICA. ENKIDU MADE IT.
OK, LET'S CALL THIS MR ENKIDU AND TELL HIM TO COME HERE STRAIGHT AWAY. WHAT'S THE PROBLEM?
AHEM, URIA.. ENKIDU IS A RATHER SPECIAL CASE. HE ONLY COMES WHEN HE WANTS TO. LET ME EXPLAIN.
LET'S TRY AND CALL HIM ANYWAY.

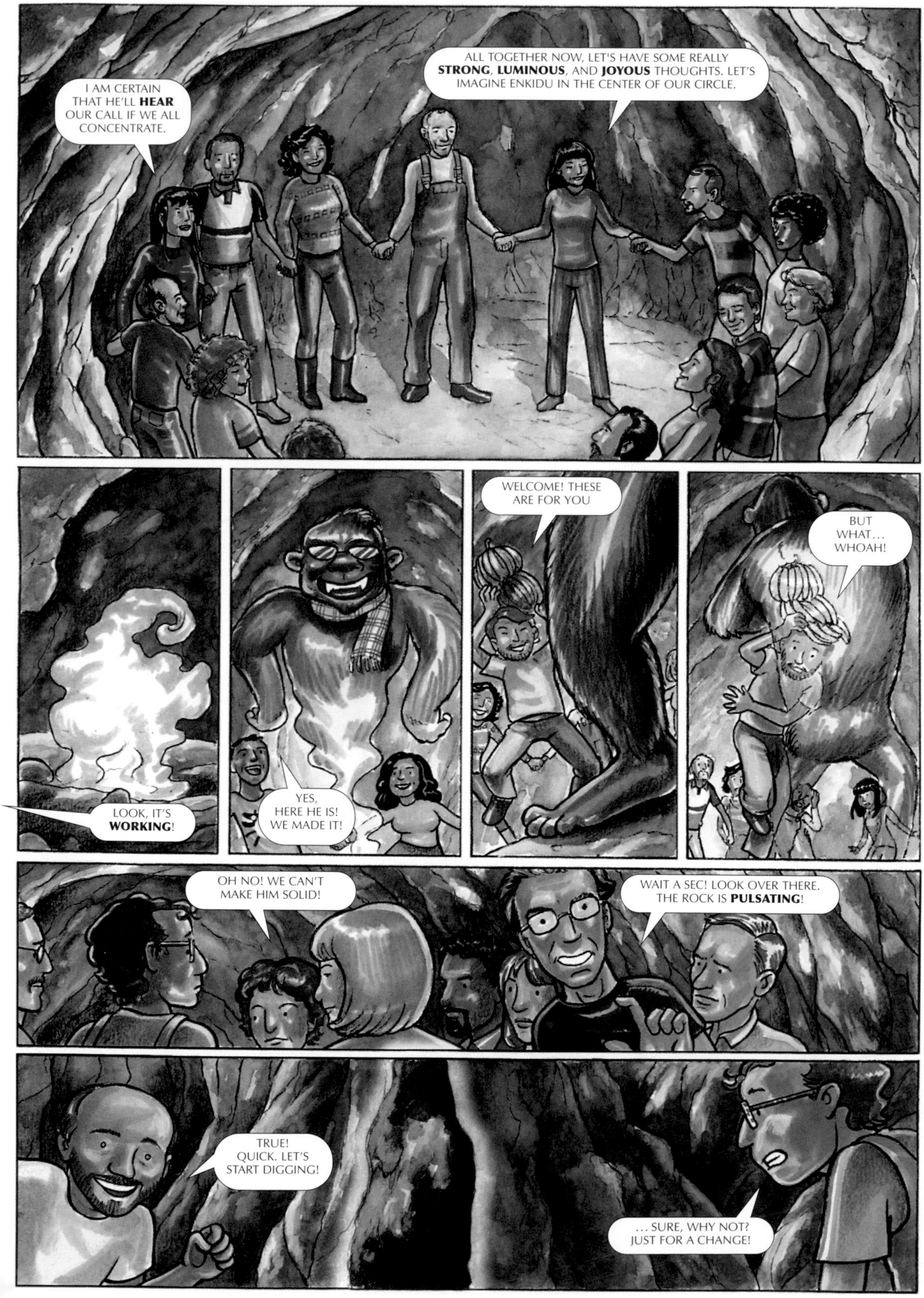
I AM CERTAIN THAT HE'LL **HEAR** OUR CALL IF WE ALL CONCENTRATE.
ALL TOGETHER NOW, LET'S HAVE SOME REALLY **STRONG**, **LUMINOUS**, AND **JOYOUS** THOUGHTS. LET'S IMAGINE ENKIDU IN THE CENTER OF OUR CIRCLE.
LOOK, IT'S **WORKING**!
YES, HERE HE IS! WE MADE IT!
WELCOME! THESE ARE FOR YOU
BUT WHAT… WHOAH!
OH NO! WE CAN'T MAKE HIM SOLID!
WAIT A SEC! LOOK OVER THERE. THE ROCK IS **PULSATING**!
TRUE! QUICK. LET'S START DIGGING!
…SURE, WHY NOT? JUST FOR A CHANGE!

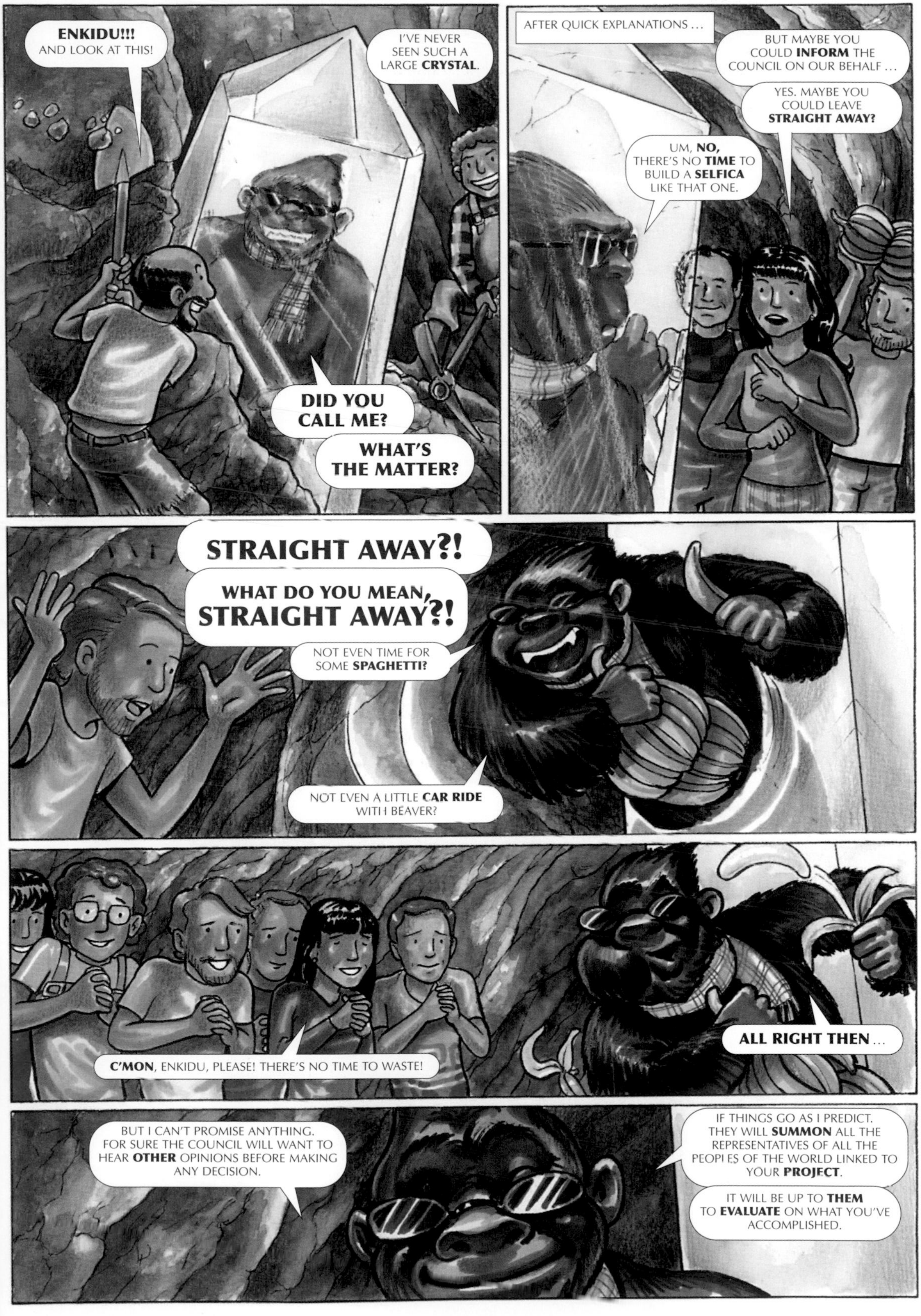
ENKIDU!!! AND LOOK AT THIS!
I'VE NEVER SEEN SUCH A LARGE CRYSTAL.
DID YOU CALL ME?
WHAT'S THE MATTER?
AFTER QUICK EXPLANATIONS …
BUT MAYBE YOU COULD INFORM THE COUNCIL ON OUR BEHALF …
YES. MAYBE YOU COULD LEAVE STRAIGHT AWAY?
UM, NO, THERE'S NO TIME TO BUILD A SELFICA LIKE THAT ONE.
STRAIGHT AWAY?!
WHAT DO YOU MEAN, STRAIGHT AWAY?!
NOT EVEN TIME FOR SOME SPAGHETTI?
NOT EVEN A LITTLE CAR RIDE WITH BEAVER?
C'MON, ENKIDU, PLEASE! THERE'S NO TIME TO WASTE!
ALL RIGHT THEN …
BUT I CAN'T PROMISE ANYTHING. FOR SURE THE COUNCIL WILL WANT TO HEAR OTHER OPINIONS BEFORE MAKING ANY DECISION.
IF THINGS GO AS I PREDICT. THEY WILL SUMMON ALL THE REPRESENTATIVES OF ALL THE PEOPLES OF THE WORLD LINKED TO YOUR PROJECT.
IT WILL BE UP TO THEM TO EVALUATE ON WHAT YOU'VE ACCOMPLISHED.

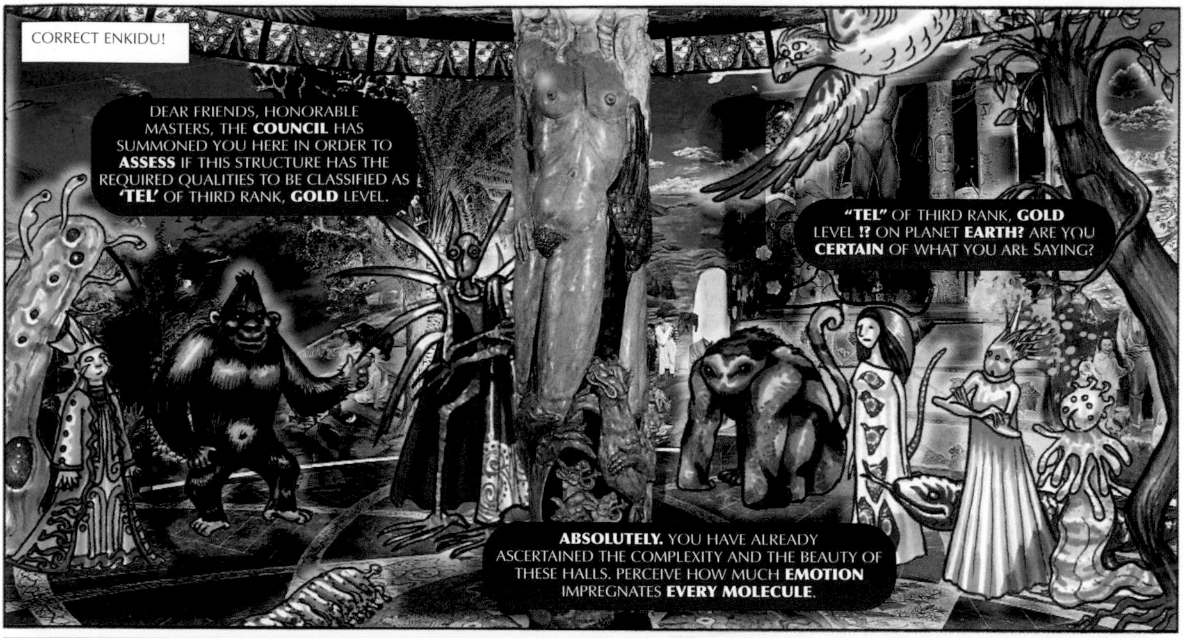
CORRECT ENKIDU!
DEAR FRIENDS, HONORABLE MASTERS, THE **COUNCIL** HAS SUMMONED YOU HERE IN ORDER TO **ASSESS** IF THIS STRUCTURE HAS THE REQUIRED QUALITIES TO BE CLASSIFIED AS **'TEL'** OF THIRD RANK, **GOLD** LEVEL.
"TEL" OF THIRD RANK, **GOLD** LEVEL **!?** ON PLANET **EARTH?** ARE YOU **CERTAIN** OF WHAT YOU ARE SAYING?
ABSOLUTELY. YOU HAVE ALREADY ASCERTAINED THE COMPLEXITY AND THE BEAUTY OF THESE HALLS. PERCEIVE HOW MUCH **EMOTION** IMPREGNATES **EVERY MOLECULE**.

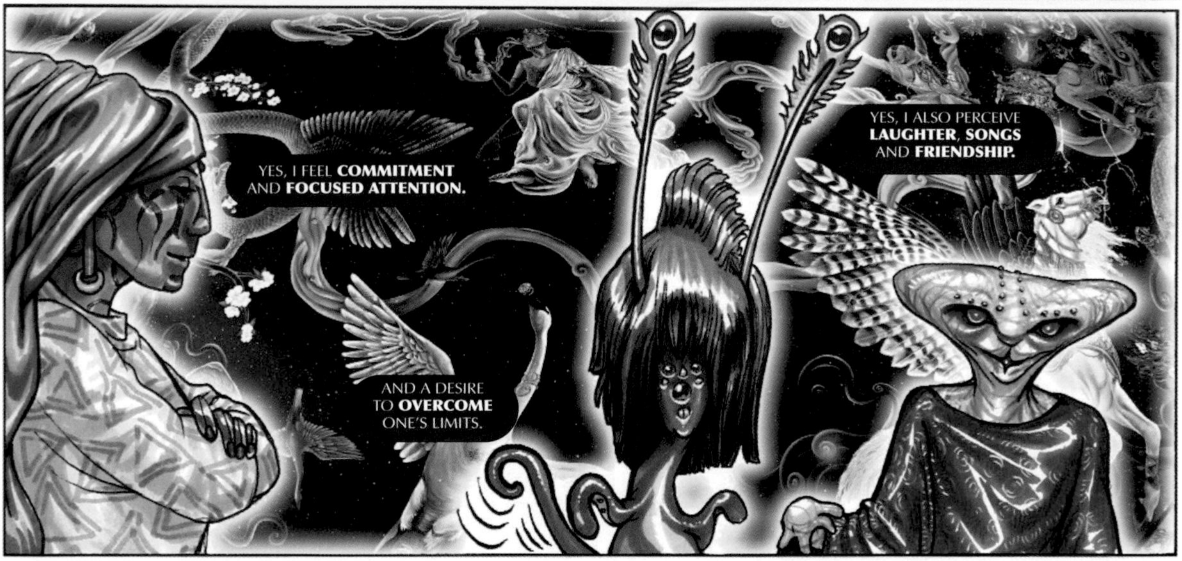
YES, I FEEL **COMMITMENT** AND **FOCUSED ATTENTION.**
AND A DESIRE TO **OVERCOME** ONE'S LIMITS.
YES, I ALSO PERCEIVE **LAUGHTER**, **SONGS** AND **FRIENDSHIP.**

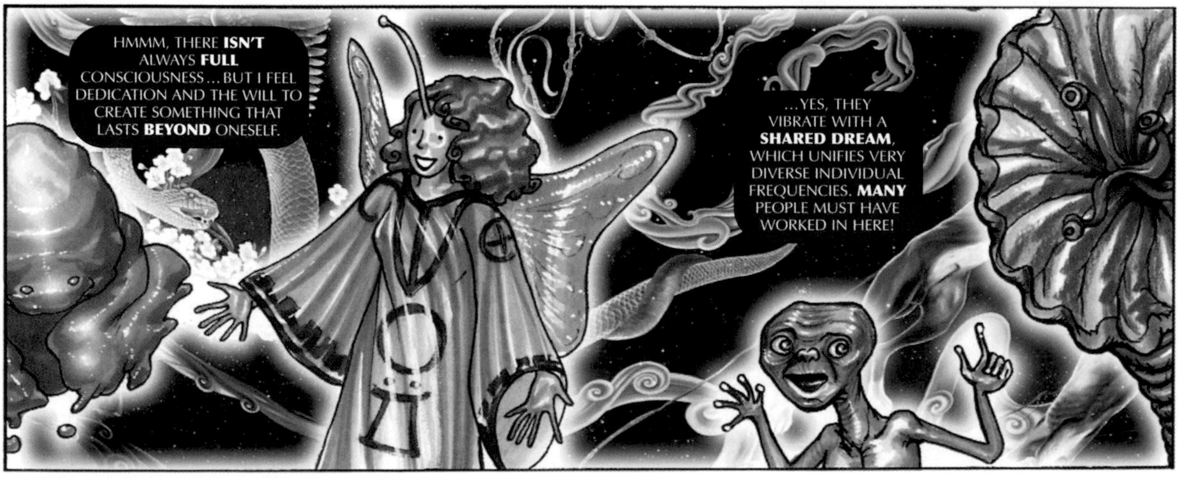
HMMM, THERE **ISN'T** ALWAYS **FULL** CONSCIOUSNESS… BUT I FEEL DEDICATION AND THE WILL TO CREATE SOMETHING THAT LASTS **BEYOND** ONESELF.
…YES, THEY VIBRATE WITH A **SHARED DREAM**, WHICH UNIFIES VERY DIVERSE INDIVIDUAL FREQUENCIES. **MANY** PEOPLE MUST HAVE WORKED IN HERE!

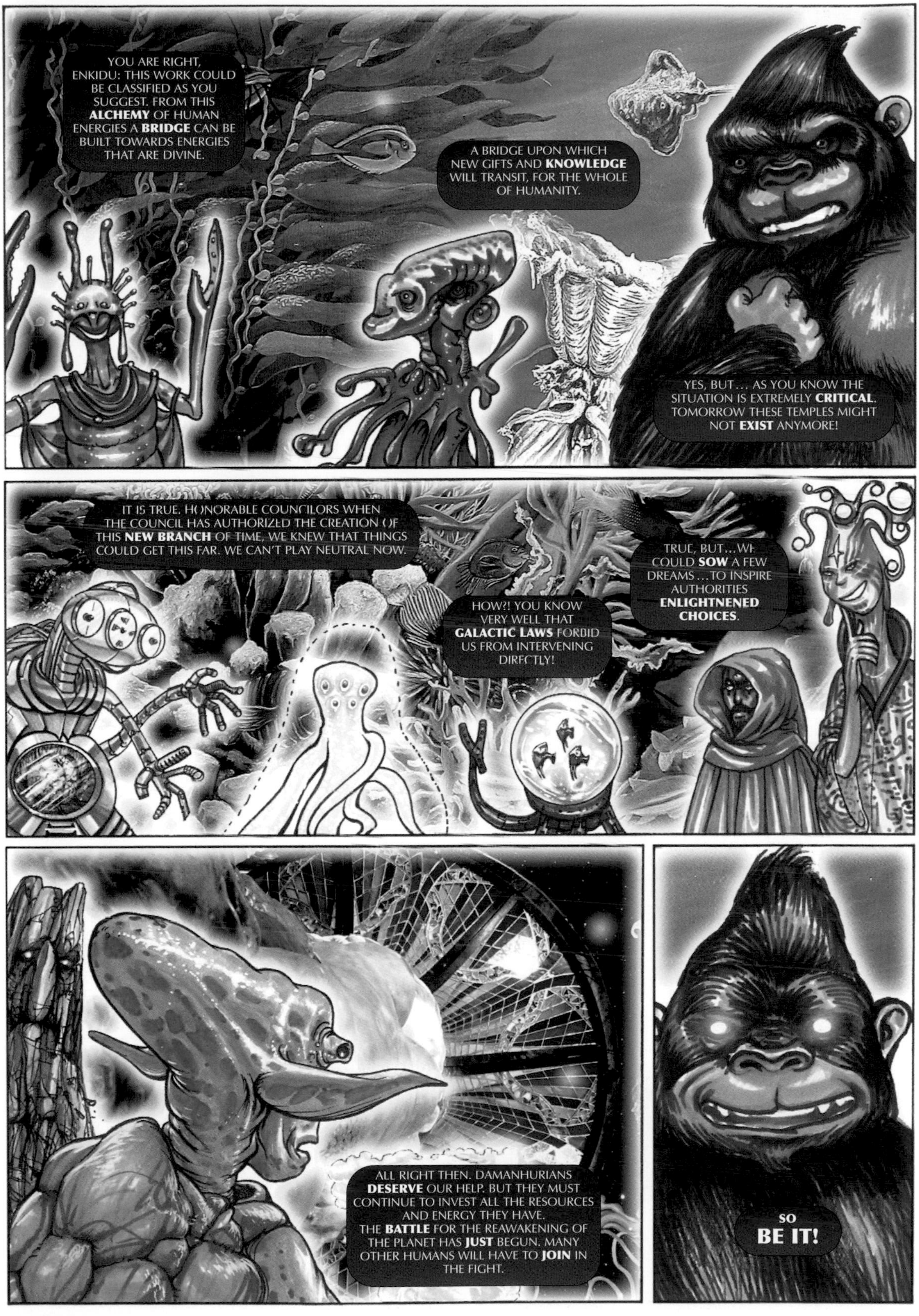
YOU ARE RIGHT, ENKIDU: THIS WORK COULD BE CLASSIFIED AS YOU SUGGEST. FROM THIS **ALCHEMY** OF HUMAN ENERGIES A **BRIDGE** CAN BE BUILT TOWARDS ENERGIES THAT ARE DIVINE.
A BRIDGE UPON WHICH NEW GIFTS AND **KNOWLEDGE** WILL TRANSIT, FOR THE WHOLE OF HUMANITY.
YES, BUT... AS YOU KNOW THE SITUATION IS EXTREMELY **CRITICAL**. TOMORROW THESE TEMPLES MIGHT NOT **EXIST** ANYMORE!
IT IS TRUE. HONORABLE COUNCILORS WHEN THE COUNCIL HAS AUTHORIZED THE CREATION OF THIS **NEW BRANCH** OF TIME, WE KNEW THAT THINGS COULD GET THIS FAR. WE CAN'T PLAY NEUTRAL NOW.
HOW?! YOU KNOW VERY WELL THAT **GALACTIC LAWS** FORBID US FROM INTERVENING DIRECTLY!
TRUE, BUT...WE COULD **SOW** A FEW DREAMS...TO INSPIRE AUTHORITIES **ENLIGHTNENED CHOICES**.
ALL RIGHT THEN. DAMANHURIANS **DESERVE** OUR HELP. BUT THEY MUST CONTINUE TO INVEST ALL THE RESOURCES AND ENERGY THEY HAVE. THE **BATTLE** FOR THE REAWAKENING OF THE PLANET HAS **JUST** BEGUN. MANY OTHER HUMANS WILL HAVE TO **JOIN** IN THE FIGHT.
SO **BE IT!**

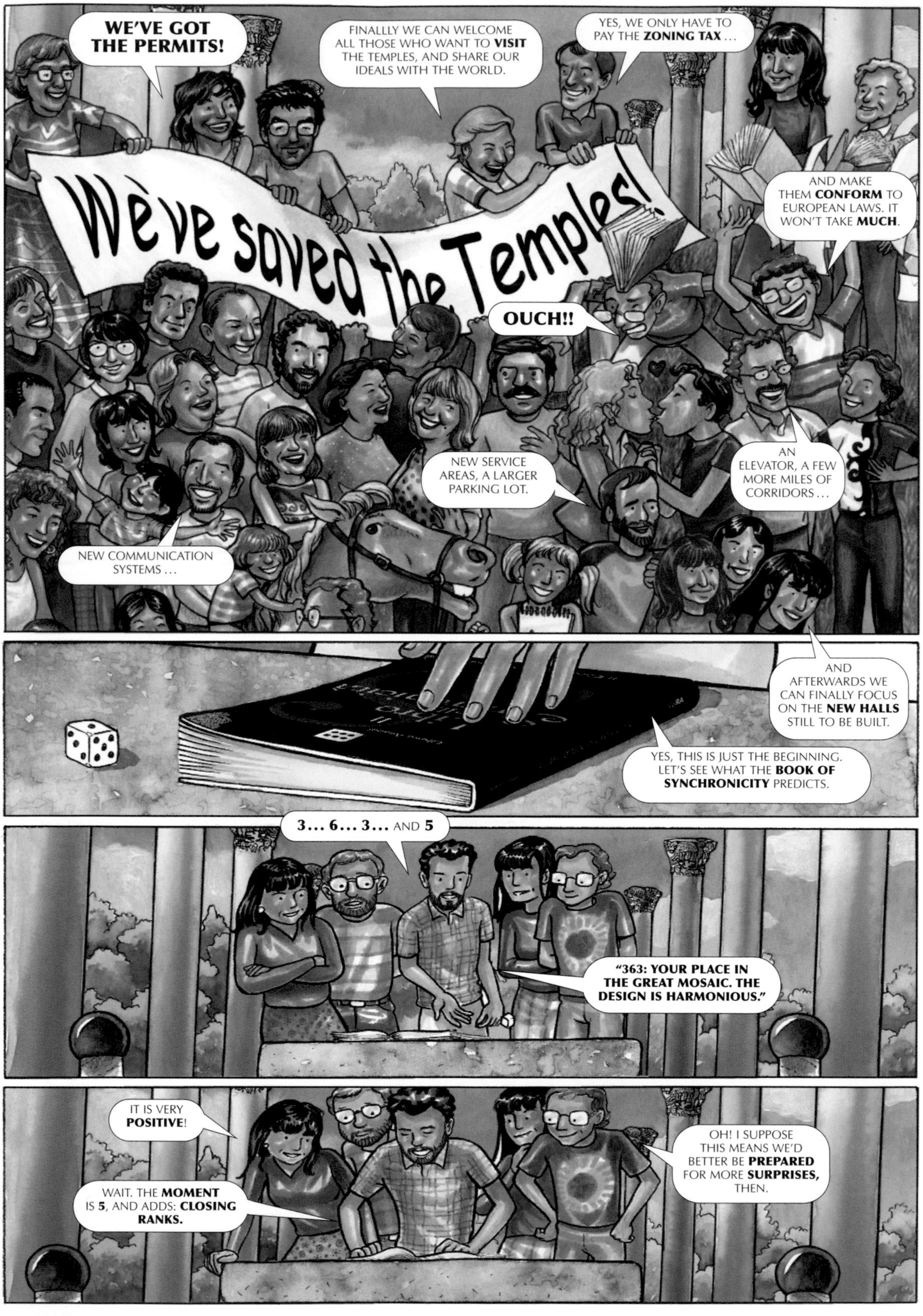
WE'VE GOT THE PERMITS!
We've saved the Temples!
FINALLY WE CAN WELCOME ALL THOSE WHO WANT TO VISIT THE TEMPLES, AND SHARE OUR IDEALS WITH THE WORLD.
YES, WE ONLY HAVE TO PAY THE ZONING TAX . . .
AND MAKE THEM CONFORM TO EUROPEAN LAWS. IT WON'T TAKE MUCH.
OUCH!!
NEW COMMUNICATION SYSTEMS . . .
NEW SERVICE AREAS, A LARGER PARKING LOT.
AN ELEVATOR, A FEW MORE MILES OF CORRIDORS . . .
AND AFTERWARDS WE CAN FINALLY FOCUS ON THE NEW HALLS STILL TO BE BUILT.
YES, THIS IS JUST THE BEGINNING. LET'S SEE WHAT THE BOOK OF SYNCHRONICITY PREDICTS.
3… 6… 3… AND 5
"363: YOUR PLACE IN THE GREAT MOSAIC. THE DESIGN IS HARMONIOUS."
IT IS VERY POSITIVE!
WAIT. THE MOMENT IS 5, AND ADDS: CLOSING RANKS.
OH! I SUPPOSE THIS MEANS WE'D BETTER BE PREPARED FOR MORE SURPRISES, THEN.

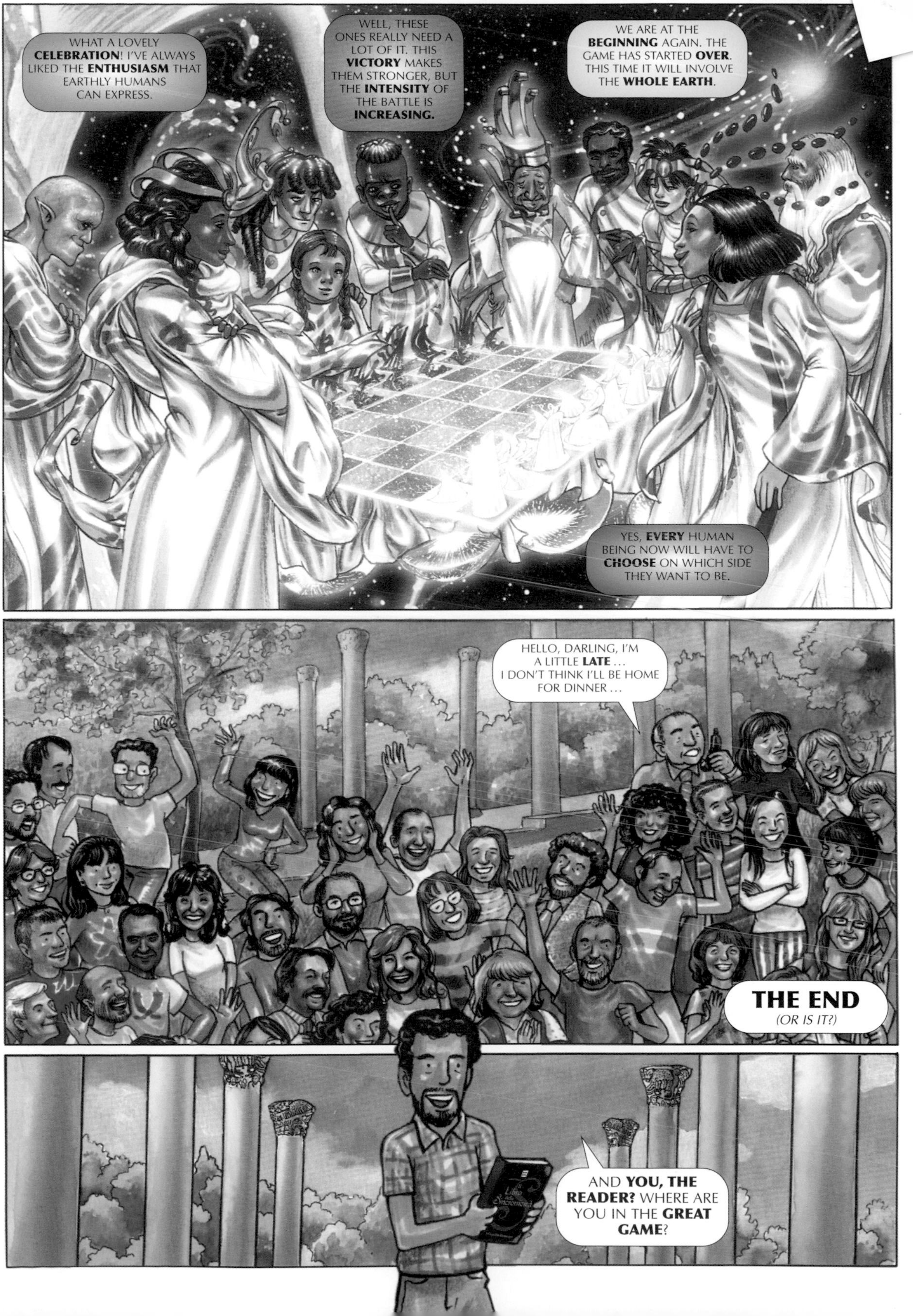
WHAT A LOVELY **CELEBRATION**! I'VE ALWAYS LIKED THE **ENTHUSIASM** THAT EARTHLY HUMANS CAN EXPRESS.
WELL, THESE ONES REALLY NEED A LOT OF IT. THIS **VICTORY** MAKES THEM STRONGER, BUT THE **INTENSITY** OF THE BATTLE IS **INCREASING.**
WE ARE AT THE **BEGINNING** AGAIN. THE GAME HAS STARTED **OVER**. THIS TIME IT WILL INVOLVE THE **WHOLE EARTH**.
YES, **EVERY** HUMAN BEING NOW WILL HAVE TO **CHOOSE** ON WHICH SIDE THEY WANT TO BE.
HELLO, DARLING, I'M A LITTLE **LATE** … I DON'T THINK I'LL BE HOME FOR DINNER …
THE END
(OR IS IT?)
AND **YOU, THE READER?** WHERE ARE YOU IN THE **GREAT GAME**?

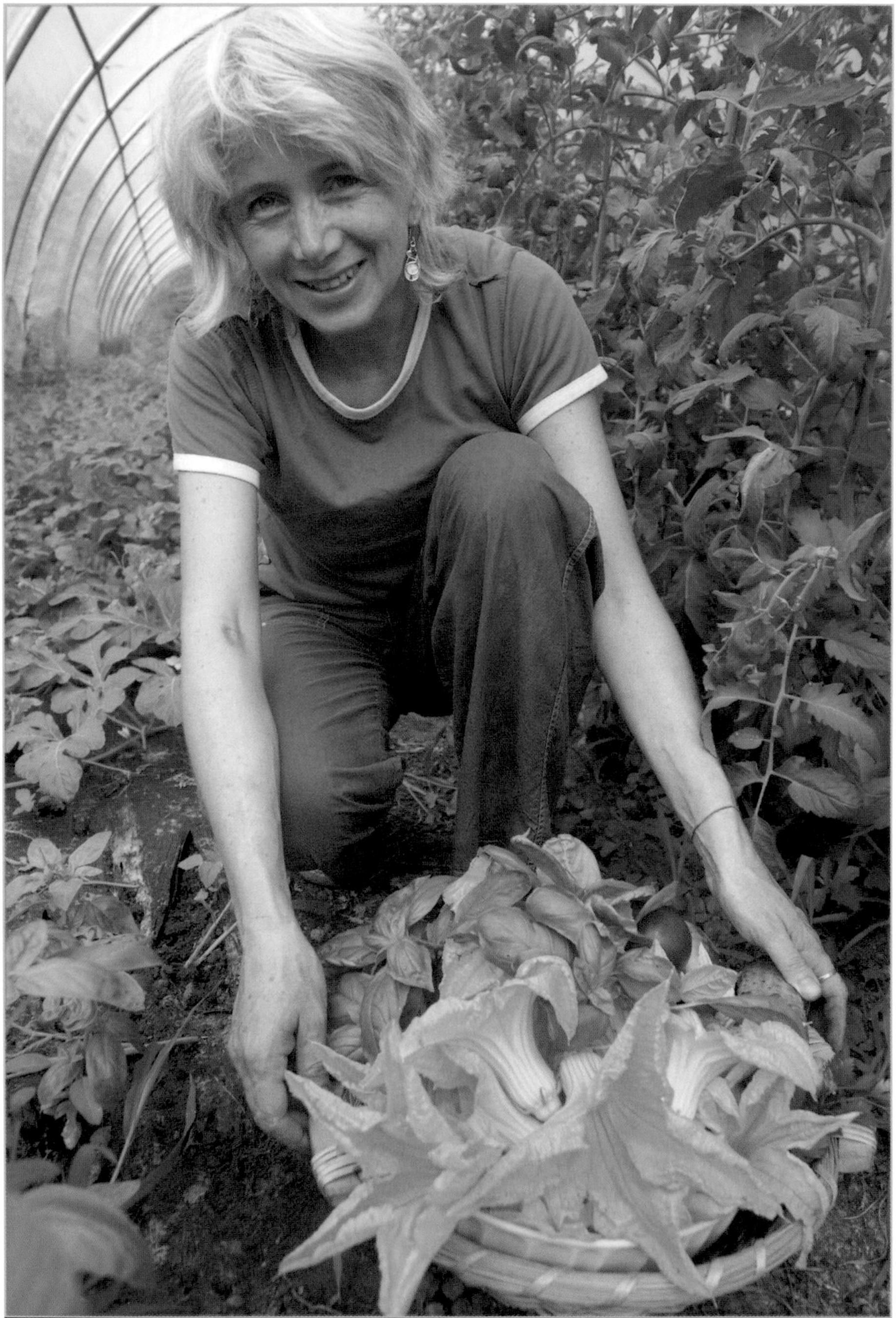

Organic farming at Pejda

A Fantastic Story
and a Beautiful Comic

Q & A with Massimo Introvigne on Sharing
Damanhur's Spiritual Vision

Massimo Introvigne, a Turin sociologist, is the director and one of the founders of the Center for the Study of New Religions. CESNUR also studies contemporary communal and neospiritual movements, and their impact on social life. Author of several dozens of books published in several languages on this topic, Introvigne is considered one of the most prominent world scholars on new religions. He also studies the history of popular comics, and is a cofounder of CESPOC (Center for Studies on Popular Culture).

Q: *You have followed our endeavor to communicate the experience of Damanhur through the unusual means of a comic book with great interest, even visiting our atelier at Damanhur Crea on several occasions. Why?*

A: I am a specialist in new religious and spiritual movements, but I also have an interest in popular culture. Besides directing CESNUR, the Center for Studies on New Religions, since 1988, I am also a member of the executive committee and curator of the library of CESPOC, the Center for Studies on Popular Culture, which has a series of thematic collections of the most important popular pamphlets and comic books in Italy. So, I must confess that I found this occasion of combining these interests of mine irresistible.

It is not the first time that a vision of the spiritual world has been transmitted through comics. Without even mentioning the ample production within traditional religions (remember the Italian Catholic magazine *Il Vittorioso*), The Family (a movement also known in the past as the Children of God), the Mormons, the Hare Krishna, the African Church founded in Congo by Simon Kimbangu (1889–1951) and almost all the religious movements in Japan—a country where comics are considered reading for adults and not primarily for children—have all communicated their ideas through comics, often with great success. Nevertheless, the experience of Damanhur seems to me absolutely unique.

Q: *Why?*

A: As with other products of Damanhur—from glass to cheese—it strikes me that *Checkmate to Time* seeks a certain standard of quality and excellence. In general, on the other hand, spiritual or religious comics do not have a good reputation. Specialists tend to dismiss them as a minor genre, in which all the focus is on content, while form leaves a lot to be desired. This is not always the case, but very often the bad quality of these kinds of productions justify the critics' judgments. In your case, however, it seems to me that the care put into the lines and drawings are definitely superior. As is the case with other Damanhurian activities, some could even see in it the influence of the vast social, economic, and cultural movement that is trying to reinvent the province of Turin and the Piedmont region from a center of mass production to a center of excellence in a number of fields. From this point of view, the pathway that has brought about the transformation of an ex-Olivetti factory into the Damanhur Crea center seems to me to have a powerful symbolic value. Or perhaps it is simply the result of the meeting of some talented people.

Q: *How do you evaluate our experiment in the context of contemporary Italian and international comic books?*

A: The person being interviewed should give answers and not ask questions, but I should like to know if and how much Jean-Paul Appel-Guéry [the founder of Iso-Zen, the French spiritual commune] has influenced you. I know that at a certain point he went to Damanhur and—besides other groups into spiritual UFO research, which no longer exist or have been replaced by new, more "elastic" organizations such as Iso-Zen and Siderella— he has produced good quality comic books, working with well-known authors like Moebius [the French comic artist Jean Giraud]. Strangely enough, ever since Iso-Zen and Siderella became the focus of big "anti-cult" campaigns of the '90s, when the press refer to Appel-Guéry as a "guru" they now say the most negative things about him, but when people speak about his comics in the specialized press, the reviews all become very positive. I seem to see something of Appel-Guéry (and also of Moebius) in the more surrealist and fantastic pages of your book. All the same, if these previous works have been a reference point, we must remember that they refer to a French/Belgian school which permits surrealist tendencies but does not forget that what made the fortune of that school is the use of a "clear line." [The *ligne claire* or "clear line" is a style of drawing pioneered by Hergé, the Belgian creator of *The Adventures of Tintin*.] The precision of the drawing serves to make the text highly legible, quite different from some American and Japanese comics, which are very trying for the reader.

This new book on Damanhur has this combination: the easily readable surrealist and science-fiction pages combine with other pages which remain in the very heart of the *ligne claire* tradition. For example, the self-portrait of Esperide, or the stories of the childhood of Falco remind us of an Italian comic book that has been translated into many languages, *W.I.T.C.H.* Numerous critics have written that the *ligne claire* style can be combined very well with stories where the paranormal and magic are present. Certainly it has not yet been exploited to the full. I would add that, unlike in many American or Japanese books, and similarly to *W.I.T.C.H.*—even though these are real people and not imaginary ones—the story is told smilingly, with a certain sense of irony . . . which, indeed, is a characteristic of Damanhur in general.

Q: *What do you mean by that?*

A: For many years I have been wondering about the reasons for Damanhur's success. For sure it has had its "apostates" (the term is not insulting, but technical: in sociology, it indicates the ex-members who leave a movement and then became its critics and detractors), its own polemics, and its attacks, but all in all, Damanhur has responded more than well, losing a smaller number of members than many other groups, and has demonstrated a remarkable stability.

In a series of articles, I defined the founder of Damanhur as having a "non-charismatic charisma." As can be seen also in the comic, the citizens of Damanhur certainly consider Oberto Airaudi a person out of the ordinary. Of course, as you state yourselves, the reader of a text like this one must always keep in mind that a dimension of dreaming is entwined with one of reality; it is quite a stretch to go from [the Italian politician] Vittorio Sgarbi, scarcely hidden behind a transparent pseudonym, to the gorilla Enkidu—an interesting contribution from the epic poem of Gilgamesh, although transposed in a theosophical and science-fiction sense. However, readers are constantly provoked to ask themselves where, in their experience, do dreaming and playing end and where does reality begin? And is a general answer at all possible, or rather, can one only find this answer within oneself? And yet, at a certain point, there always emerges a liberating smile, a self-ironic wink, an invitation not to take oneself too seriously. It is in this sense that I speak of a "non-charismatic charisma." There are spiritual leaders who exercise their charisma by multiplying the signs that separate them from their followers, which underline their characteristics of being special and unique. I have met many such leaders. They speak in oracular tones, or only move around surrounded by followers who, for example, hold an umbrella over their head, so that such a banal thing as the sun does not disturb the holy head of the Master. It is true that often all this works well, and that there is a certain type of follower who actually looks for a Master of that kind. But in Damanhur the charisma is "non-charismatic" in the sense that it is never disconnected from a dimension of playfulness, which dilutes any tension that could be perceived as oppressive even before it arises. As tension is the greatest enemy of the chances for a community to last long-term, this could provide an explanation for the nonephemeral character of Damanhur (and history teaches us that many such communities are ephemeral). I say "an" explanation and not "the" explanation—there are, for sure, other factors like the success of various enterprises that secure for Damanhur the economic stability that other communities have either lost, or never reached.

Q: *In your opinion, how can a person read this comic, if they do not identify with the experience of Damanhur?*

A: The question could be: How do *I* read it? I have religious and spiritual ideas, which are certainly not those of Damanhur. I think that the answer is twofold. Those who know Damanhur know that it is a very relevant reality, especially in Piedmont (but now not only there), while those who don't know Damanhur may underestimate it. Whoever is interested in the social, economic, and political life of Piedmont—let alone its culture and spirituality—must absolutely try to understand what Damanhur is. In this sense, this comic is also a very precious instrument for those who do not share Damanhur's vision of the world. It probably helps us to understand it better than more voluminous books, or sociological works or articles do (mine included, of course).

On the other hand, for those who do not know Damanhur, the text can be read at a very different level, appreciating its quality as a fantastic story and a beautiful comic. For many, the two levels of reading will be enjoyed together.

Q: *Frankly, is there anything that you did not enjoy?*

A: Yes—the way in which the link is represented between the "discovery" of the Temples of Humankind and a plot involving a cardinal in the Vatican. I would like to declare beforehand that, in my opinion (but it's a subjective opinion), the fact that the Temples of Humankind came to light, has been—in the long term and everything considered—positive in the history of Damanhur, because it opened up a new phase in which the temples have become a resource for more than the Damanhurians. It helped to insert the temples in the context of a richer and more fecund interaction between Damanhur and the surrounding region. But I would like to add that—besides the "apostate," whose activities and motivations are shown in the comic—the theme of a Vatican plot and the evil cardinal is a bit trite, both from a point of view of substance and from its representation in literature or comic books. Of course, in this comic the cardinal is the first to realize that on themes such as how to behave in relation to religious or "nonconventional" spiritual minorities, various attitudes coexist within the Catholic Church (so partially saving himself from being a mere stereotype). It is still an ongoing debate.

In fact, it is certainly not difficult to find, also in the case of Damanhur, Catholic people or organizations which, without any critical thinking, have accepted the "anticult" rhetoric. This rhetoric is, in turn, based on the idea of a conspiracy, a Great Plot of the Cults to damage the Church and society, naively reducing into one unity a series of different and incompatible positions. I understand your resentment, which is founded on objective historical facts, towards those who have adopted such a position and have also taken action accordingly. But I should like to add that one must not confuse the "anticult" maneuvers, which ask the State to limit the free competition of spiritual and religious visions of the world, with a critique based on doctrinal reasons, such as those that a Catholic would have of the experience of Damanhur according to his or her faith. Unlike the former, the latter are an expression—not a limitation—of the freedom of religion and spiritual research. It seems to me that in the Third Millennium we must privilege the positions of respectful dialogue (and of course also those of respectful controversy) that avoid all Great Plot rhetoric and try, first of all, to understand their interlocutor without hiding doctrinal differences and so not slipping into relativism. This is the spirit that, I believe, has animated us in this interview, and I would be pleased if it could also inspire many of the readers of this comic book.

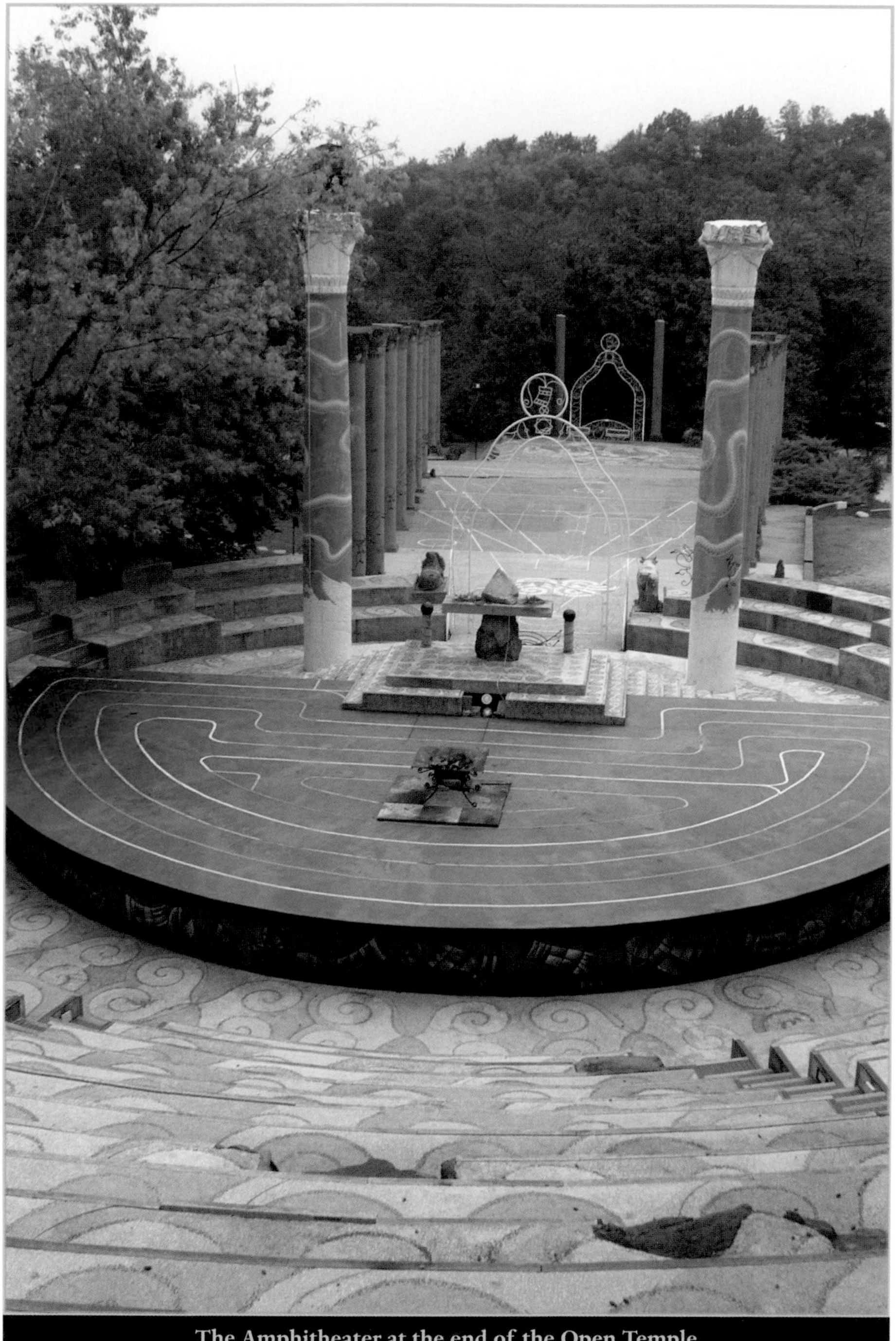
The Amphitheater at the end of the Open Temple

RECOMMENDED READING

Airaudi, Oberto, *The Book of Synchronicity: The Game of Divination*. Berkeley: North Atlantic Books, 2007

Ananas, Esperide, *Damanhur: Temples of Humankind*. New York: CoSM Press, 2006

Dejamour, Adam and Gabrielle, *Damanhur Guide: Valchiusella Valley*. Vidracco: Comitato ValdiChy, 2006

Merrifield, Jeff, *Damanhur: The Story of the Extraordinary Italian Artistic and Spiritual Community*. Santa Cruz: Hanford Mead Publishers, 2006

ACKNOWLEDGMENTS

Many people are to be thanked at the end of a work like this.

Thanks to Falco for the inspiration, the encouragement, and the insights he has given us. Most of all, thanks for allowing us to freely embroider his character and his story.

Thanks to Gambero Finocchio Selvatico for his infinite patience in accepting the frequent changes in the manuscript, the drawings, and the lettering, and to Albatros for the graphics of the pages of "Characters and Actors" and those of the police visit to the Temples.

Thanks to Roberto Benzi for authorization to use some of his pictures of the Temples, and to Orso Lichene for the historical pictures of the building phases.

Thanks to Quetzal and Coyote-Franco de Giorgis for some of the pictures of the Journey.

Thanks to Formica Coriandolo and Jo, Elsa, David, and Zac Pearl who with love and patience have examined the whole work and given precious suggestions.

Thanks to Professor Massimo Introvigne for his interesting contribution and his precious suggestions, and to Richard Grossinger for his insightful and inspiring essay. Thanks to Hisae Matsuda, who with loving care has been invaluable in composing the complex puzzle of the English version of this book.

Thanks to Dawn Aldredge for collaborating with Esperide Ananas years ago, when they worked together on the first manuscript of the story of the Temples.

Last but not least, thanks to all those who have contributed a memory, a photo, an anecdote: too many to be able to quote them all.

the Authors and the Artists

CONTRIBUTORS

ESPERIDE ANANAS is Damanhur's Communications Director. STAMBECCO PESCO is editor in chief of the community's publishing house, ValRa. Artist CINZIA DI FELICE is a well-known graphic novelist. Illustrators APE SOIA and PANGOLINO TULIPANO collaborated on artistic projects for more than twenty years, including art for the Temples of Humankind. All live in Damanhur.

MASSIMO INTROVIGNE, a Turin sociologist, is the director and one of the founders of the Center for the Study of New Religions. CESNUR also studies contemporary communal and neospiritual movements, and their impact on social life. Author of many books published in several languages on this topic, Introvigne is considered one of the most prominent world scholars on new religions. He also studies the history of popular pamphlets and comics, and is a cofounder of CESPOC (Center for Studies on Popular Culture).

Since the issuing of *Solar Journal: Oecological Sections* by Black Sparrow Press in 1970, RICHARD GROSSINGER has published some twenty-five books, most of them with his own press, North Atlantic Books and Frog Books, but also titles with Harper, Doubleday, Sierra Club Books, J.P. Tarcher, among others. These have ranged from extremely long explorations of science, culture, and spirituality *(The Night Sky, Planet Medicine, Embryogenesis)* to memoirs and nonfiction novels *(New Moon, Out of Babylon)* to experimental prose *(Book of the Earth and Sky, Spaces Wild and Tame)* and science fiction *(Mars: A Science Fiction Vision)*. Grossinger received a PhD in anthropology from the University of Michigan in 1975 and lives with his wife Lindy Hough in Berkeley, California.

Theater performance in the Open Temple at Damjl

INDEX

Painting class in Damjl

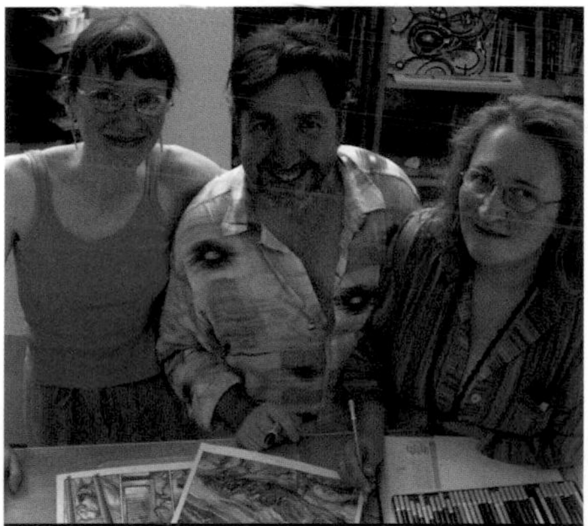

Comic book artists Cinzia di Felice, Ape Soia, and Pangolino Tulipano

**Doctors Formichiere Carota
and Daina Albicocca**

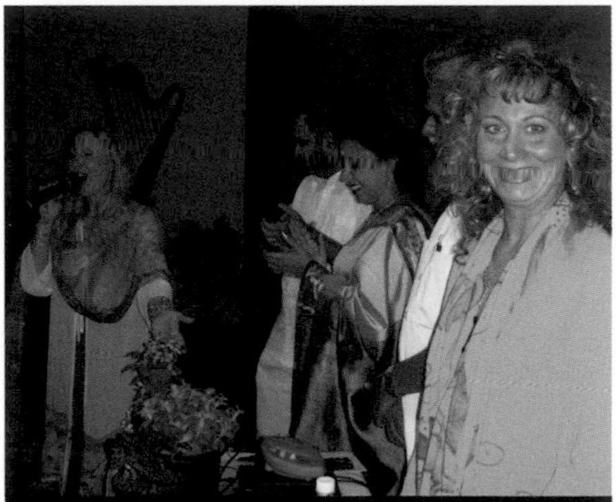

Music of the Plants concert in Chennai, India, February 2008

Children of Damanhur's dance school taking a bow after a performance
at Damanhur Crea

Fashion show of Damanhurian eco-clothing at Damanhur Crea

The hill from Vidracco to Damjl—an easy scenic hike
to the ancient tower "Cives" on top

Home of the Dendera nucleo

A Damanhurian wedding
in the Open Temple

Le Arti glass workshop
at Damanhur Crea

The Open Temple at Damjl at night

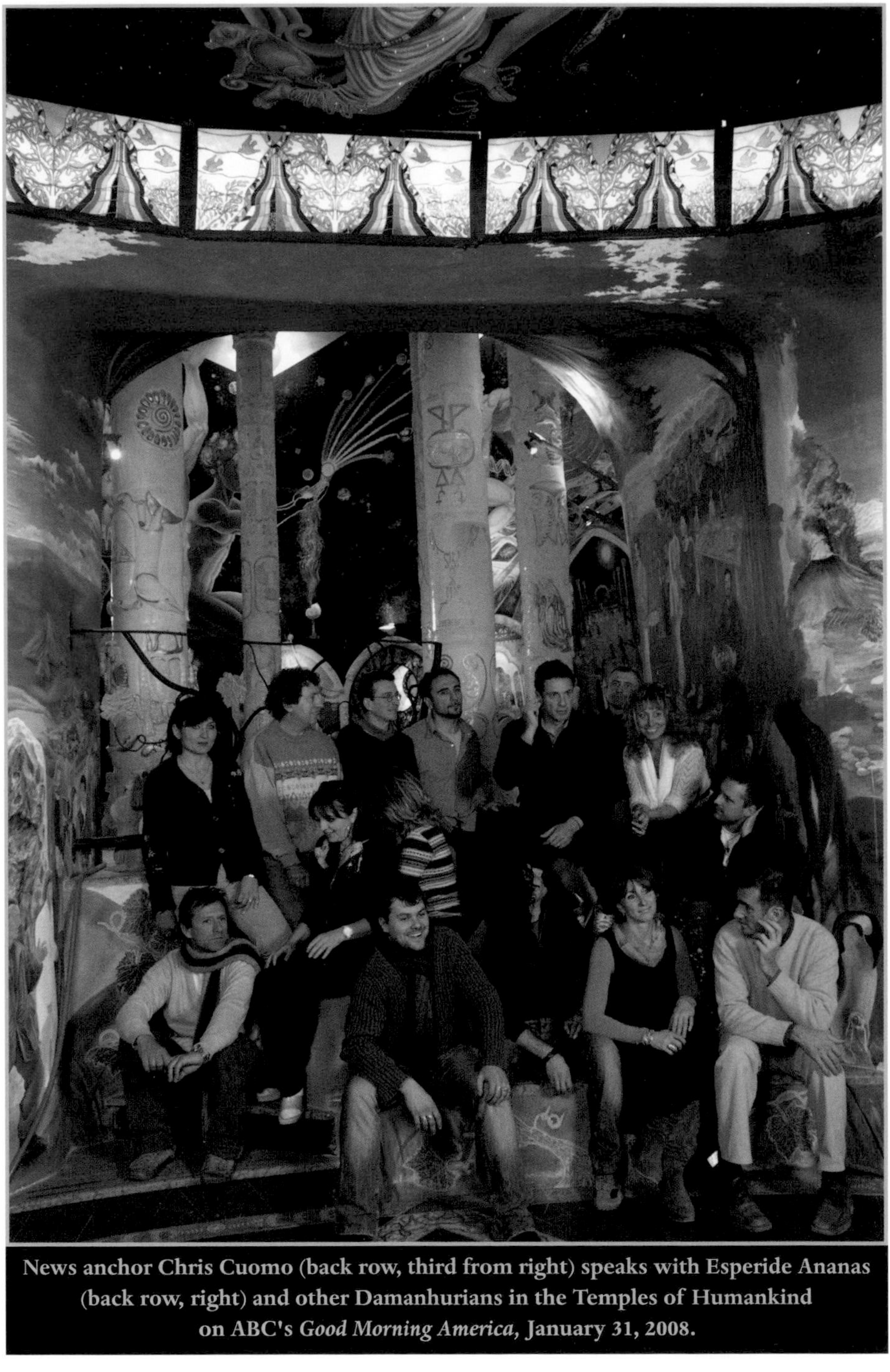

News anchor Chris Cuomo (back row, third from right) speaks with Esperide Ananas (back row, right) and other Damanhurians in the Temples of Humankind on ABC's *Good Morning America,* January 31, 2008.